These were nights when men remembered their God, nights when only the dark form of another Ranger to your front shared your loneliness. There were hours of moving through the blackness, taut hours with every sense and nerve straining to locate the enemy before he found us. Each sound of night magnified in the imagination with men, listening . . . listening, then satisfied, whispering inwardly, "Yea though I walk through the valley of the shadow of death, I will fear no evil," and continuing on.

RANGERS IN KOREA

Robert W. Black

IVY BOOKS • NEW YORK

Ivy Books
Published by Ballantine Books
Copyright © 1989 by Robert W. Black

Library of Congress Catalog Card Number: 89-91424

ISBN 0-8041-0213-9

Manufactured in the United States of America

First Edition: December 1989

Map by Shelly Shapiro

To my wife Barbara.
Her love, support, and sacrifice
made this work possible.

Preface

The night was so cold, water froze in the canteens. The snow lay thick on the ground, its crust hard and brilliant under a hunter's moon. To the small force of Americans moving deep behind enemy lines, the slightest sound was magnified, each shadow coming alive as senses strained to separate reality from illusion. Though seeking to avoid enemy contact prior to arrival at their objective, some fighting had been necessary to penetrate the enemy line. An aroused foe could be waiting, allowing them to come deeper into a trap from which there would be no escape.

They continued on, moving as silently as nature would allow. They avoided both hamlets and isolated huts, but the village dogs had sensed the Americans' presence, and the night silence was marred by their barks of alarm. In the rude huts of a Korean village, the men of the enemy headquarters were at rest. The night watch looked to their comfort. With their savage reputation for barbarity against wounded and prisoners, the North Koreans were sure no United Nations force would risk a deep raid and possible capture, and so they slept.

It would be the sleep of death.

The Americans were in the town before the enemy was aware of them, and the calm was shattered by the full-throated roar of American weapons. From out of the night came an all-volunteer force, its roots deep in American military tradition; the Airborne Rangers attacked, the North Koreans died.

To be a Ranger is to be a part of American history. From as early as the 1600s, American Ranger units, men born in the

1

New World, saw action: from the hardwood forests of New England, the valleys and mountains of Virginia, and the piny bottoms of Georgia, the American Ranger led the way westward. Manned by volunteers, many of whom were skilled woodsmen who had known danger since boyhood, the Rangers were hardy and independent. Rangers were frequently required to furnish their own arms and equipment, and they went into battle expecting and usually receiving little support from others.

From the Atlantic to the Pacific the Rangers rendered service far out of proportion to their small numbers. Fighting in more wars than any regiment of the United States Army, the Rangers proved versatile, serving as long-range reconnaissance units, scouts, raiders, and light infantry. The Rangers were representative of a young and vibrant nation on the move: their discipline was of the forest rather than the parade ground, and they attracted leaders of initiative and daring, leaders who set a standard of going beyond the expected.

But however useful they were in war, peacetime brought the Rangers scorn from the regular Army establishment and they were rapidly disbanded. In 1891, at the close of the Indian Wars, it appeared the proud name Ranger would disappear from the lexicon of the U.S. Army, but in World War II the Rangers returned to again prove their worth. Then came war in Korea . . .

This is the history of a select group of American volunteers who served during the first American war against the Communist menace. There were eighteen Ranger companies formed during the Korean War, seventeen of which were parachutists, or in Army terminology, "Airborne."

They were a small, elite group. During a time when the United Nations forces numbered over 500,000 men, there were less than 700 Airborne Rangers fighting across the width of the Korean peninsula, in front of every U.S. Army division engaged. Other Ranger companies went where duty required them to serve. In the United States, Germany, and Japan, these select troops set a standard of excellence for the U.S. Army. In time they would play a major role in the development of the Ranger Department, spreading Ranger leadership and philosophy throughout the Army, ultimately becoming a fundamental force in the birth of Special Forces (the Green Berets).

This history is being written in the warmth of an old, Pennsylvania farmhouse, on land once owned by an Indian fighter. There is a continuity here: surrounded by the remembrance of war, there is peace. This book is a chronicle of many people, and inevitably some will be overlooked and others may feel their contribution is ignored or slighted. This is an effort to break down the walls of silence, and, as in war, one does the best one can with the information at hand.

I am indebted to many people—to Rangers Jack Cambra and Richard Pittenger, who provided morning report data; to Ranger Herm Boldt and his wife Lois, who devoted years of their lives to finding our comrades, and to Barney Gill, who so ably assisted them. Ranger Howard K. Davis taught me the wonders of word processing and, with his wife Nancy, provided enthusiastic support. Rangers Andrew Bartlett, Bob Channon, Horton Coker, Emmett Fike, Frank Forbes, Ralph Puckett, and Larry Thibodeaux provided much useful information.

Also of great assistance were the staffs of the United States Army Military History Institute, Carlisle Barracks, Pennsylvania; the Center for Military History in Washington, D.C.; and the modern Military Field Branch of the National Archives in Suitland, Maryland.

And finally, my thanks to the Korean War Rangers who provided cassette tapes or letters of their Ranger memories.

Robert W. Black
Willow Crossing House
18 November 1985

Introduction

When used in its military sense, *Ranger* is an American word. The Ranger came into being when early settlers in the New World found that in order to survive they had to blend European discipline and weaponry with the knowledge the American Indian had of distance, terrain, and the tactics of the raid. Since the early 1600s the name Ranger has been woven into the fabric of American history.

The Rangers have always been few in number. An all-volunteer force, they specialize in combat behind enemy lines, performing long-range reconnaissance, ambushes, and raids. They have often been used as shock troops or "Spearheaders" to lead assaults.

During the Korean War these men, who for three centuries went into action by land and water, added a new dimension by also going into battle from the air. Eighteen Ranger companies were formed during the Korean War. Seventeen of these companies were parachutists, or "Airborne" in Army parlance. Seven companies fought in Korea, the mix being one 112-man Ranger company to an infantry division of seventeen to twenty thousand men. The Rangers did "out front" work: scouting, patrolling, raids, and spearheads. These men destroyed an enemy division headquarters, made the first combat jump in Ranger history, and participated in the first defeat of Chinese forces during the war. When the U.N. forces in Korea numbered over 500,000 men, less then 700 Rangers were fighting to the front of every American infantry division on line. They were volunteers for the Army, the Airborne, the Rangers, and for combat. It was dangerous work, and the companies suffered from forty to ninety percent casualties. One of the companies was the only all-black Ranger unit the Army has ever had.

This is their history. How they came to be, their organization and training, their performance in training and combat, and the long-lasting effect these men have had on the U.S. Army.

Chapter 1

In the dark early morning hours of Sunday, 25 June 1950, soldiers of the Republic of Korea huddled at their positions near the 38th parallel. The summer monsoon was beginning; the night rains had been heavy, and the men looked forward to the rising of the sun. Many did not live to see it. At 0400 hours flashes on the horizon heralded the arrival of a new and much more devastating storm—a slashing hail of shrapnel followed by the thunder of Soviet-built T-34 tanks.

A highly trained army of 90,000 North Koreans, well equipped by their Soviet backers and supported by armor and air, fell upon a poorly trained South Korean force of 65,000 men, ill equipped by their American sponsors and without armor or air support.

The Korean War had begun.

The ancient land that was destined to become a battlefield was somewhat equivalent in size to Great Britain or the state of Minnesota. The Korean peninsula, which projects southward from Manchuria, is 500 miles long with a width that varies from 125 to 200 miles, bounded on the east by the Sea of Japan, on the west by the Yellow Sea, and on the south by the Korean Strait. At its southern tip Korea is within 120 miles of Japan.

Seasonal reversal of the direction of the prevailing wind gives Korea long, cold winters and hot and humid summers, with a monsoon season that lasts from June until September. The terrain is difficult to traverse, often impassable to wheeled and tracked vehicles. Less than eighteen percent is flatland, space that is primarily used as rice paddies which, when flooded, swallow an infantryman's boot in deep mud. Most of the rivers flow swiftly. Korea is a rugged, mountainous country whose peaks rise to nine thousand feet, with slopes that are steep and collared with offshooting razorback ridges. To the infantryman, travel in Korea seemed a continuous climb.

From A.D. 935 to 1932 the Koryo Dynasty (which gave the country its western name) ruled, but because of its proximity to China and Japan, Korea suffered frequent invasion. In 1910 Korea was annexed by Japan. In 1945, following the unconditional surrender of the Japanese, Korea was occupied by U.S. forces for six days.

At the close of World War II the mood in the United States was that with the advent of peace, military preparedness was no longer needed. The American military was emasculated. To the men in the Kremlin the end of World War II presented an opportunity to continue the march toward world communism. This goal was furthered when, in 1949, Chinese Communist armies under Mao Tse-Tung crushed the Nationalist Army forces of Chiang Kai-Shek and drove them from the mainland.

While these ominous events were developing to the north, Korea found itself a house divided. Despite agreeing that Korea should be free and independent, Soviet leadership had long since trained the Korean Communist cadre that was to do the bidding of Moscow.

To Americans (anxious to return to civilian pursuits) the major problem regarding Korea seemed to be the determination of a line north of which the Russians would accept Japanese surrender, while U.S. forces took the surrender in the south. The line agreed upon had no relationship to terrain or military position; it was lifted from the surface of a map, a device used by map markers to show degrees of latitude on the earth's surface. The ancient land and its people were divided by an imaginary line known as the 38th parallel.[1]

Soon, however, this imaginary line became brutal reality. While the north contained the smaller number of people—nine million, as opposed to twenty-one million inhabitants in the south—it also held the industry that was critical to the prosperity of the agricultural south. The Communists began to turn the 38th parallel into a barrier behind which their cadre could develop a military power capable of uniting the Korean peninsula on Communist terms. The seizure of Korea would be a major step in ousting American influence from Japan, and could eventually lead to a Communist Asia.

In the summer of 1948 governments were formed on both sides of the 38th parallel, with Syngman Rhee elected president in the south and Kim Il Sung established as premier in the north. Throughout the remainder of 1948 and 1949, tensions between the north and south continued to increase; Communist-inspired uprisings continually flared in the South and border problems were frequent. On 30 June 1949 all major U.S. forces, with the exception of a military advisory group consisting of approximately five hundred men, were withdrawn from South Korea. On 10 June 1950 the North Koreans proposed to the United Nations that unifying elections be held to select a legislature representative of both the north and the south. Fifteen days after that proposal, the North Koreans, claiming they had been attacked, suddenly launched an invasion. Within three days of crossing the 38th parallel, they had seized the South Korean capitol of Seoul. The South Korean Army had no armor and no heavy artillery or air power with which to oppose them.

With the Soviets absent due to a boycott by their delegation, the United Nations was able to take action. On 27 June 1950 the Security Council passed a cease-fire resolution and directed the North Koreans to withdraw. The directive went unheeded by the north. With South Korean forces in a desperate situation, President Harry S. Truman ordered U.S. Naval and Air Forces to support the South Koreans. Early hopes that air and sea power would suffice were quickly dashed. The ferocious North Korean attack was aided by an incredible blunder by the South Korean military.[2] Critical bridges over the Han River were destroyed by the South Koreans, denying their own forces a route of withdrawal. Large numbers of South Korean soldiers and the bulk of their heavy equipment were lost as a result.

On July 1, 406 men of the 24th Infantry Division arrived in Korea from Japan, the vanguard of the American army. On July 5, near Osan, the small force of Americans engaged an enemy force of superior numbers supported by T-34 tanks equipped with 85mm guns. After a brief, valiant fight, the Americans were driven from position. This began a series of delaying actions as newly arriving, ill-equipped and ill-trained American garrison forces from Japan were thrown into the fight.

On July 7 the U.N. agreed to a unified command in Korea to be controlled by the United States, the principal supplier of men and material. Gen. Douglas MacArthur was appointed Supreme Commander.

From the outset the North Koreans proved skilled at infiltration, and took full advantage of agents and guides planted prior to the war or raised from dissident factions. Americans had difficulty identifying friend from foe as refugees flooded the roads. North Korean units, sometimes dressed in civilian garb, would filter around or through American positions, reassemble, then strike from the rear or at objectives farther south.

By July 8 the North Koreans were at the 37th parallel and more American forces were arriving, including the 25th Infantry Division and the 1st Cavalry Division from Japan. On July 13 Gen. Walton H. Walker took command of the American Eighth Army, but inexorably, American and South Korean forces were pressed southward and eastward.

Mid-July found the remainder of the 24th Infantry, the 25th Infantry, and 1st Cavalry divisions in Korea employing troops more accustomed to garrison than the field in a desperate bid to stop the North Korean advance. By the end of the month the Americans and South Koreans had been pushed into the Naktong perimeter—a defensive line along the Naktong river—where four ROK and three U.S. divisions faced eleven North Korean divisions. By 1 August 1950 the North Koreans had cleared the eastern half of the peninsula and bathed their feet in the waters at the southern tip of Korea.

While being forced into a shrinking perimeter, the U.N. forces fought off attack after attack, losing territory but using the advantage of interior lines while building up ground, naval, and air forces. It was a race, with the North Koreans trying to drive the United Nations Forces into the sea before the American buildup, pouring men and material into the deep-water port of Pusan on the southeast tip of Korea, that could succeed.

Both sides were beset by problems. Americans who had suddenly been taken from the soft garrison life to a desperate battlefield situation were further confused when their president kept referring to the fighting as "police action" or a "conflict," unwilling to call Korea the bloody war that it was. The American people were equally confused. There was a general lack of interest on the part of the public.

The North Koreans, originally bold, became hesitant and more tentative in their attacks as resistance increased. The 2nd Infantry Division, a brigade of Marines, and the 5th Regimental Combat Team arrived within the first three days of August, and the British would be coming, their 27th Brigade arriving from Hong Kong toward the end of the month. But still the world waited, expecting to hear at any moment that the Americans had been driven into the sea and Korea conquered by the Communists. The U.N. forces were fighting within an ever shrinking perimeter while hundreds of thousands of refugees, infiltrated by North Korean soldiers disguised as civilians, flooded the roads to Pusan. Enemy infiltration, rear-area sniping, and attacks continued while the defensive perimeter shrank and an understandable eagerness to take the offensive prevailed in American headquarters. One expression of this spirit was a call for volunteers for hazardous duty. A company of Rangers was about to be formed.

Chapter 2

At the outbreak of the Korean War the United States Army was a brown-shoe army, an army of khaki uniforms in summer and wool, olive drab, in winter. Haircuts were twenty-five cents and a stamp three cents, recruits earned seventy-five dollars, and a master sergeant with over thirty years' service had a base pay of $294 a month. The Army resembled the false-front Main Street of a frontier town on a Hollywood movie set, gutted by a nation that less than a decade after Pearl Harbor had forgotten the lessons of unpreparedness. It was an army that consisted of only eight divisions, whose regiments were short of manpower, equipment, and training funds. Where the Germans and Japanese failed, the U.S. Congress succeeded; the mighty American army of 1945 was stripped to bare bones by 1950.

It was an army looking back to past victories, confident that American initiative would prevail in the future. Being unprepared for war was an American tradition fully observed in the summer and fall of 1950; once again thousands of young men would trade their lives for time. War had come swiftly, and as in the past, men hurried to rectify the mistake of being unready.

Under a warm July sun Lt. Col. (later Brigadier General) John Hugh McGee reported for duty with Headquarters, Eighth United States Army at Taegu, Korea.[1] Thousands of refugees sought shelter in the city, enemy patrols had reached the edge of the airfield, and Communist agents were marking targets inside the city, firing flares by which observers could adjust artillery. Shortly, the North Koreans would break through the defenses between Taegu and Pohang known as the Naktong perimeter, on the east coast of Korea. Eighth Army staff labeled the area of intrusion "the Pohang pocket."

Assigned to Eighth Army G-3 Operations, McGee was ordered to prepare a study for the conduct of guerrilla operations in North Korea; this soon became an instruction to organize a unit for operations behind enemy lines in the Pohang pocket. His background had prepared him well for the assignment. A 1931 graduate of the United States Military Academy, McGee was in the Philippines when the Japanese attacked Pearl Harbor and was serving in southeastern Mindanao when surrender came. Two years a prisoner of war, McGee escaped from a prison ship in the Basilan Strait, joined a guerrilla organization, and subsequently took charge of a group of survivors from a torpedoed Japanese prison ship. McGee was evacuated by submarine and closed out his World War II experience as commanding officer of the 169th Infantry, 43rd Division.

While passing through Japan en route to assignment in Korea, he had been involved in the screening of Army volunteers for special missions. Now McGee returned to Japan and the replacement depot at Camp Drake armed with a Table of Organization and equipment for a WWII Ranger company. He was looking for young officers with leadership ability and the volunteer spirit. McGee selected Lt. Ralph Puckett, Jr. of Tifton, Georgia, as company commander of the new unit.[2] "Puck," as he was known to his classmates, was tall, slender as a reed, an accomplished boxer, and so anxious to be a Ranger that he told McGee he would serve as a squad leader if necessary to get accepted. The World War II organization of a Ranger company called for two platoons. Lt. Charles N. Bunn of Springfield, Illinois, would head the first platoon; Lt. Bernard Cummings, Jr. of Denver, Colorado, the second. Though short on experience, these young officers were all 1949 graduates of West Point and had vitality—they would need it, for in the next several weeks of organization there was little time for sleep.

McGee's instructions to Puckett were to screen men of service units and those in the replacement stream. Infantry units in the Far East had sufficient problems trying to fill their own ranks, and McGee had already selected sixty likely candidates. Feeling like characters in a Kipling story, the three lieutenants began seeking out men for their as-yet-unnamed unit. Hundreds of personnel records were screened, and this review, if found favorable, would result in a man being called to a group interview.

The meeting would begin with the statement, "If you are not willing to volunteer for anything dangerous, you are free to leave the room now." That was sufficient to deter a third of the soldiers called. Those who remained were interviewed on an individual basis, cautioned not to discuss the interview, and dismissed. The process of separating men from their parent units would then begin. It took a week for orders to be prepared and forwarded, restricting the volunteers to their current assignments to await further orders. A relative few of those interviewed received orders to report to Camp Drake.

A small staff had been working under McGee's direction, gathering supplies, weapons, and ammunition; with men and material coming together, it was time to give birth to the organization. General Orders 237 from Headquarters, Eighth Army, dated 24 August 1950, officially formed the unit with the designation Eighth Army Ranger Company and authorized strength of three officers and seventy-three enlisted men. Physical training began immediately. While the three young lieutenants had little troop experience, they were all graduates of the Airborne school, and as rated paratroopers, they understood the importance of fitness. That there were other paratroopers within the company, as well as men who had earned the Combat Infantryman's Badge in World War II, made the task slightly easier. Cpl. Earl Cronin of Ohio had fought in Europe, meeting the Russians at the end of the war; Cpl. Harland F. Morrissey had fought as a member of the 1st Marine Parachute Battalion and earned a Silver Star. There were also men who had little experience in the infantry: PFC William Judy had been a mechanic in an engineer unit, Cpl. George Mikez came from duty with a signal depot. Experienced or not, trained or not, the volunteer spirit brought the men together.

On August 26 the men received assignments to platoons, and the rigorous physical training resulted in one man being returned to his former unit, the first of several men who failed in training. On August 28 the company departed Camp Drake by train en route to Camp Mower near the port city of Sasebo. On September 1 the company boarded the Japanese ferry *Koan Maru* and sailed for Pusan, Korea.

Chapter 3

The tide that flows also ebbs, and early September found Maj. Gen. William Kean's 25th Division punishing North Korean forces in battle at Masan. The North Koreans sustained some 12,000 casualties. On August 15, the U.S. X Corps landed 170 miles behind North Korean lines at Inchon, and the following day the U.N. forces rose from the perimeter at Pusan and began to push back the stunned and shattered North Korean Army. Linkup between the breakout forces of Eighth Army and X Corps occurred at Suwon on August 26.

The morning of September 2 the Eighth Army Rangers were in Pusan, where, after a three-hour wait, they boarded a vintage Korean train that wheezed and puffed steam from every pore but successfully brought them to a rendezvous with trucks. The men were driven to an isolated area south of a small village named Kijang, where they established their camp on a hill, one they would become so familiar with, they would dub it "Ranger Hill." Under the command of Colonel McGee, the Eighth Army Ranger Training Center was established. Seven weeks were allocated to training, at the end of which time the company was to be prepared to undertake the following missions:

 a. Raids
 b. Reconnaissance patrolling
 c. Combat patrolling
 d. Motorized detachment
 e. Trail blocks

Training was continuous, lasting from before dawn until long after sunset. As garrison fat turned to muscle, more men left the unit. A few others were accepted. One was James Beatty, known as "the Flea" because of his small stature. Beatty would become Ralph Puckett's driver and radio operator. No vehicles were initially provided, however—the Eighth Army Ranger Company was not authorized vehicles, nor did they have a unit mess, being dependent on a nearby battalion for their food.

While men of the Eighth Army Ranger Company sweated on Ranger Hill, other events were occurring at General Headquarters, United Nations command. By General Order 7, dated 5 September 1950, an organization named the Special Activities Group was formed. One of the missions the activating order gave the unit's commanding officer was to organize, train, and prepare for employment a group of specially qualified United Nations Command units and individuals for such raiding, commando, intelligence, and other operations as might be directed by the commander-in-chief. Col. Louis B. Ely, an artillery officer, was appointed commanding officer. Units attached to his command were:

a. Provisional Raider Company, Headquarters and Service Group, General Headquarters, Far East command (approximately 300 men)
b. Royal Marine Commando, United Kingdom (It would be the 41st, with 225 men.)
c. Royal Navy Volunteer Group, United Kingdom (twelve men)
d. United States Marine Corps Provisional Raider Company, Fleet Marine Forces, Pacific (203 men)

The units of the Special Activities group would undergo sixty days of intensive training at Camp McGill near Yokosuka, Japan, where they would be joined by approximately three hundred selected South Koreans for training in raids and guerrilla operations. They served well as part of the cover and deception plan for the Inchon invasion when they were used in the Kunsan area in the first days of battle.

* * *

The incredible success of the North Korean Army at infiltration caused concern at the highest levels of the U.S. Army. The North Koreans had obscured the rules of war. In a nation of refugees, every man, woman, and child was a potential spy, saboteur, or disguised member of a military unit. Infiltration was constant; large bands of pre-positioned guerrillas roamed the rear area establishing ambushes and roadblocks and assassinating South Korean leaders.

The implications were not lost on Army Chief of Staff J. Lawton Collins. On return from his August 1950 visit to Korea and Japan, where he attended General MacArthur's Inchon invasion conference, Collins sent a memorandum to the Department of the Army G-3—who was the general staff officer responsible for plans, operations, and training. The document reviewed North Korean success by infiltration and set forth the need to establish a test organization to provide American forces a similar capability. His command guidance placed restrictions on unit size and organizational employment, instructing the staff to plan for one company per division.[1] The mission was "to infiltrate through enemy lines and attack command posts, artillery, tank parks, and key communications centers or facilities." Supply and administration, the document stated, should be held to a minimum, and unit size should not exceed one hundred men. Those selected were to be volunteers of high intelligence. Organized into three platoons, each consisting of three squads of ten men each, the company would be armed with light, automatic weapons, with machine-gun-mounted jeeps to provide maximum mobility. Collins's memo had been titled, "Organization of Marauder Companies." Study by the staff resulted in the elimination of the jeeps and the requirement that the unit be Airborne, and the name was changed from Marauder to Ranger.

The uncoordinated efforts by the Eighth Army in Korea, the United Nations Command in Japan, and the Department of the Army in Washington, were a knee-jerk response to the North Korean success at operations behind U.N. lines. There was not a U.S. Army plan or doctrine at the beginning of the Korean War for a school or even a unit at cadre strength that would specialize in a form of warfare Americans had excelled at since the seventeenth century—the raid.[2]

In a 30 November 1950 interview with famed radio commentator Elmer Davis, General Collins called fighting in Korea

". . . a throwback to old-time warfare more comparable to that of our frontier Indian days fighting than to modern war."

Davis asked, "Do these tactics require revision in the tactical training of our own troops or is Korea a special case?"

General Collins replied:

"Well, we have learned some new lessons in Korea, although in general our own tactical doctrines have proved eminently sound. One of the changes that we found necessary as a result of the Korean experience is a reactivation of Ranger units. A Ranger unit is a group of specially trained men designed to infiltrate within enemy positions. This is one of the major tactical developments, in my judgment, out of this war: the successful use of specially trained and designed Korean units to infiltrate back of our lines, attack command posts, artillery positions, communications centers. We are going to do the same thing, and we have already put in motion the organization of special units of that character. General MacArthur had done so on his own initiative, of course, at once, and we picked it up here at home and are aiding now in the development of such units, which we are sending to Korea as rapidly as they are trained."

As the three officers and sixty-three enlisted men of the Eighth Army Ranger Company sweated in simulated combat patrols that at any moment could become reality, the war moved at a rapid pace.

Sometimes in panic, sometimes grudgingly, the U.N. forces retreated until they were fighting in a perimeter the size of the city of Los Angeles. In the early days of the war it was the Russian T-34 tanks that seemed unstoppable.[3] But American air and naval power bought time and reduced the number of enemy tanks available for combat. At the same time, by ship and by plane, young American soldiers arrived—some just recruits barely out of basic training—and were hurriedly issued weapons that were often still in cosmoline, and without time for indoctrination or training, were thrown into battle. It was a meat grinder, and they paid a terrible price, but they lived up to their commander's words. The Eighth Army commander, Gen. Walton Walker, had announced his resolve, saying ". . . there will be no more retreating, withdrawal, or readjustment of the lines or any other term you choose . . .'' and by September 15 the area known as the Pusan perimeter contained a force anxious to break out, anxious to be the hammer on the anvil of the Inchon invasion.

The plan to destroy the North Korean Army had been formulated in the mind of General MacArthur in the first week of the North Korean invasion. On a hill overlooking Seoul, MacArthur, recognizing that ground must be traded for time, conceived the possibility of using American air and naval forces and his own great experience in amphibious warfare in an end run. The operation would strike deep in the rear of the North Korean Army, severing their logistical umbilical cord and placing the enemy between the U.N. forces landing at Inchon and those breaking out from the Pusan perimeter. The objections of the Joint Chiefs of Staff and his own advisers did not deter him. A student of military history, he remembered Wolfe's audacious and victorious strike against Montcalm on the heights of Quebec in 1759. If the staff felt it could not be done, thought MacArthur, so the enemy was likely to reason. On 15 September 1950 the invasion at the port of Inchon began.

While the guns of Joint Task Force Seven pounded Inchon, an officer was reporting to the chief of staff, Office of the Chief of Army Field Forces, Fort Monroe, Virginia. Col. John Gibson Van Houten had been personally selected by General Collins to head the new Ranger training program.[4]

Born 11 March 1904 at Macon, Georgia, Van Houten received his education at the University of Georgia at Athens, graduating in 1926 with a degree in Agriculture and a commission as a 2nd lieutenant in the cavalry reserve. The same year, he was commissioned in the regular Army, Infantry. In the years preceding World War II he served with various Infantry regiments in New York, the Philippines, and Texas. He also had three years of duty with the Civilian Conservation Corps. With the outbreak of World War II he served in combat with the 9th Infantry Division as chief of staff, regimental commander, and assistant division commander. At the outbreak of the Korean War he was serving on the faculty of the Command and General Staff College and Army War College at Fort Leavenworth, Kansas.

Van Houten was an able officer but without experience in Ranger operations. That experience came in the form of the executive officer appointed by Department of the Army, Col. Edwin Walker.[5] Walker had served as a regimental commander in the 1st Special Service Force, a special operations unit that had distinguished itself during World War II. His bravery and devotion to his men was widely recognized. Walker was a combat soldier with little interest in garrison protocol. One officer said Walker did not care if the barracks were filled with trash cans, it was how things went in the field that mattered.

On September 17 Walker joined Van Houten at Fort Monroe, and after two days of joint briefings, they separated, Van Houten traveling to Washington, D.C., to make further arrangements, and Walker going to Fort Benning, Georgia, to do the same. It was a crash program, necessitated by the rapid pace of the war. Fort Benning was the logical location as it was the center of infantry activities, the home of the infantry school. While arrangements were made for barracks and training areas, personnel records were being screened for those who had served with the six Ranger battalions or the 1st Special Service Force or the 5307th Composite Unit Provisional (Merrill's Marauders) during World War II. Men were sought who could use their experience to put together the toughest training course in the Army. As leaders were being selected, the call went out for volunteers to serve as Rangers. The requirement that these be qualified Airborne personnel narrowed the selection base. The 11th Airborne Division at Fort Campbell, Kentucky, had been significantly reduced in strength to fill the 187th Airborne Regimental Combat Team for duty in Korea, so the 82nd Airborne Division at Fort Bragg, North Carolina, became the ideal recruiting pool.

Signs at Fort Bragg named the 82nd Airborne Division "America's Guard of Honor." It was common knowledge among the men that if war came, the 82nd would be the first to fight; that was why most of them were in the 82nd. The movie *Battleground*, a story of the Battle of the Bulge, had recently played at the post theater, exciting the imagination, but for the young, well-conditioned, and motivated paratrooper, there was little to do—men had their fights and frolics at Combat Alley in the town of Fayetteville, or if without funds, as most young soldiers usually were, stayed in the barracks. Sitting on wooden footlockers at the end of steel cots, they polished their Corcoran jump boots again and again. The boots were a badge of achievement. The rag, the water, and Kiwi polish were an intimate part of barracks life; men polished and talked about when the orders would come to go to war. The orders did not come, and each day the band would parade the division area playing the division fight song that began, "We're all-American and proud to be. We are the Soldiers of Liberty." Men went to training or pulled guard duty or "ash and trash" detail or sweated in the mess halls on K.P. War offered a chance to escape the routine of garrison life. When the news came that the North Koreans had invaded South Korea, the men reacted with enthusiasm at the prospect of mobilization, but the 82nd did not move.

The young, eager soldiers were not aware that though the American army had been gutted by the demands of war in Korea, Europe rested uneasily under the threat of invasion by a massive Soviet Army that had not been demobilized. The 82nd Airborne Division was the strategic reserve that the United States held back from Korea in case Europe again became a battleground. But the men of the 11th and 82nd Airborne Divisions were not prepared to wait for action that might never come. With the announcement that Airborne Ranger units were being formed for combat, and volunteers were needed, long lines formed—in the 82nd Airborne Division estimates ran as high as five thousand volunteers. These were regular Army soldiers, men who had volunteered for the Army and the Airborne. They had a wide variety of skills as light and heavy weapons infantrymen, and some served in artillery, or signal corps, or medical units. They brought to the Rangers a wide experience that would enable them to instruct each other and to overcome problems beyond the skills of most units.[6]

Many of the original officers were volunteers, but some were not. A few were shunted off from replacement depots or from units that did not want them. One gallant officer, who was later killed in action, was sent to the Rangers because he had received a parking ticket.

The interviews with the enlisted volunteers were conducted by officers chosen but a few hours earlier to serve as Ranger company commanders. As in colonial times, Ranger officers themselves selected the men they would lead in combat. They were pleasantly surprised to find that a number of noncommissioned officers had combat experience from World War II. There were privates, twenty and twenty-one years old, who had already served a three-year hitch in the Army or Marines. Their boyhood had occurred during a time of great national patriotism; service was expected, and the services did not make an extensive age check. Some Ranger volunteers in World War II had packed an unused razor and faced the recruiter at age sixteen.

Goaded by the spur of war, the selection process moved with incredible swiftness. On September 20, just five days after Van Houten had received his orders, the first group of volunteers arrived at Fort Benning. The facilities of the Infantry School were used to establish a Ranger training "section," but a message and verbal orders from the commanding general of the Third Army resulted in the organization of the Ranger Training Center (Airborne), 3340th Army Service Unit, effective 29 September 1950.

The headquarters detachment was established with a strength of twenty-two officers and thirty-four enlisted men. Also activated on the 29th were the 1st, 2nd, 3rd, and 4th Ranger infantry companies (Airborne). Unlike the Eighth Army Ranger Company which was initially a Table of Distribution unit (usually organized for temporary usage within a theater), these companies would be the lineal descendants of Ranger units of World War II—the 1st Ranger Infantry Company from Company A, of the 1st Ranger Infantry Battalion; 2nd Company from Company A, 2nd Ranger Battalion; 3rd and 4th companies respectively from companies A of the 3rd and 4th Ranger battalions. This practice would continue with each of the fifteen Ranger infantry companies (Airborne) designated as Table of Organization and Equipment units (see Appendix A).

Chapter 4

The exhilaration of victory was in the air as U.N. forces drove in hot pursuit after the fleeing North Koreans. By October 10 the allies were across the 38th parallel. On the east coast, Wonsan fell, by October 18, Hamhung and Hungnam were taken, and the following day the North Korean capitol of Pyongyang.

But suddenly the victory march hit a sour note. The Chinese had warned that an advance by anyone but Koreans past the 38th parallel would trigger their involvement. The threat was not taken seriously by General MacArthur or, indeed, by the governments of the United Nations forces. Chinese involvement now was possible, but considered too late to be effective. The opportunity was at hand to settle the Korean question. The United Nations now intended to drive to the Yalu River and reunite Korea.

At the same time a Ranger reorganization was at hand in Korea. General Order 106, issued by Headquarters, Eighth Army on 8 October 1950, changed the designation of the Eighth Army Ranger Company to the Eighth Army Ranger Company, 8213th Army unit. The company was also reorganized under Table of Distribution 301–1498, 19 September 1950, with three officers and seventy-four enlisted men. A Table of Distribution unit is considered a temporary unit organized in-theater. It has no lineage, and its campaigns and honors could not accrue to the Rangers. This action would cause much resentment in the years to come.

At the Ranger Training Center, Fort Benning, Georgia, train-

ing began on 2 October 1950 for nineteen officers and 314 enlisted men. These were organized into three companies and were
comprised of men whose race was listed as "white." On October 9 another company consisting of five officers and 135 enlisted men began training—this unit was comprised of "negro"
Airborne volunteers. Initially designated as the 4th Company,
it would be redesignated as the 2nd. It would be the only black
Ranger unit in the history of the Unites States Army.[1]

Company commanders were assigned as follows:

1st Ranger Company	Capt. John Striegel
2nd Ranger Company	1st Lt. Warren E. Allen
3rd Ranger Company	Capt. Jesse M. Tidwell
4th Ranger Company	Capt. Dorsey B. Anderson

A Ranger company was initially intended to have a strength
of five officers and 110 men. Table of Organization and Equipment number 7–87 dated 17 October 1950 set the authorization
(with augmentation) at five officers and 107 enlisted men. By
comparison, line infantry companies of the period had six officers and 212 men. Each Ranger company was organized into a
company headquarters and three rifle platoons of thirty-three
men each. All platoons were further divided into a platoon headquarters and three squads each of ten men. Normal squad armament was two Browning Automatic Rifles, four M-1 rifles, and
four M-2 carbines.[2] Thirty-six submachine guns (.45-caliber)
were also available for issue. Crew-served weapons were in
abundance, including nine 3.5-inch rocket launchers; nine
60mm mortars; three .30-caliber, air-cooled machine guns; and
three 57mm recoilless rifles. Crew-served weapons were kept
at company level and issued according to mission requirements.
Such armament produced a volume of firepower that line infantry units would later marvel at, but the men learned quickly that
it was muscle power that carried this prodigious weaponry and
the vast amount of ammunition it required.

The Ranger Training Center was established eight miles from
the main post area, near Harmony Church. The infantry center
provided administrative support and, for three days, the instructors. Soon men with Ranger experience from World War II be-

gan to arrive—Maj. George Monsarrat, Maj. Jack Street, Capt. Jack Snyder, and TSgt. Joseph Cournoyer were among these.[3] Lt. Col. Samuel Cromwell was assigned as adjutant, and Lt. Col. Henry Koepcke would be the director of training. Infantry instructors also began to arrive. Maj. Herman Zimmerman ("Powder-Happy Herman"), a bemedaled combat engineer from WWII, taught demolitions in a manner that made the subject a favorite of the Rangers. When Rangers arrived for the class, Zimmerman would set off explosive charges around them—a powerful attention-getting device. The initial training cycle was set at six weeks. What began as a forty-eight-hour training week quickly rose to sixty hours, not including time for maintenance of equipment and weapons. Training was rigorous: demolitions, sabotage, land navigation, hand-to-hand combat, communications, U.S. and foreign weapons, artillery, and air and naval fire support were blended with constant physical challenge. The day began with a five-mile run and calisthenics. Long-distance marching with full equipment was routine; fatigue jackets would turn black with perspiration and the body salt would crystallize on the cloth. Drinking water was discouraged—it was considered a mark of manliness to come back with a full canteen.[4] Van Houten's goal with such strenuous training was "to prepare a company to move from forty to fifty miles cross-country in twelve to eighteen hours, depending upon the terrain."[5]

Exhaustion was a soldier's constant companion, and there was loud complaint from muscles that had taken previous training in stride. A quarter-ton truck with a white flag attached followed close behind the sweating Rangers. If a man felt the training was beyond his capability, he had only to go sit in the vehicle—no questions were asked or comments made. He would be driven away and his belongings moved from the Ranger barracks before the company returned. No one was forced to be a Ranger, the desire had to come from within. Those who failed were returned to the Airborne division from whence they came. Van Houten's staff, many of whom were familiar with the drop-out rate in Airborne training, had allowed a thirty percent over strength. It would be needed, as there were also injuries that reduced strength.

Occasionally morning classes were held indoors, but these were a rarity; Rangering is an outdoor experience. The bark of

commands before dawn, the Ranger yell, the crunch of boots
striking gravel in unison—these were the choral sounds in the
Ranger area. Swinging out on a long march, the singers of each
platoon would break into "Jodie Cadence" and the men would
respond as one:

"You had a good home but you left."
"You're right!"

Competition was the first law of the Ranger Training Center.
From company commander to rear-rank private, everyone was
convinced their company was superior in every way to any other
company. Platoons vied with one another, as did squads within
the platoons, yet the magic of being a Ranger brought instantaneous cooperation when required. Things were different in the
Rangers. Gone were the Friday-night G.I. parties to scrub the
barracks floor and latrines. Gone were the standby inspections
with cardboard-stiff uniforms. In the Rangers each man took
care of his own area and equipment; if it wasn't as it should be,
he was shamed or dismissed. Ranger officers were also different
from those of other units. When the 8th Airborne Rangers were
issued weapons in cosmoline, the company officers worked side
by side with the men until the weapons were clean. By not
holding Friday-night G.I. parties and Saturday-morning standby
inspection, the men were able to don full field equipment and
spend more time on long-distance speed marches.

On a long night march, one young Ranger was roused from
sleep by bright lights and found himself leaning forward against
the bumper of a 2½-ton truck that had stopped on the road to
keep from running over him. The rest of the company had properly concealed themselves in the roadside ditches. His face red
under camouflage paint, the Ranger hurried to join his comrades.

The men were proud of being volunteers, those who sought
a challenge, and the most frequent response to the question
"Why do you want to be a Ranger?" was, "I want to be part
of the best."

November 1950. At the movies one could see John Wayne
and Maureen O'Hara in *Rio Grande*, Randolph Scott and Ruth
Roman starring in *Colt 45*, and Bob Hope and Lucille Ball mak-

ing people laugh in *Fancy Pants*. On the radio one could hear the controversial Drew Pearson or the the rapid-fire news delivery of Walter Winchell. Louella Parsons provided the gossip from Hollywood.

Those few Rangers who had access to a newspaper would have found themselves described in glowing terms. They were known as "the Army's happy hatchetmen," "the Masters of stealth," "an Army Bowery brawler," and "Rougher then a stucco bathtub."

The training schedule brought more sweat then ego satisfaction. A typical day's schedule:

> A.M.—Company day attack w/air and artillery
> P.M.—Company day attack w/air and artillery
> Night—Company ground raid
> Company night airborne raid
> Company return to friendly lines

(Travel to and from training areas by foot march)

"What is an Airborne Ranger?" asked a letter from home.
"Tired," was the response.

A popular saying among the men was, "It doesn't matter, I'm going to be sick anyway."

On November 13, with the first training cycle completed, General Burress (commander of the infantry center) and Colonel Van Houten faced the initial four Airborne Ranger companies on French Field, made their congratulatory remarks, and awarded Ranger shoulder insignia to each company commander to issue to the men. General Burress presented a Ranger guidon to the 1st Ranger Company. Like the units, the guidon was unique, featuring the parachute and the word *Ranger*.

Initial planning had called for one Ranger company to be supplied to each infantry division in Korea. There was great emphasis on getting a test Airborne Ranger company into battle, whose success in Korea would result in a policy review regarding the others. On 19 October 1950 the deployments branch of the operations division of the Department of the Army G-3 had directed one of the initial four Airborne Ranger companies to be assigned to Korea, two to Europe, and one to remain at

Benning to help train new Rangers. The Chinese entry into the war changed these priorities.

Five officers and 119 men of the 1st Ranger Company departed Fort Benning by train for the San Francisco Port of Embarkation on November 15. The 72nd Army Band played them off to war, concluding with the song "Now Is the Hour." As the train was departing, a vehicle pulled alongside with a member of the staff who had some good news for Sgt. Reginald King—his wife had just given birth to a baby girl.

On the following day the Ranger Training Center made preparations to receive trainees into the 5th, 6th, 7th, and 8th Companies, and company commanders were assigned to each unit. The 5th Ranger Company was commanded by Capt. John C. Scagnelli, the 6th by Capt. James S. Cain, the 7th by Capt. Robert W. Eikenberry, and the 8th by Capt. James A. Herbert.[6] An extra platoon of forty-four black enlisted men and two officers would be assigned to 8th Company. While preparations were made for the new companies, 2nd and 4th companies conducted showdown inspections and training on foreign weapons.

The first large increment of volunteers arrived at 0600 on November 23, Thanksgiving Day, at the Columbus, Georgia, railway station from Fort Bragg. For the next two days the men who would comprise the second training cycle hastened to complete administrative processing. The training cycle began on November 27 with physical and weapons training; 2nd and 4th companies continued preparations for overseas shipment and received replacements from 3rd Company, which would remain behind to assist in demonstration and training details.

In Korea training time for the Eighth Army Ranger Company had been cut short by the breakout of United Nations forces from the Pusan perimeter; the war seemed to be hurrying to a close, and every man available that could hasten that purpose was needed. On October 8 lieutenants Puckett, Bunn, and Cummings had been promoted to 1st lieutenant, and two days later Lieutenant Puckett was leading a quartering party to the Tropic Lightning Division. The Eighth Army Rangers would come under 25th Infantry Division control at Taejon.[7]

Sweeping northward rapidly, the United Nations forces were leaving behind them pockets of enemy resistance. It would be the mission of the Eighth Army Rangers to track down and eliminate the enemy that remained in the vicinity of Taejon. Approximately thirty-two miles from Taejon the Rangers joined the 25th Division Reconnaissance Company at the village of Poun and commenced operations. Lieutenant Bunn's 1st platoon established a base at a nearby hamlet, while Lieutenant Cummings's 2nd platoon and the company headquarters operated from Poun. Working closely with the 25th Division Reconnaissance Company, the Ranger platoons engaged in active patrolling and began capturing demoralized enemy soldiers. A strong sense of comradeship quickly emerged. On October 17 a South Korean police unit, unaware that the Rangers were operating in the area, opened fire on a Ranger patrol. Cpl. Harutoku Kimura had the unwanted distinction of being the first Ranger casualty of the war. The wound to his arm was slight and he soon returned to duty.

Chapter 5

As November began, the U.N. soldiers pushed on into ever higher mountains where the cold was becoming a serious hardship, an unrelenting enemy that found its way through every defense. The push was on to end the war by Christmas, but the signs were ominous. There were constant firefights and reports of contact with Chinese ground and air forces, and on November 8 the first battle fought entirely by jet aircraft occurred over Sinuiju. More U.N. forces continued to arrive in Korea: the American 3rd Infantry Division, along with battalions from Thailand, the Netherlands, and France.

For the Eighth Army Rangers, patrols and road blocks continued until November 4, when the unit began a movement by road and rail of approximately 175 miles to Kaesong, where they were billeted in a warehouse close to 25th Division Headquarters. Unit strength was three officers, sixty-two enlisted men, and nine Koreans. Kaesong was memorable because it was there that the men had their first hot baths since arriving in Korea. The bath house had a tile basin that could hold five men at a time, and though the water could not be changed easily, the prospect of a warm soak made it a popular place.

On November 10 the Eighth Army Rangers joined Task Force Johnson, whose mission was to conduct mopping-up operations in the Munsan-ni and Uijongbu areas. The Rangers engaged in heavy patrolling but made no contact at Munsan, but in the Uijongbu area the hunting was better. On the edge of a village the Rangers located an approximate squad of enemy soldiers in full uniform. The Communists ran into heavy brush, but Sergeant Morrissey, who was serving as point man for the Rangers patrol, killed one with his automatic rifle—the first of many enemies the Rangers would dispatch.

The cold was intense. On one night march a Ranger located four chickens, which he saved in a sack, hoping to eat them later; they were frozen solid by dawn.

On November 21 the Eighth Army Ranger Company began a motor march toward Kunuri, North Korea, and by 1600 the following day they reached Yong-po-dong, where the 25th Infantry Division was preparing to launch an offensive. But the zone of attack for the division was too wide for a two-regiment front and too narrow for a three-regiment front. The solution was to form a task force to spearhead the attack, and so the 89th Medium Tank Battalion was once again attached to the division; its commander, Lt. Col. Welborn G. Dolvin, had a fighting reputation. Task Force Dolvin was formed under 25th Infantry Division Operations Order #15 on 21 November 1950. The Eighth Army Ranger Company joined Task Force Dolvin on November 22. The task force consisted of:

Company B 89th Medium Tank Battalion with the 1st platoon, 8213th (Eighth Army) Ranger Company, attached.
Company E 27th Infantry Regiment with the Assault Gun Platoon, 89th Medium Tank Battalion, attached.
Company B 35th Infantry Regiment with the 1st platoon, Company B 89th Medium Tank Battalion, attached.
25th Reconnaissance Company
Company C 65th Engineer Combat Battalion
Reconnaissance Platoon, 89th Medium Tank Battalion

On Thanksgiving Day, November 23, while a briefing of all task-force commanders was held and the men checked and prepared weapons and equipment for the attack, Ranger patrols were sent forward five thousand yards without contact. At noon a liaison officer arrived with orders; H-hour would be 1000 hours on November 24.

The attack kicked off on time, with the Rangers in the center, riding on the tanks of Company B of the 89th Tank Battalion. Company B of the 35th Infantry was on the left flank and Com-

pany E of the 27th Infantry on the right. As the attack started,
two Americans from the 8th Cavalry Regiment approached the
Rangers and stated they had been held prisoner and released by
Chinese Communist forces. They said there were twenty-eight
other prisoners some five thousand yards forward. The task force
continued ahead without contact until 1320 hours, when the
other prisoners were located and sent to the rear.

By 1400 hours the task force had achieved its initial objective.
The tanks came under fire and buttoned up while the Rangers
leaped to the ground and attacked toward Hill 224, with the 2nd
platoon leading the assault. Chinese fire mortally wounded PFC
Joe C. Romero. The assault continued when the Rangers were
suddenly fired upon by the tanks of B Company 89th Tank Battalion. Sgt. Mackey McKinnon and PFC William J. Murphy
were killed, and Sergeant Cagley, Corporal Anderson, Corporal
Tabata, and three of nine Koreans with the company, wounded.
Puckett ran to the tanks and got them to lift their fire.

The Rangers continued the attack and seized their objective.
Enemy patrols were observed in the dimming evening light, but
there was no contact. The task force assumed defensive positions for the night of November 24–25.

In the morning the attack resumed. Task Force Dolvin advanced north to the west of the Chongchon River, with the
Rangers and Company B of the 89th Tank Battalion in the center. The infantry companies had switched flanks. Heavy fighting
was soon encountered. At 1000 hours the southwest portion of
Objective 7 was captured after heavy fighting by Company B,
35th Infantry Regiment. Simultaneously, Company E of the 27th
Infantry Regiment and the 89th Tank Battalion's assault-gun platoon took Objective 10. After the seizure of these two flanking
objectives, the Rangers and Company B 89th Tank Battalion
moved through the center and took Objective 8 (Hill 205). Sergeant Hoagland, Corporal Dzurcanin, and Corporal Landers
were wounded in the attack. Enemy forces were encountered in
strength and intense small arms fire was being received from
high ground to the southeast.

The cold was abetted by a driving wind, and close behind it
came the Chinese, counterattacking along the flanks of the
Chongchon River. As night settled under a brilliant moon, the
Chinese overran a platoon of Company E, 27th Infantry. Other
elements of the task force also came under attack. The Chinese

sent forward scouts that were fluent in English; pretending to be American officers or members of adjoining units, they would engage the Americans in long-range conversation. Deceived, some Americans would reveal their positions and even their numerical strength.

The Rangers had dug into the frozen ground and were in the process of being resupplied when, at about 2200 hours, the night air was rent by the sound of drums, bugles, and whistles. Swarms of Chinese rose from the earth in a frontal attack on the Ranger position. In a foxhole in the 1st platoon area, PFC Billy Walls had just taken off his boots and changed socks. Walls was normally a machine gunner but for this operation was using a Browning Automatic Rifle. The boots would have to wait; standing in his stockings, Walls opened fire.

The Chinese attack was met by heavy fire from the Rangers and the skillfull use of artillery by Lieutenant Puckett. By 2250 hours the first attack was beaten off. Several of the Rangers had been wounded, including Lieutenant Puckett, who was hit in the right shoulder. He refused evacuation.

Amid the noise of battle, one of the South Koreans kept calling out, "May I surrender, please?" Walls fired a few shots in his direction and the Korean was quiet.

By 2300 hours another battalion-size Chinese attack struck the Rangers, while other units of the task force also came under heavy attack. The Chinese had arrived in strength, and the dreams of a Christmas victory parade down the Ginza in Tokyo had vanished. This was a new war.

The second attack was beaten back by the Rangers, as was a third. In each attack the Chinese committed additional forces, and the fighting raged at hand-grenade range. Lieutenant Puckett was again wounded, but continued to lead an aggressive defense. The fourth and fifth attacks were also repulsed, but the Rangers were down to their last rounds of ammunitions. Someone yelled, "Fix bayonets and prepare for counterattack." Some Rangers who had exhausted their ammunition were already fighting with the bayonet, for the Chinese were already inside the perimeter. PFC Fraccola was wounded by a Chinese who approached him from behind.

Chinese grenade attacks were heavy and constant. A Ranger tried to pick up a Chinese grenade and throw it back, but it exploded in his hands. In agony and shock, the man kept sobbing over and over, "I tried to get rid of it and it went off."

Shortly before 0300 hours on November 26, the Chinese made their sixth attack, this time overrunning the Ranger position. Merrill Casner recalls hearing a black Ranger named Wilbert Clanton roaring in rage as he fought to the death surrounded by Chinese soldiers. Puckett was shot through the chest and unable to move. The Chinese swarmed over the hill, bayoneting and shooting men in their holes. As Ranger Merrill Casner lay wounded, a Chinese soldier put a rifle against his head and pulled the trigger, but by amazing good fortune, Casner received only a scalp wound and faked death until the opportunity came to get off the hill.

Over the noise of battle a Ranger kept repeating a rosary over a rifle that was jamming, and his voice could be heard saying, "Holy Mother of . . . *God damn this rifle!*"

Ranger Judy located Corporal Pollack and Ranger Walls, telling them the position was overrun and Lieutenant Puckett seriously wounded. While Judy went to locate platoon sergeant Morrissey, Pollock and Walls moved near the crest of the hill, where Judy had said they could find Puckett. They encountered three Chinese and killed them before the Chinese could fire. The two men found Puckett on his hands and knees, and since the Chinese were close upon them, Walls picked up Puckett, slung him over his shoulder, and began to run. Pollock provided covering fire, holding the Chinese at bay until they reached a small draw. Exhausted, Walls placed Puckett on the ground.

"Is he still with us?" Pollock asked.

"I'm not going to leave you," Puckett responded.

The draw was filled with brush and trees, and the Chinese were directly above the three men, firing down the slope of the hill. Unable to carry Puckett, the exhausted Walls and Pollock dragged the wounded officer down the ravine. It was almost daylight when they reached the bottom of the hill, where they were found by Sergeant Morrissey and other men alerted by Ranger Judy. Taken to an aid station, Puckett secured a radio and continued to call in artillery on the Chinese.

Others did not make it from the hill. Some were men who had fallen trying to provide covering fire so that their comrades might withdraw. Lt. Barnard Cummings, Jr.; Rangers Sumner

Kubinak, Ernest Nowlin, and the nineteen-year-old Librado Luna were among this number.

Of the fifty-eight men listed on the company morning report for 26 November 1950, twenty-eight were casualties. Eleven of these never returned and their bodies were not recovered.

Task Force Dolvin continued to receive heavy attacks. On November 26 the commanding general of the 25th Infantry Division formed a new task force under the command of Brigadier General Wilson, and Task Force Dolvin became a component of this new force. At 1200 hours the remaining Rangers were moved to the 25th Infantry Division's forward headquarters as a security force, and this duty continued until December 9 while the company received replacements and welcomed the return of men lightly wounded.

While the Eighth Army Ranger Company was undergoing its November ordeal by fire, the 1st Ranger Infantry Company (Airborne) was moving to war. The train ride to the West Coast was uneventful, but during a brief layover in Texas, transportation officers cautioned the company commander, Capt. John ''Black Jack'' Striegel, not to allow his men from the train as some might prefer going AWOL rather than going to war. Striegel laughed and told his men to enjoy themselves and make it back in time for the train's departure. All were on board when the train pulled out.

The company arrived at Camp Stoneman, California on November 18 and began the final preparations for passage overseas. They were inoculated and issued new fatigues without markings. For several days, when marching back to their barracks, the Rangers received catcalls from soldiers in a nearby barracks. After receiving permission from Lt. Mayo Heath to conduct a class in manners, the 1st platoon left the line of march and went through the offending barracks like a whirlwind. Those of the opposition who could leaped from windows and ran; the rest went down before the Ranger onslaught. It was over in a matter of seconds. Leaving a shambles behind them, the Rangers double-timed back to rejoin the column.

On November 25 the 1st Ranger Company embarked on the troopship USNS *C.G. Morton*. Embarkation began at 1300 hours, and at 1630 hours the ship weighed anchor and sailed. The Rangers were only one small contingent of the troops on board destined for Korea, and their difference from the other outfits was immediately apparent. Shortly after departure an announcement came over the ship's loudspeaker that the North Koreans were on the run and the war would be over before the ship docked. The troops were jubilant, shouting with joy and pounding each other on the back, but the Rangers were tight-lipped and sullen, angry at being denied their chance at battle.

Little time had passed before another announcement was made: the Chinese had entered the conflict and it was a whole new war. Now the Rangers leaped and shouted for joy while the other soldiers were despondent. The Rangers spent the rest of voyage in physical training and weapons preparation. While en route, the Rangers gave instruction in weapons and self-protection to medical personnel, including doctors. Later, in Korea, some would see these medics again and be told the training had saved their lives.

Chapter 6

Through the biting wind and swirling snow, in scenes that were reminiscent of Napoleon's retreat from Moscow, the trek back from the Yalu began. On December 6, X Corps was extracted from Wonsan by sea and sailed south to land at Pohang and Pusan. On December 23, the feisty Gen. Walton Walker was killed in a vehicle accident while on his way to present an award to the Commonwealth Brigade. A Greek battalion and a Canadian brigade arrived in Korea during December, and the month closed with the Chinese attacking south across the 38th parallel. X Corps became part of Eighth Army, with Lt. Gen. Matthew B. Ridgeway taking command.

On December 5 Capt. John P. Vann was assigned as company commander of the Eighth Army Rangers.[1] Vann, who would years later find fame and death in Vietnam, was from Norfolk, Virginia. In World War II he had served as a navigator on a B-29 bomber, and in 1946 he wanted the opportunity to serve in the Airborne, so he requested and received a commission in the infantry. He had arrived in Korea with the 25th Infantry Division in July 1950.

With the groundwork laid by the capable Puckett, Vann began reorganizing the company. The Eighth Army Ranger Company, 8213th Army Unit, carried the additional unwieldy title of "Bulk Authorization Unit," and, as such, it was reorganized effective December 10 under Table of Organization and Equipment 7-87, to bring the unit to an authorized strength of five officers and 107 enlisted men.[2] This action would bring the company a strength comparable to the units being formed at Fort Benning, adding much-needed mess personnel and an executive officer.

On December 9 the company was distributed among the division's tracked and wheeled vehicles and road-marched eighty-six miles southwest to Kaesong, South Korea. On December 13 the company moved south another thirty-eight miles, to the vicinity of Seoul, where two additional officers were assigned: 1st Lt. Glenn W. Metcalf and 2nd Lt. Dick M. Stiles. The company now had seventy-nine men assigned, sixty-eight present for duty.

On December 16 the Eighth Army Ranger Company was attached to the Turkish Armed Forces Command for operational control. The Turkish Brigade had the responsibility for security of Kangwha Island, at the mouth of the Han River. On December 18 the Rangers established outposts and patrols on the island. Amphibious vehicles known as a DUKW were used for transport to and from the island and for waterborne patrols.[3] Refugees continued to pour south from North Korea, attempting to escape the Chinese, and even on Kangwha Island the refugees were a major problem. For men who had lived by foraging what they ate, it was good duty on Kwangwa Island; chickens, and therefore eggs, were available, and a man could occasionally have a fire and a hot bath.

The Rangers were unaware that Kangwha Island already had a footnote in American history. In June 1871 a five-ship American squadron arrived in Korean waters to open trade and investigate the sinking of an American merchant ship. When fired upon by the guns of the fortress of Kangwha, American marines and sailors had stormed and seized the fort.

On December 9 the *Morton* docked at Yokohama and the 1st Rangers moved by train to Camp Zama, where they completed processing, received cold-weather gear, and checked weapons and equipment. At 1730 hours on December 16 they departed Japan, traveling the 150 miles to Pusan by ferry.

Arriving in Korea at 0700 hours on December 17, the company spent the night in a warehouse and was flown to Kimpo airport at Seoul the next day. From there they entrucked to the central front, where on December 23 the 1st Ranger Company was attached to the 2nd (Indianhead) Infantry Division and then further attached to the 3rd Battalion, 23rd Infantry Regiment.

Regrettably, their beloved commander Captain Striegel was

stricken by hepatitis; he tried to hide his illness but was so desperately sick that he had to be evacuated. Striegel would rejoin his command, but he was too sick to function in a leadership role. Lt. Alfred Herman assumed command on 6 January 1951. He was a twenty-eight-year-old native of St. Louis, and a 1945 graduate of West Point. Nicknamed "Scratch" by his classmates, Herman was an expert pistol shooter and an accomplished musician.

The 2nd Infantry Division included the 9th Infantry Regiment, the 23rd Infantry Regiment with attached French Volunteer Battalion, and the 38th Infantry Regiment with attached Netherlands Volunteer Battalion. The French and Dutch forces had arrived in early December. The division had suffered major personnel and material losses during heavy fighting in November—in fact the 2nd Division lost more men in the Korean War than in WWI or WWII. Assigned an Eighth Army reserve mission, the division was engaged in reequipping and training new personnel in an area around the town of Chjungju when the Rangers arrived.

The lean, logistical structure of a Ranger company made itself immediately apparent. There was no mess section, so the Rangers had to be satellited on other units for food. This problem would be corrected, but not before hungry Rangers were enraged and other commands, themselves short of supplies, complained bitterly at the additional burden of feeding the Rangers.

Billeted in an old schoolhouse made memorable by the miserable cold, Christmas Day 1950 the Rangers enjoyed what would be their last hot meal for some time. They were in a feisty mood, calling the cooks who fed them "legs," the sometimes derogatory term for non-Airborne personnel. As men from the various units gathered for Christmas dinner, they would call out their home states, which led Mark Goyen, a Ranger from Illinois, to an enjoyable reunion with a soldier from his hometown.[4]

By the end of December the 2nd Division was back in action, assigned to the Hoengsong–Wonju area. Wonju was the center of the American line and an important rail and road center, with five significant supply routes. Working to the front of the 23rd and 38th regiments, the 1st Ranger Company began a period of heavy patrol activity. On New Year's Eve a four-man patrol led by SSgt. Reginald King and consisting of Sgt. Norman A.

Grimm, Cpl. George Lublinski, and PFC John Spence, was trapped and captured by the Communists. Sergeant King would never see the child whose birth had been announced as his train left Fort Benning; he died under torture. Rangers Grimm and Spence died in a Chinese prison camp. Lublinski, who had been born in Poland, was taken away by Russian officers and vanished.

The end of December 1950 found two additional Ranger companies arriving in Korea: The 2nd and 4th Ranger Infantry companies (Airborne). These companies—one black, the other white—had trained together and established a deep and abiding friendship. The 2nd Rangers—with five officers and 116 enlisted men—and the 4th Rangers—with four officers and 118 enlisted men—had departed Fort Benning by train for Camp Stoneman at 0730 hours on December 3.

While en route to California, an incident occurred that gave the two companies a special name. A Ranger, who had been born and raised in the city, was gazing out the window as the train rolled through Texas, when he suddenly let out a cry of amazement and began to bellow. "Look—look at the buffalo!" Other Rangers gathering around were amazed to find that the man was pointing at a herd of steers. From that point on men of the 2nd and 4th Rangers referred to themselves as "buffaloes" or used the word buffalo to mean anything from "Hello" to "Bug Off."

On December 9 the two companies departed San Francisco aboard the USS *General H. W. Butner*, stopping briefly at Pearl Harbor and disembarking at Yokohama, Japan, at 1400 Hours on December 24. The 2nd and 4th Rangers left Camp Zama, Japan, six days later and flew from Tachikawa Air Force Base, Japan, to Kimpo Air Force Base in Seoul. On December 31 the 2nd Ranger Company was attached to the 7th Infantry Division, and the 4th Ranger Company to Saber (1st Cavalry Division) headquarters at Seoul. The 4th Rangers startled the 1st Cavalry and the Koreans by taking their morning run through the streets of the Korean capital.

Colonel Van Houten, Lt. Col. James Adams, Maj. John Singlaub, and other officers of the Ranger Training Center visited the infantry divisions in Korea and made every effort to acquaint members of the division staffs with the capabilities and limitations of a Ranger company.[5] Despite this effort, a true appreciation of Ranger company capabilities was rare. The G-3 section (Operations) of a line infantry division is an extremely busy place; its primary concern is attacking or defending along the division front. It takes time and experience to plan operations to be conducted behind enemy lines; neither of these were to be found in most divisions. The 2nd Infantry Division staff made the most concerted effort to properly employ the Rangers, while the leaders of the 1st Cavalry Division were the least able to grasp the potential of the Rangers. Much to their disgust, the highly trained and motivated men of the 4th Rangers began performing rear-area security missions.

More then a month later, Colonel Van Houten would write a letter to General Collins that contained an excerpt of a letter written by a former Fort Benning public information officer in Korea:

> And today, I wandered through the 4th Ranger Company's area to get a few stories. From Fort Benning, they came directly to the 1st Cavalry for assignment as an attached unit. In retrospect, I cannot remember being so impressed with the sheer doggedness and cold, anxious anticipation of battle from a group of men. Without exception these men are savagely craving a fight with the Communists—the sooner, the better—something out of a Warner Brothers movie, but I rather imagine there is nothing superficial or false about their determined expressions. Each of them has shaved his head in the old Indian fashion (a strip of fuzz on top of the head) and they constantly carry two hand grenades, a pistol, and a switchblade knife. In our area they have left an indelible impression with their tough do-or-die attitude. Whenever a move is required, they heap massive loads upon their backs and stride across the snow and hills with as little effort as would be required to light a match. If and when they are given a mission to get behind the enemy and create a bit of havoc, I fear the Commies are going to be searching frantically for some solution to stop this new American menace.

Van Houten added an insert: ". . . and their impatience is beginning to show around the jaws . . ."

For many men of the second cycle, Christmas 1950 was preembarkation leave. Just in time to impress the girls back home, the daily bulletin of the Ranger Training Center for December 23 carried this announcement:

> The new Ranger Background for parachutists insignia is now on sale at the Ranger Training Center exchange. The selling price is eight cents per background.

The approved, oval background had a black center surrounded with gold, but many men had taken to wearing an oval with a black background and red center. The red, white, and black colors of the 1st Ranger Battalion of WWII had a strong attraction for the men, while to the student of Ranger history, black and gold had no meaning.

On December 26 a report was prepared at the Ranger Training Center that sought to change the policy of assigning one Ranger company per infantry division. The staff study was a masterful document prepared by men knowledgeable of the capabilities of Ranger units. The officers who prepared the report worked against a serious handicap. The directive issued by the Department of the Army on 7 September 1950 had specified, "There is a requirement for one such company per infantry division." Faced with that instruction, a study to determine "the best organization, command and staff relationship needed to achieve the maximum effectiveness from Ranger units" was hamstrung. Still, the Ranger Training Center tried.

Opposing views on the role of Ranger units were discussed. One school favored their use as shock troops, spearheading attacks; another envisioned the Ranger role as penetration of enemy lines and operations to the enemy rear. It was assumed that "to be surrounded by the enemy may be a normal operating procedure . . ."

The use of Raider platoons in World War II infantry divisions was reviewed. Experience proved these units became a catchall for missions that should have been assigned to rifle companies. There was a gentle reminder that during World War II, Ranger units were primarily controlled at headquarters level rather than by a division. This resulted in the opinion that there were many advantages to organizing Ranger units on a battalion or larger-task-force basis. The reasoning behind this idea included:

a. A field-grade commanding officer could provide adequate representation to any headquarters to which the unit was attached.
b. Such a unit would have an adequate staff to plan Ranger missions.
c. The unit would be administratively self sufficient.

Throughout the study, those who prepared the report made frequent statements that demonstrated a desire for operational control at a higher level than a division headquarters. The opinion was made clear that Ranger battalions (three Ranger companies with a small battalion headquarters and staff) were the most plausible form of organization. The problems foreseen in the staff study by the Ranger Training Center quickly came to pass, but Army Chief of Staff General Collins had specified one Ranger company per infantry division—and so it remained.

Chapter 7

As 1950 came to a close the Chinese came on, conquering Seoul and Wonju. Despite these defeats, General Collins claimed 200,000 casualties inflicted on the Chinese in January, and while this figure is open to question, there is no doubt the enemy paid a heavy price for their victories. They had become overextended on the drive south and suffered from constant pounding by American air and artillery, and, beginning in early January, the Communists were forced to withdraw the main body of their troops to regroup and refit. As always, they screened their activity with aggressive reconnaissance forces.

By mid-month they were beginning to look less formidable. With overextended supply lines and terrible suffering from the elements, it was the turn of the Chinese to be on the down side of the seesaw. Operation THUNDERBOLT was scheduled as a strong, Eighth Army reconnaissance in force to test the Chinese screen prior to a major U.N. attack. Part of the plan scheduled a Ranger company to parachute behind retreating Chinese forces to cut off the route of withdrawal of some senior Chinese officers. The 1st Ranger Company was alerted, but the orders were not issued. Later, Far East Command staff officers in a document to the Department of the Army dated May 19, would claim that "because of the treatment generally accorded prisoners in Korea, particularly by the NKPA, General Ridgeway while in Command of Eighth Army refused to permit the employment of Ranger Companies in deep penetrations." American Airborne doctrine of the period was that the Airborne landings behind enemy lines must be in at least regimental combat-team strength and linkup with ground forces accomplished within seventy-two hours.

On 25 January 1951, U.N. forces attacked north, meeting only delaying actions by the enemy. Seoul, Inchon, and Wonju were recaptured, but Chinese resistance soon stiffened, and by the end of the month the U.N. advance was at a crawl.

On the first day of the new year, the Eighth Army Rangers left their island and at 1900 hours began moving to Pupyong, then on via Seoul and Sinchon-ni to Chonan.

On January 2 patrols from the 1st Rangers went six miles west on the railroad line from Yongdong Station, then established an outpost near a bridge. Sgt. Jerome O'Leary was killed while on railroad-line patrol. O'Leary had found a hand-propelled railway cart and decided to reenter the Ranger positions by pumping his way down the tracks. The noise prevented his hearing the sentry's challenge, and in the darkness, he was shot and killed.

To miss a challenge was to court death. Ranger officers were frequently called to higher headquarters for briefing, which necessitated their reentering the perimeter after dark and passing the challenge of those on guard. One dark night when the sign was "Night" and the countersign "Hawk," a Ranger officer began to enter the perimeter:

"Night," hissed a voice from the gloom.

"Sky," the officer replied.

"Night!" insisted the voice.

"Bird?" the officer queried hopefully.

The soft click of a safety being pushed forward was followed by a voice heavy with threat. *"Night!"*

The Ranger officer exploded with rage, cursing and shouting at the top of his lungs.

"Pass, sir," the voice said in the darkness. "I recognize you."

In early 1951 even the work, sweat, and proven performance it took to become a Ranger were not enough to earn a black man equal treatment in the U.S. Army. Change was coming, but slowly.

Shortly after the 2nd Rangers arrived in Korea, a 7th Infantry Division report contained the following:

Policy reassignment of colored personnel reiterated by G-1, X Corps, after concurrence by Eighth Army: Colored troops who arrive in the division, if they have proper MOS's, [Military Occupational Specialties] will be assigned to the 2nd Ranger Co. Others who are assigned to the division in error may be returned to the Eighth Army Replacement Bn. Personnel will not be mixed within units. If Ranger Company becomes greatly over strength, another Company will be formed.

The intent was obvious: the 2nd Ranger Company was to become an instrument of segregation for the 7th Infantry Division. But the 2nd Ranger Company had no intention of becoming merely a replacement depot. While the Army sorted out its policy on integration, the 2nd Rangers compiled a remarkable combat record—and did so while training the men it had been sent for useful service with other units.

January found the 2nd Rangers on the move. The 7th Division, which consisted of the 17th, 31st, and 32nd infantry regiments, was en route from Yongchon to Wonju via Tanyang, with the mission of blocking enemy threats from the northeast. Traveling 130 miles from Yongchon to Changnim-ni via Andong, the 2nd Rangers arrived on January 5. The area was a hotbed of guerrilla activity. At 0235, January 7, twenty Koreans attempted to pass a Ranger roadblock. They were fired on and dispersed. At 0630 an enemy guerrilla force, approximately 150 strong, attacked a nearby medical aid station and the 2nd Ranger command post. The Rangers broke the enemy attack at both locations. SFC Isaac Baker was killed and Rangers Webb, Paulding, and Small were wounded. Guerrilla attacks became so frequent that 7th Division refused to allow Korean civilians in the Tanyang area. The policy for Koreans in the vicinity of Tanyang was, "Move after darkness and you get shot."

The 4th Rangers were serving security duty for the division command post of the 1st Cavalry Division and later the 82nd Field Artillery Battalion. The 1st Cav was in reserve in and around Seoul. During the enemy drive south, division headquarters was displaced rearward, but the Ranger company was ordered to remain in position till transportation was sent. No food had been left for the Rangers, though stacks of equipment, including mess hall supplies, had been left burning; still, the hungry Rangers scavenged large cans of chipped beef and sweet potatoes. While some of his friends opened the cans, Ranger Frank Forbes went in search of a container that would serve as a mixing bowl. He soon found a long metal tube cut in half lengthwise. Washing it out with snow, Forbes hurried back with his prize. The food was placed in the container, mixed, and placed over a fire. The men used their canteen cups to transfer the piping hot food to their mess kits and the feast began. It did not last long. A sharp-eyed Ranger took a long look at the container and said, "That is a urine trough from a latrine."

Fifteen hours went by while the Rangers watched U.N. forces stream south. When there was no one else but a battalion of the 21st Infantry to their front, Captain Anderson offered 4th Company to fight with them. Unfortunately, the cavalry trucks came at that time with instructions for the Rangers to rejoin the division.

On January 7 three North Korean divisions attacked 2nd Division positions around the critical communications center of Wonju. Fighting a delaying action, the 1st Rangers were engaged in blowing bridges and rail lines.

January 8 saw the Eighth Army Rangers on the move once more, this time on a motor march of some seventy-four miles to Nonsan. The 25th Division intended to move its headquarters and trains into this area. The Rangers were given the mission of clearing the area of guerrillas and providing security. The company now had 123 enlisted men assigned.

At 0945 hours on January 9 a 1st Ranger patrol led by Sergeant Robertson encountered an enemy force near Chungchon and engaged. Lieutenant Herman estimated enemy strength at two hundred and committed the 2nd and 3rd platoons. The battle was fought in snow-covered woods of black-boled trees banked by deep drifts. Men fought with frozen extremities, and weapons that frequently jammed. Their exhausted breath rose white against the gray winter air as they struggled from position to position. The shooting continued into the afternoon, when both sides broke contact and withdrew. A number of the enemy had been seen to fall, but the outcome was inconclusive. Rangers Kenneth "Nick" Delfine and Fred Heedt were wounded, their blood crimson against the new snow. Ranger medic Howard K. Davis distinguished himself by crossing three hundred yards of open ground under heavy fire to come to the assistance of the wounded.[1]

The 2nd Rangers were also in action on January 9. Its 3rd platoon was on patrol near the village of Changnim-ni when, at approximately 0900 hours, they engaged an enemy force in a firefight that lasted until 1445 hours. Ranger Sherman Daniels was wounded.

On January 11 the 2nd Rangers were designated as the counterattack force for the Tanyang Defense Plan, which called for American and ROK forces to hold the Mun'gyong and Tanyang passes of the Han-Naktong watershed.

The constant cold, driving wind, and deep snow brought misery that severely tested every soldier's endurance. Units reported men fainting from the cold; mortar barrels froze and cracked; the coffee in canteen cups became brown ice. Still, the Rangers, often dressed in white coveralls, patrolled the front.

Every effort was made to deprive the enemy of sanctuary from American air power and the freezing temperatures; across the front, village after village was set afire to deny the enemy shelter. Concerned that war correspondents eager for a story might seize on this to raise controversy, American commanders were told to refrain from using the term "scorched earth" with reporters and to speak instead in terms of "clearing fields of fire." The United Nations soldiers devoutly hoped the Chinese would all be deprived of shelter and freeze.

Enemy infiltration and deception was constant, and the slightest unwariness could bring injury or death. On the evening of January 11 a 1st Ranger patrol entered a mountain village where Ranger Horace "Bud" Harding approached a woman squatting in front of a hut. His rifle slung over his shoulder, Harding stopped and said, "Hello, mama-san." The woman fired a pistol into Harding's chest, killing him. Retribution was immediate.

The company closed, cleared the village of infiltrators, and took up positions among the houses. Forward outposts were kept throughout the night, and at first light on January 12, a squad-size reconnaissance patrol was dispatched. Crossing a mountain, the patrol was halfway down the other side when they were suddenly taken under fire and pinned in position by the Communists.

When reinforcements arrived, Rangers Clifton and Dahl drew

fire on themselves by repeatedly moving into open areas until
fired upon and then scrambling back to cover. By this technique
they were able to distract the enemy, allowing the patrol to break
free.

January 12 was a day of frustration for the Eighth Army Rangers. Two platoons were moving through a defile at 1440 hours
when they were ambushed by enemy guerrillas. Rangers John
Mitchell, Jr. and Joseph R. Lauzon were killed, and nine Rangers were wounded, including lieutenants Stiles and Simenson.
The enemy lost fifteen. The Rangers were unable to reach the
bodies of Mitchell and Lauzon, and when they were eventually
recovered, they were found to be badly mutilated.

At 0730 hours on January 14 the 2nd Ranger Company entered the village of Majori-ri with the mission of taking possession of the village then following another American unit in
continuing the attack. The 2nd Rangers found the village occupied by a large enemy force, and a furious fight ensued. The
Rangers accomplished their mission and drove the enemy from
the town, but the Chinese retaliated by ambushing the other
American force in a mountain draw and counterattacking. During the day Rangers Richard Glover, J. T. Holley, Milton Johnson, Frank King, Jr., Charles D. Scott, Robert St. Thomas,
Herman L. Rembert, and Lawrence Williams were killed. Lt.
Bernard Pryor, and Rangers Andres, Boatwright, Harold Johnson, Lanier, Davis, Estell, Aikens, William Thomas, and SFC
Donald West were wounded.

As the Chinese counterattack pushed the Americans back,
Ranger William E. Rhodes of Bridgeport, Connecticut, was one
of the covering force. Rhodes was firing when he realized that
he was the only one of the covering force left alive and that the
Chinese were coming right at him. Rhodes, who was nicknamed
"the Thin Man," played dead. The Chinese, who were taking
items from the dead Americans, took from Rhodes his rifle,
watch, and cartridge belt, then moved off. Rhodes waited about
thirty minutes, then began to move back toward friendly lines.
After walking and running for some time, he was fired upon
again, and again played dead. This time the Chinese stripped
him of his boots, socks, wallet, parka, and cap. Rhodes tried
again and made it to a small Korean village where he hid out
for three days under the care of a friendly, elderly Korean cou-

ple. On the third night, American troops entered the village, and Rhodes returned to the 2nd Rangers. Several days later, the 2nd Rangers moved some twelve miles and established headquarters in Tanyang. For the remainder of the month they were employed in searching out enemy guerrillas. On January 29 they were attached to the 17th RCT.

Meanwhile, the 4th Rangers had been ordered to Taegu; there was a feeling of action in the air as Airborne equipment was drawn from the 187th RCT, and the company embarked upon a rigorous training schedule. Eighth Army had planned a parachute assault on a guerrilla headquarters, but after several weeks of preparation which reached the point where the 4th Rangers were waiting to board the aircraft, the mission was cancelled—intelligence could not pinpoint the enemy location.

On January 16, while on ambush five to six thousand meters in front of the 38th Regiment, the 1st Rangers received orders to proceed forward to the vicinity of the Wonju–Chechon road or until they made contact. A battery of the 25th Field Artillery was displaced forward to support the mission. The 1st Rangers moved forward on their deep scout. One of the early missions was to investigate a report of thirty-one Chinese soldiers at the town of Kirichi. The Ranger report stated dryly, "Remained overnight, saw thirty-one women, no Chinese Communist forces." They continued on their way, returning on January 19 with a prisoner. There was scant opportunity for the 1st Rangers to rest, as they were promptly attached to the 9th Infantry Regiment to patrol to the north and northeast. The 2nd Division enjoined the 9th Infantry Regiment to "use them to the fullest."

From January 20 to 31 the 1st Rangers made deep patrols by day and night in the vicinity of Sillim-ni. On January 27 Sgt. Wallace Dobbie was wounded near Song Nam-ni and evacuated. The situation was fluid: jeeps purloined near Pusan were outfitted with machine guns, giving the men additional mobility and firepower. Lieutenant Herman wanted a jeep rigged with a bell and an enemy skull on the front bumper as a challenge to the enemy.

On January 28 a mobile patrol of the 1st Rangers located an enemy force of at least two platoons. Establishing a blocking position, the Rangers attacked and dispersed the enemy. Later that same day the company was passing through a destroyed Korean town, near the center of which was the rubble of a bank with only its vault left intact. The temptation was too great to resist. Employing a 3.5-inch rocket launcher and explosives, the Rangers opened the bank vault, which contained a large amount of Korean won. Of the conversation that surrounded this incident, little is remembered save for the one-liner delivered by the company commander. "Put *my* money in the jeep."

Claims to ownership of the money, however, were immaterial. Before the Rangers returned, the jeep was ambushed. Cpl. Charles Yates was wounded and PFC Eunis Waters was captured and would die in a Communist prison camp. The shot-up vehicle had been stripped of weapons, equipment, and money.

In late January the 1st Rangers patrolled an area east of Chipyong-ni known as the "twin tunnels." Possession of the ground around these railroad tunnels was hotly contested. Patrolling through the long, dark tunnels was part of the Ranger mission and an eerie experience.

On January 30 the Eighth Army Ranger Company traveled some eighty-eight miles by motor convoy from Nonsan to Suwon, where they assumed duties as a security force for 25th Infantry Division Tactical Headquarters.

The beginning of January 1951 saw activities at the Ranger Training Center in Fort Benning reach a solid footing. It was now evident the war would be continuing, and the training was constantly improving as procedures were developed. The 3rd, 5th, 6th, 7th, and 8th Ranger companies were commencing their fifth week of training. It was a particularly cold winter even in Georgia; to strip to undershorts and swim Victory Pond while its edges were rimmed with ice left a memory more lasting than many combat experiences.

On some nights, during the brief interval between the end of daylight training and the beginning of the night exercises, there was time for a cheery campfire. Men sat close, warming their hands and singing:

> *I'm a Ranger born*
> *I'm a Ranger bred*
> *And when I die*
> *I'll be a Ranger dead!*

Foreign officers frequently visited Fort Benning, coming from Thailand, Italy, and Greece to see how Rangers trained. Officers of the training center often traveled to the Far East Command, assessing the training, performance, and utilization of the Ranger companies. Maj. John Singlaub of the S-3 section played a prime role in these reports, and Colonel Van Houten himself traveled to Korea in December 1950.

As the infantry divisions of the National Guard were called into federal service, prompt steps were taken to recruit and train volunteers from these divisions to serve in Ranger companies. After completion of training, these companies would be attached to the division from which the men were recruited.

On January 5 the 9th, 10th, and 11th Ranger infantry companies (Airborne) were activated. The 9th Ranger Company was left unmanned for a few days. The 10th Ranger Company was drawn from and designated for the 45th Infantry Division (Oklahoma National Guard), and the 11th Ranger Company was drawn from and for the 40th Infantry Division (California National Guard).

The initial volunteers for the first nine Ranger companies were primarily regular Army; all were qualified parachutists. Along with the extension of the Ranger concept to the newly activated National Guard divisions came the requirement to hone down the large number of volunteers to approximately 190 men for each company. This contingent would be sent initially to Airborne school as a company; those who completed would continue as a company through Ranger training. The excess number allowed for those who would not succeed.

The final week of the second training cycle commenced on 8 January 1951. The unofficial but descriptive title was, "Hell Week." It opened with a low-level night parachute jump deep in simulated enemy territory.

Between 1900 and 2400 hours the 3rd, 5th, 6th, 7th, and 8th Ranger companies exited aircraft over Lee Field drop zone. The night was moonless. Hunched over by the tightly drawn straps of their T-7 parachutes, their weapons strapped in Griswald containers by their sides, the Rangers sat in the dimly lit bellies of the roaring aircraft, waiting for the sequence of commands that went: "Get ready—Stand up—Hook up—Sound off for equipment check—Stand in the door—" and, on the green light, "Go!"

In rapid succession the men exited the aircraft, with the last man (the "stick pusher") running after the pack. Static lines, which were hooked to the cable in the interior of the aircraft, stretched taut under the weight of each falling body, tearing the cover from the parachute and withdrawing it from its pack. For a brief instant the Ranger, falling at a speed of 120 miles per hour, was attached in umbilical-cord fashion through parachute and static line to the aircraft, then the cords attached to the "bridal loop" at the top of the parachute broke free and the Ranger was literally "Airborne."

To me, this night jump was like stepping from a lighted room into a dark one without a floor. When the opening shock came, I looked up to check my canopy—and suddenly struck the earth with a force that rattled my teeth. I did not feel I had ten feet of falling space to spare. The aircraft had come in low, under two hundred feet, to escape radar detection, pulling up only just before the drop. Engine trouble and pilot nervousness prevented some of the planes from reaching the planned drop altitude. In the event of trouble there was neither time nor space to use the reserve parachute. Twenty-two Rangers were injured that night, some so badly they would never recover. Ronald E. Sullivan of the 8th Rangers was killed when his parachute malfunctioned.

One day, two men from the first three companies to go to Korea were returned to the Ranger Training Center in disgrace. They had gone AWOL on the West Coast, gotten drunk, and missed the shipment. These men were placed in a pup tent in the containment area, were addressed as "dog," forbidden to associate with Rangers, and during the time they remained before being busted out, they were ridiculed as scum unfit to be among men.

At Camp Polk, Louisiana, the 45th Infantry Division completed the selection process for the men who would form the 10th Ranger Infantry Company (Airborne). Six hundred men had volunteered. They were put through a thorough, strenuous program which narrowed the number to 191, of which 73 were National Guardsmen, 15 were regular army enlistees, and 103 were from among the selectees used to fill out the 45th Division. In early January 186 of these men left Fort Polk to begin training. The 10th Rangers would be under the command of Capt. Charles E. Spragins, a regular Army officer who had been in training at the Ranger Training Center.[2]

Meanwhile, at Camp Cooke, California, the 40th Infantry Division had completed their elimination process and chosen 197 volunteers to begin Airborne and Ranger training. The unit would be commanded by Capt. Rudolph M. Jones.

Each volunteer was required to sign a paper that contained the following words:

> I volunteer for Ranger Training and duty. I further volunteer to perform frequent aircraft flight, glider flight, parachute jumps, and to participate in realistic combat training while receiving Airborne and/or Ranger Traning and performing Ranger duty. I understand that I will continue to be eligible for parachutists' pay.
>
> ....
>   (Name)

For the 10th and 11th Rangers (and those who followed them) the first test was to make it through the four-week basic Airborne training, or "jump school," as it was more popularly known. Effective January 7, the 10th Ranger Company and the 11th Ranger Company were attached to Company E, Airborne Battalion, Student Training Regiment. Their training began January 14.

Activities at jump school were geared around mental alertness, rapid and correct response. Men were taught the basic principles of the aircraft, how to exit it in flight (some said *fright*), and how to execute a parachute landing-fall to reduce injury. The first steps in the training were jumps from the thirty-four-foot-high towers. Thirty-four feet is a height that does not seem terrifying, until a recruit stands in the door of the tower and makes the mistake of looking down. After properly performing jumps from the tower and riding the cable down to earthen mounds, the trainees advanced to 250-foot towers. With the parachute open in a ring, the would-be paratrooper entered his harness and was lifted skyward. Somewhere near the top, he bounced gently to a halt, and with a whir of machinery, the chute and trooper were lifted a few more feet and released. Then and direct the parachute away from the steel tower. Having done that, it was expected that a first-class parachute landing-fall would be accomplished when one reached earth.

Everything was done at double-time to the shouts and snarls of the instructors. These men seemed to have the eyes of eagles and the temperaments of rabid wolves. The push-up was the constant reminder of error or its possibility.

"Drop and give me ten!"

"Hit it!"

"Grab the clay!"

Instructors were able to impart new meaning to the language with a wide variety of pet sayings such as, "Daddy, Daddy, Daddy—bull pussy!" and the ever popular, "Shit fire!" To novice parachutists all these expressions meant one thing: assume the leaning rest position and start pushing yourself away from the red Georgia clay.

Some men paid an extra price. Emmett Fike of the 10th Rangers stood six feet five inches tall, and his trouser legs were too short to remain properly tucked in his boots in paratrooper fashion. (Rubber bands, chains, condoms, and the wide variety of devices experienced paratroopers used to blouse their boots were forbidden in jump school.) Each time his trousers pulled free of his boots, Fike found himself facedown, pushing off the earth. In desperation he sewed the bottoms of his trouser legs to the tops of his socks. The ruse lasted but a short time; when the humorless instructor found out, the man put Fike back in the leaning rest position.[3]

The sixth and final week of the second Ranger training cycle at Fort Benning ended on January 13. In addition to the 3rd, 5th, 6th, and 8th companies being available for overseas shipment, all surplus personnel from these four companies were transferred to the 7th Ranger Company. The 7th was informally designated as the Ranger holding company, pending the beginning of the third training cycle. Six Ranger officers and ninety enlisted men were available for replacements. The 5th Rangers had Mohawk haircuts. When the opportunity presented itself, they would sit in a circle at the small Ranger post exchange drinking beer and throwing the empty cans at anyone who entered the PX. No one who was not a Ranger was permitted entrance.

At 0900 hours on January 18 the advance parties for the 3rd,

5th, and 8th Rangers departed Fort Benning, en route to Camp Carson, Colorado. The three companies were scheduled for mountain and cold-weather training for four weeks before deployment to Korea. At 1000 hours the 6th Rangers made an extra jump, as availability of aircraft for parachuting in Europe was questionable. At 1710 hours, on French Field, a graduation parade was held and each of the companies received their guidons from Colonel Van Houten.

On January 20 the 3rd, 5th, and 8th Ranger companies departed Fort Benning by troop train to Camp Carson. The same afternoon five Ranger officers and sixty-nine enlisted men departed for Korea as replacements. The 3rd, 5th, and 8th Rangers held going-away celebrations where youthful spirits held sway. In 5th Company the bill for damages was $1,200.

Each Ranger company commander had considerable leeway in shaping his command, and the companies would often take on the personalities of their commanders. Some saw their commands as highly efficient killing machines and maintained strict discipline. Some stressed individual initiative. There was even a school of thought that Rangers were like pirates or freebooters, that anything outside the company was fair game. The only loyalty that mattered was within the company. It is not the purpose of this work to compare the performance of the various companies who fought in Korea; all fought well, and all found discipline necessary to success.

On January 22 Lt. Col. Henry Koepcke, Jr., left Fort Benning to attend a training conference at Army Field Forces, then proceeded to Camp Pickett, Virginia, to discuss the screening of volunteers for the next cycle of Ranger training, scheduled to commence on March 19.

On January 29 Colonel Van Houten made his first parachute jump.

The 6th Ranger Company (after making four parachute jumps during their final week at Benning) departed on January 31. Five officers and 118 enlisted Rangers left Columbus, Georgia, by commercial train for the New York port of embarkation via Fort Dix. The 6th was commanded by Capt. James S. "Sugar" Cain. A member of the 1st Special Service Force in World War II, Cain had won a battlefield commission in 1944. The executive officer was Capt. Eldred E. "Red" Weber, who had served with both the 1st Ranger Battalion and the 1st Special Service Force in World War II. Completing this triad of outstanding leadership was 1st Sgt. Joseph Dye. A member of the 1st Ranger Battalion in World War II, Dye participated in the Dieppe raid and campaigns in North Africa, Sicily, and Italy. Despite its strong leadership, however, the 6th Company had a serious morale problem. The men of the 6th Rangers had volunteered to fight in Korea, and to be ordered to the defense of Europe was a terrible blow. Some very tough men openly wept when duty prevented them from going to battle. But procurement of Ranger volunteers from the U.S.-based armies was going slowly, so another call was made to the 82nd Airborne Division for 202 more volunteers.

A troop train, it has been observed, is an instrument invented by the devil. The train that carried the 3rd, 5th, and 8th companies to Camp Carson was no exception. Its rolling stock was antiquated, filthy, and devoid of comfort to the point that would have made a Spartan wince. If the war was a priority, it was not noticeable; the troop train was shunted into sidings to free the tracks for a never-ending procession of locals and slow-moving freights that were apparently deemed of greater importance. It was on this trip that the Rangers began their practice of lowing like cattle to express their displeasure.

The experience of these Ranger companies on the trip to Colorado, and their training there, differed little from those Ranger companies that followed, except that it was winter in the Colorado mountains when these three companies arrived. By its nature, war and preparation for it is a "hurry up and wait" experience. Boredom is the soldier's frequent companion. During the long train ride, Rangers played cards, wrote letters, and talked, but it was not sufficient to break the monotony. Soon small groups of Rangers were slipping away from the train at each stop, arriving unannounced at local bars and taverns. These dusty bands of grim-faced men would, to the astonishment of the local clientele, toss down whatever was available and disappear as quickly as they came. Frequently, refreshment the Army calls "class VI" was brought back to their comrades. The parties grew raucous as the train crawled through the night. There was a lot of bragging about what was in store for the Chinese when the Rangers hit the battlefield.

At one lonely way station a two-man combat patrol was dispatched to capture a quantity of beer. The pair was successful, but before they could reboard the train it suddenly began to move. Refusing to discard their precious cargo, the two Rangers raced down the tracks in pursuit of the train. It was a grueling run made under the eyes of a supportive and critical audience, but at length the booty reached outstretched hands and the exhausted heroes were dragged aboard.

The desolation of the Texas outback provided an opportunity some men could not resist, and they honed their marksmanship by firing their weapons out of the train windows at a variety of objects.

The Rangers arrived at Camp Carson at night and were out with the dawn for their morning five-mile run. Men from other sections of the country were astounded at the area's natural beauty. The mountains seemed to rise forever, and that first sight was the beginning of a love affair between the Rangers and the high country. But that morning run also quickly brought home a significant difference: what had become routine in Georgia was difficult in the high altitudes of Colorado. Getting the lungs acclimated to reduced oxygen was the first barrier to be crossed in mountain and cold-weather training.

New cold-weather equipment was issued, and the men found it difficult to pack away the beloved Corcoran jump boots. Ankle-high hiking boots with eyelets and metal hooks were used in the mountains, their soles and heels deep-lugged for traction. The boots were worn in conjunction with a short canvas legging. Thermal underwear, fur-lined pile caps and parkas, trigger-finger mittens, and shoe packs were part of the issue, as were rucksacks, pack boards, and two-man mountain tents with white interiors, which could be heated with a candle.

Rangers accustomed to long-distance horizontal marching now began to master the techniques of vertical movement. Day after day they climbed mountains ranging from six to ten thousand feet in elevation. They forded swift-flowing mountain streams and hiked in and out of draws, ravines, and canyons. Training included the uses of ice axe and piton, rappeling, and the technique of walking in snow shoes. The names Cheyenne Mountain, St. Peter's Dome, and Rock Creek Canyon became as familiar to the Rangers as the landmarks of their home communities.

as familiar to the Rangers as the landmarks of their home communities.

The cold was ever-present, and temperatures of 25 to 35 degrees below zero were commonplace. As with the lack of oxygen, cold took getting used to. Strange things happened to metal; as Captain Herbert, commander of the 8th Rangers was chopping wood, the steel head of the axe exploded.

While learning new techniques, the men continued to practice the old. There was first aid, field artillery adjustment, communications, map and compass, and weapons training—and, as always, the long speed march under heavy packs.

Constant movement called for individual rations that could be quickly prepared. The Trail Frigid Ration consisted of one meat bar, ten cigarettes, one soup packet; packets of tea, coffee, cream, and sugar; iron rations, matches, and enough toilet paper for one bowel movement per day. The quantity of this last item was sufficient, as the meat bar was usable only as a sap or pry and the remainder of the ration was insufficient to leave any waste product. Normal functions were inhibited by the extreme cold. It took an act of courage to drop one's trousers in such a climate. One Ranger went a week before doing so, and the legend is that his piteous cries still resound among the hills.

Snow meant being wet, cold, and routinely miserable. Rangers learned early to protect their boots when curling up in the warm and snug mountain sleeping bag. Many men slept cuddled next to their boots; to leave them exposed was to risk marching with feet encased in cast iron the next morning.

There was seldom protection from weather, and the route to the objective was always over the most difficult terrain. Sleeping on steep mountainsides often required tying the bag to a rock or tree. The following morning men uncurled at the bottom of their sleeping bags and began to work their way back up to find the opening.

In the mountains there was never a set time for rest. After a long, cold march that lasted till well after dark, a Ranger decided he would remove all his wet clothing and put it in the bottom of the sleeping bag. He reasoned that while he slept nude, body heat would dry his clothes. All preparations were made. With a contented sigh the nude man zipped up the bag. Suddenly he was jarred from his rest by the platoon sergeant's cry of, "Everybody on your feet, we're moving out—*right now*!"

slopes canned heat would be broken out and snow melted to
make coffee and soup. As darkness fell, the Rangers would watch
the lights of Colorado Springs come on.

Down in the lowland, on a sunny day, a speed march ended
at a series of corrals. "Our new home," cried a delighted
Ranger, while others mooed and stamped their feet. The ap-
pearance of some weatherbeaten cowboys in Army garb soon
brought silence. "This here," one cowpoke said, pointing to a
large object behind him, "is what the Army calls a quadruped,
but you Rangers can call it a mule." Farm boys in our ranks
sniggered while city dwellers took notes. We learned that these
"cowboys" were members of the 35th Quartermaster (pack)
Company. Along with the 4th Field Artillery Battalion (pack),
they formed the last of the mule skinners in the U.S. Army.[4]
Like the Rangers, they were a different breed of men. Their
average PFC looked to be forty-five years of age, with worn
face and callused hands. It was difficult to determine how much
of their instruction was fact, as opposed to being for their own
amusement. Mule and Ranger were soon joined in an uneasy
relationship.

"When you are in the high country," one instructor said,
"never forget that the supplies this mule carries on his back can
mean the difference between life and death to you."

"How much can he carry?" a Ranger asked.

"About three hundred pounds."

"Lazy bastard!" the shoulder-weary Ranger snapped.

"Remember this," the instructor said, spitting a stream of
tobacco juice to one side. "Never, never look a mule in the
eye."

"Why not?" a wide-eyed innocent asked.

"Because if you do," the instructor opined, "the mule will
know he is smarter than you are, and when that happens it's all
over."

With disbelieving laughter, the Rangers went about the business of learning myriad rope, halter, and other barnyard accessories. Soon the mules were being packed and led about, and
very quickly the Rangers were heading up Cheyenne Mountain.
The long trek upward was pandemonium as men cursed and
snarled, dragging both mule and supplies up the steep slope.
Some men nursed bruises from kicks and bites or ran to and fro
in pursuit of cantankerous beasts whose dark hearts held not an

Some men nursed bruises from kicks and bites or ran to and fro in pursuit of cantankerous beasts whose dark hearts held not an ounce of cooperation. Farm lads bit the mules' ears and twisted tails, while those raised in the city gazed on in horror.

One Ranger mulled over the instructor's last advice in his mind and came to the conclusion that he did not believe him. "You're not smarter than I am," he snarled, and, turning, fixed the mule with a long, cold stare. The mule gazed back, his eyes black, opaque, a long dark tunnel of nothingness. The Ranger tensed and summoned a mad fire in his eyes. The mule gave no sign of recognition. The man relaxed. Suddenly the mule loosed a tremendous bray. Coming off the ground with all four feet, it launched a devastating kick rearward, bared teeth resembling the blade of a guillotine, and jerked the lead rope from the startled Ranger's hand. There was a spray of dust and gravel as the mule charged down the hill. An hour passed before they met again. The mule was fresh, and its muzzle wore the haughty look of the victor. Exhausted, keenly aware of the difference between the civilian and the Army mule, the Ranger apologized and promised good treatment. The mule had made his point. With dignity intact, it permitted its lead rope to be grasped, and Ranger and mule headed toward the high country. The Ranger kept his face and eyes looking to the front. I remember the episode clearly, for I was that Ranger, and I was sure I had seen that mule smile.

There were the usual hijinks performed by young men bursting with vitality. Neighboring units who had so little pride in their guidons as to leave them out at night found them missing, detour signs showed up in strange places, street signs were changed about. A small demolitions charge removed the corner of a building.

In Colorado Springs groups of Rangers established favorite watering holes. The Brass Rail, Navaho Hogan, Caravan Club, Covered Wagon, and House of Oscar each had a group of Rangers who defended their turf against all comers. The military police began to travel in packs; like wild dogs, they had learned they were not effective operating singly, and they were quick to use their clubs. One Ranger made the mistake of sassing the M.P.s in their den. When he came to on their orderly-room floor, he found he had been scalped: his red, white, and blue

Airborne patch had been torn from his cap and tacked, along
with similar patches, above the military-police bulletin board.

Rumor had it that the 5th Rangers received seventy-eight de-
linquency reports for their last night in Colorado Springs. The
5th began to affect the wearing of a small gold earring, but this
was not popular with the other companies. When a Ranger of
8th Company showed up with a gold earring, Captain Herbert
burned it off by the sheer fire in his voice.

The social event of the season was the wedding of Lt. Berkeley Strong, platoon leader, 3rd platoon, 8th Rangers. But he had
little time for a honeymoon. One of the men had fallen asleep
in the bathtub of a downtown hotel, leaving the water running.
As water obeys the law of gravity, a first-floor dress shop suffered greatly, and Lieutenant Strong supervised the settlement.

The last march was a long one at a rapid pace through snow
from Camp Hale to Camp Carson with an infiltration course on
the end. On Tuesday, 27 February 1951, the 3rd, 5th, and 8th
Ranger companies entrained for Camp Stoneman. A military
band played "So Long, It's Been Good to Know You." As the
train pulled away, Lieutenant Strong's bride stood by the train
waving farewell. This poignant scene brought home the realiza-
tion that like those Rangers who had gone before, the 3rd, 5th,
and 8th would soon know war.

Chapter 8

The February rounds of stroke and counterstroke opened with a Chinese counterattack to the north of Yoju. U.N. forces responded by regaining Inchon and the Kimpo airfield in Seoul. On February 13 Chinese armies launched a massive attack in central Korea, but at Chipyong-ni they tasted defeat. At 1000 hours on February 21 the U.N. forces struck back with Operation KILLER. Slowly, against stiff resistance and heavy rain, the U.N. forces pushed the enemy back, cutting off Hoengsong and killing large numbers of the enemy.

The beginning of the month found the 1st Rangers in Wonju for maintenance and rest. Their respite was brief, and on February 3 they were back in action, patrolling to the front of the 38th Regiment. When a search of their patrol area brought no enemy contact, the company employed one platoon as a decoy sitting around fires while the other two remained in hiding. The Communists took the bait and were punished in a short, sharp firefight; they fled with the Rangers in pursuit. Several stream crossings in the intense cold made it necessary to discontinue the chase and return to friendly lines. There were no Ranger casualties.

The following night the 1st Ranger Company closed in to an assembly area near Hoengsong. The move was made to facilitate a daring operation, a raid on a North Korean headquarters located nine miles behind enemy lines at the town of Changmal. Planning for the raid was jointly conducted between 2nd Infantry Division G-3, the 38th Infantry Regiment, and Lt. Alfred Herman, 1st Ranger Company commander.

Because the objective was in mountainous terrain, beyond the transmission range of the company radios, it was decided that the raiding party would communicate by means of a light, fixed-wing aircraft equipped with an SCR 300 radio. The plane would pass over the Ranger route of march at 1700 hours on February 6 and at 0900 hours the following day. The Rangers gave specific instructions that the plane not circle and reveal their position, so overhead flight would be on a straight line. Contact would be made on the second pass.

At 1352 hours on February 6 the 1st Ranger Company, its leaders well-briefed on the location of known enemy positions, crossed the line of departure. The route required and received a masterpiece of land navigation. The most difficult terrain was employed, as the Rangers moved by compass azimuth from landmark to landmark. The men traveled light, the bulk of their load being ammunition, with riflemen carrying two bandoliers plus three to six hand grenades. To enable leaders to exercise better fire control, all ammunition was tracer.

Near the town of Songbau the company left two squads to cover them from the ridgeline while they moved along a valley floor. On the ridgeline the covering force came under attack. While pinning the enemy with fire, the remainder of the force moved to the flank of the enemy and killed them. Sgt. John Girolimo of Binghamton, New York, distinguished himself in this action.

The movement north continued through the darkening night. It was a long, grueling march in sub-zero temperatures and deep snow, under a starlit sky. Ranger Mark Goyen remembers that in places the slopes were so steep and slick that the Rangers slid down them, using their bodies as toboggans. There were several crossings of ice-cold streams, but there was no respite from the misery of marching in wet boots. In the darkness they could hear enemy forces moving nearby, but the Rangers continued on the mission. A source of constant concern was the barking of dogs, more alert than their Communist masters.

Nearing Changmal, one platoon went forward while the remainder of the company remained in reserve. Numerous lights were seen within the houses, and the Rangers were close enough to hear enemy soldiers talking and laughing. The company interpreter identified the voices as North Korean and said that there were "many, many." At that moment the Rangers were challenged by an enemy guard. Lieutenants Herman and Green fired their carbines, and Sgt. William Cole threw a fragmentation grenade into a building. The attack was on.

From a range estimated to be as close as fifteen feet, the 1st Rangers opened fire. The crash of grenades and the roar of small-arms fire ripped the night. The 38th Infantry Regiment report to the 2nd Division states that the enemy were caught "coming out of windows, doors, and everywhere." Lieutenant Herman reported ". . . they came running out of those huts like bees out of a hive, only many of them did not get out."

The Ranger tracer ammunition streaked the sky with red. Lines of fire stitched across a squad of enemy soldiers trying to get out of a hut. Their bodies fell in the shadows. The Rangers' firepower was devastating; squad leader Anthony "Luke" Lukasik of Warren, Michigan, remembers quickly firing two bandoliers of ammunition and throwing all his grenades.[1] Men remember the night glowing bright from tracers and from buildings taking fire. They remember seeing the enemy running and falling.

With Changmal ablaze and enemy bodies littering the snow, the Rangers started home. Fire was received from flanking ridges but was eliminated by the 1st platoon. The official report shows that five enemy machine guns and three burp guns were secured in the process. Sgt. William Cole of San Diego performed yeoman service in knocking out those guns. A prisoner was also captured who stated that his battalion was quartered in the town and that he was a member of the 12th North Korean Division.

Using an alternate route that at times took them deeper into enemy territory, the 1st Rangers began their return march. Ranger casualties were only three men wounded: A squad leader had been hit in the hand, another man in the elbow, and the most seriously wounded had been hit twice in the leg.

With a long distance to go and cross-country movement hampered by the wounded, Lieutenant Herman decided to leave a small stay-behind force with the wounded near Su-dong while the remainder of the company made its way back to friendly lines. There an attempt would be made to send a helicopter in after the most seriously wounded men. The company had no communications with friendly forces, for the plan to communicate with the liaison plane had gone awry when the pilot could not locate the Rangers.

Moving back to friendly lines, the Rangers were able to evade North Korean search forces. Spotting enemy observation posts overlooking Hoengsong, the Rangers cut enemy telephone lines and returned to 38th Infantry positions, arriving at 1730 hours on February 7.

A helicopter came forward to 38th Infantry positions but developed engine trouble and could not go beyond the lines to secure the wounded man.

At 0730 hours on February 8 a Ranger patrol passed through the lines to bring back the wounded. They had not gone far when seven demoralized North Koreans surrendered to them. The prisoners stated that Changmal had been headquarters of the 1st Regiment, 12th North Korean Division, and that this regiment along with another had been quartered around the town of Changmal. The uncertainties generated by the raid had caused these two regiments to withdraw to the northwest. Encumbered by the prisoners, the patrol returned to friendly lines.

The stay-behind force—consisting of seven men of the 1st squad, 1st platoon, and the wounded—were concealed in an abandoned Korean hut. On outpost duty overlooking a nearby road was the sharp-eyed Cpl. Glen M. Hall from California.[2] Hall's instructions were to observe and report enemy movement but to take no action that would reveal the position of the squad. Those keeping watch from the house were therefore startled to hear a single shot from Hall's location. Moving warily up the hill, they were relieved to find Hall still in position. On the road below him lay a dead North Korean messenger, the wheels of his bicycle up-ended and spinning lazily beside him. Hall apologized, allowing it was a target he could not pass up. Hiding the evidence, the remainder of the squad returned to their positions, again cautioning Hall to observe but take no action.

Several hours passed before Hall's rifle spoke again and another messenger joined his ancestors. Hall's repeated firing, coupled with the nonappearance of the helicopter or any relief force, made the squad determined to take action on their own. But just at that moment a most welcome sight appeared: 1st Sgt. Romeo Castonguay. An experienced professional soldier, Castonguay hailed from Maine and had served as a cavalry officer. Concern for his men ruled his life. Displeased with efforts to assist the stay-behind force, Castonguay had come through enemy lines by himself to bring the men home.

Under Castonguay's direction the men constructed a litter and the march back to friendly positions began. In straight-line distance the route measured six miles, but straight-line distance is not descriptive of what these men endured in carrying out the wounded man. During their return through enemy territory, the squad crossed eight razorback ridges, each of which was a major obstacle.

The 1st Ranger Company raid on Changmal ranks in history with the Roger's Rangers' raid on the Saint Francis Indians and the raid of the 1st Ranger Battalion on the Italian Bersaglieri at Sened Station, North Africa.[3] Each involved a long and difficult approach march through enemy territory, a violent and successful surprise attack, and a rapid and hazardous withdrawal.

A subsequent prisoner-of-war report confirmed that Changmal had been the headquarters of the 12th North Korean Division.

A twenty-minute audio recording of interviews with men of the 1st Ranger Company, who had been asked to talk about the Changmal raid, was received by the public information officer to document the Rangers' exploits.

Early February saw the Eighth Army Rangers doing night patrols ahead of the Turkish Brigade. The patrols were hazardous, but the major difficulty was remembering the Turkish password in effect.

Despite the relatively short time three of the four Ranger companies had been in Korea, high level reports were requested on their performance. On February 6, X Corps sent a message to divisions that stated in part:

Request from EUSAK [Eighth U.S. Army Korea] in regard to Rangers, report due to EUSAK by 10 Feb. Report of operations of Rangers as organized under TO&E 7–87. Report should include method of employment, adequacy of TO&E, contemplated operations, and specific comments of commanders to which these outfits are attached.

The comments returned by the commanders reveal typical conceptions and, in the case of Major General Moore, misconceptions of Ranger capabilities.

Comments by Major General Moore, CG IX Corps:
The 4th Ranger Company, which was attached 1st Cavalry

Division, was relieved from attachment before its equipment had arrived this theater. Further, the company needed additional training, particularly physical training, before being committed to action because it had spent some six to eight weeks of inactivity while en route Korea. It therefore has not been employed on other than local security or training missions. Included in plans for employment of the Ranger company: Leave it in various ambush positions when the division withdraws to successive delaying positions. Set up ambushes in villages which guerrillas are in habit of frequenting to secure food, to destroy guerrilla forces in our rear area, and to make deep reconnaissance of enemy rear areas when front stabilized.

Comments of Major General Ruffner, CG 2nd Infantry Division:
In modifying T/Os and T/Es, care must be exercised to keep this type unit a small, compact, lightly equipped outfit which can move swiftly on foot over a considerable distance. If it becomes another rifle company, then it loses its reason for being created. It is a ready-made force for rapid, finite operations in enemy rear areas, designed to hit a particular target, destroy it, and return to base rapidly by some other route.

The performance of our attached Ranger company has been outstanding. Their devotion to duty and desire "to get the job done" is a splendid example of our American soldier's aggressive spirit and will to win. I recommend a Ranger company be organic to each infantry division.

Comments of Major General Ferenbaugh, CG 7th Infantry Division:
In view of mission assigned this division requiring its employment by battalion combat teams in tortuous mountain terrain over extended distances and widely separated sectors, it has been difficult to employ the 2nd Ranger Company entirely in its prescribed specialist role.

On every occasion, performance of 2nd Ranger Company has been highly praised by commanders who have assigned missions to the organization. Their specialized training and high esprit due to their volunteer status makes their assignment desirable to augment any fighting unit.

This unit is presently at sixty-one percent strength. No forecast indicating increase to authorized strength has been given this headquarters. In order to utilize this highly trained unit efficiently and maintain morale, qualified replacements should be made available through normal channels with same frequency as for other units of a division.

In view of outstanding performance of this unit, it is believed that one company (Ranger) for each infantry regiment with a battalion headquarters and service company for administration and logistical support would be desirable.

Comments of Major General Keen, CG 25th Infantry Division:
The present TO&E under which the Ranger company is organized is adequate wherein it is necessary that they support themselves during limited periods of time while engaged in a combat mission. But the Ranger company, as organized under TO&E 7–87, even with authorized augmentation, is dependent upon another unit for support when not engaged in combat operations.

It is contemplated that the Ranger company will continue to operate on separate day and night combat-type missions and/or in conjunction with armor or tank infantry team missions.

Although there have been a scarcity of suitable targets where Ranger-type missions could be performed, the Eighth Army Ranger Company has proven its value to this division, and it is considered that under present TO&E that the company will continue to be an essential part of the division.

It is recommended that sufficient personnel and equipment to perform necessary administration and messing facilities be authorized the Ranger company to make it self-sufficient.

Three of the four commanders spoke highly of the Rangers and wished to retain them. Major General Moore's comments on the 4th Rangers being out of condition are without foundation. All companies did regular physical training on ship. The 4th traveled with the 2nd, yet the 2nd was promptly committed to action and showed no sign of needing additional physical training. There was nothing wrong with the 4th Rangers except the need to be given a meaningful mission.

* * *

February 10 was a day of celebration for the Eighth Army Rangers. While on patrol on the road to Inchon, the Rangers were joined by the 25th Division Reconnaissance Company and both units advanced toward the port city, encountering numerous mines and booby traps left by the withdrawing Communists. By 1700 hours the Rangers and the 25th Reconnaissance Company had entered Inchon, the first units to do so. A defensive perimeter was established from which platoon-size patrols were dispatched. On February 11 the 2nd platoon encountered a Communist force near a railroad station on the outskirts, killed two and captured one of the enemy without Ranger loss.

On February 12 an event occurred that flashed along the front. The Dutch Battalion was approached by a force their sentries assumed to be enemy. The Dutch opened fire. "Don't shoot," the approaching troops yelled. "Okay. We're ROKS, okay. Okay ROKS!" Confused, the Dutch sentries allowed the force into the perimeter. The strange soldiers smiled politely and chattered away until they were close to the battalion headquarters. Suddenly they dropped the pretense of being South Korean and revealed themselves as a skilled Chinese raiding party. They killed the Dutch commander, Lieutenant Colonel den Ouden, and five headquarters personnel; fourteen other Dutch were wounded and eight were reported missing. It was said some of the Dutch were bayoneted in their sleeping bags. After the Dutch experience, it was exceptionally dangerous for South Korean troops to enter their allies' lines.

The 2nd Rangers had been frequently on the move throughout early February, answering the calls of one regiment after another in the manner of a fireman when the town is ablaze. The twelfth of February found them at Chechon attached to the 32nd Regimental Combat Team. On February 14 the Eighth Army Rangers moved twenty miles, and through the following day, they maintained security outposts and patrols at 25th Division tactical headquarters. On February 16 they moved to the vicinity of Songyolmi. The 25th Division was advancing toward the An River, and the Rangers patrolled, maintained contact on the division's right flank, and established blocking positions. By late February they could look across the frozen waters of the Han River at the point where the Pukhan River joined it from the north.

Chapter 9

A major attack by the Chinese was developing, which they called "the Fourth Phase Offensive." The blow would strike most heavily on the 8th ROK and the 2nd U.S. Infantry divisions. As the U.N. forces began to withdraw, X Corps established a new defense line with the 24th Division on the left, the 2nd Division in the center, and the 187th Airborne Regimental Combat Team on the right. The 2nd Division had assigned the 23rd Regimental Combat Team with the attached French Battalion a threefold mission: defend the Chipyong-ni area; protect the left flank of the division; and deny the enemy the use of the important road network in the vicinity of Chipyong-ni.

Chipyong-ni is a crossroads town in Central Korea. Located approximately thirty kilometers northwest of Wonju, Chipyong-ni is encircled by eight hills that reach as high as four hundred meters. In February 1951 a single railroad track ran through the town. Most of the buildings had been destroyed, and only a few brick and frame houses and the railroad station remained.

Col. Paul L. Freeman, commanding officer of the 23rd RCT, recognized that his force of approximately four thousand men was not sufficient to defend the town using the high ground which surrounded it. While these were otherwise ideal defensive positions, the high-ground perimeter was too great a distance to be covered with the men available. Freeman dug in his forces in a circular perimeter approximately two kilometers in diameter on low hills around the town. It was difficult digging, as the ground was frozen and covered with snow.

Ammunition was stockpiled for the 37th Field Artillery Battalion and B battery of the 82nd Anti-Aircraft Artillery (quad .50-caliber machine guns, half-track mounted). Registration of fire commenced. Registration involved adjusting fire (usually artillery or mortar fire) on one or more reference points before the fighting began. Firing data for other targets could then be arrived at with more speed and accuracy during the confusion of battle. Heavy patrol activity was also planned, and this resulted in a call for the Rangers.

On February 9 the 1st Ranger Company moved by truck to Chipyong-ni where it was attached to the 23rd Infantry Regiment. On arrival, Ranger Lukasik noted that American artillery pointed east, west, north, and south—a foreboding alignment.

While the 1st Rangers were occupying new positions, the 2nd Rangers, with the 7th Division, were moving from Tanyang some twenty miles to Chuchon-ni. There they would be attached to the 32nd Regimental Combat Team for the defense of Chechon. During the move one of the 2nd Rangers became an object of admiration and kidding. In the small hours of night, from his snow-covered foxhole, Ranger Herculano Dias had heard a sound closing on him that was neither the wind nor a fellow Ranger. Dias did the prudent thing and fired; the sound ceased. The next morning Dias and his friends were startled to find a cat shot to death in front of Dias's foxhole. "You is a hearin' mutha!" said one Ranger. "Anybody that could hear a cat walking on snow . . ."

At 1900 hours on February 11 the 1st Rangers left the Chipyong-ni perimeter on a combat patrol. Their mission was to penetrate the town of Miryang-ni and the high ground to the northwest and develop the location of the enemy. The company cleared the town but at 2150 hours found the enemy entrenched on a ridge west of Miryang-ni, and a sharp, hour-long firefight occurred in which the enemy employed heavy machine-gun and 82mm mortar fire.[1] The Rangers fought their way into the Chinese position and seized two prisoners before withdrawing. James O. Dance, Jr. was killed and Gordon Meanley and Roy Coffey were wounded. The company returned to friendly lines at 0140 hours on February 12.

Another casualty of this patrol was the French war correspondent Jean Marie de Premanville of Agence Press. This, the only occasion where a civilian war correspondent accompanied the Rangers on a combat mission in the Korean War, ended in tragedy, when de Premanville was hit by enemy machine-gun fire. The Rangers tore the door off a school and with this make-shift stretcher attempted to bring him to safety. His life ebbing from his wounds, de Premanville's last words were, "I came for a story and I got it."

On return from the patrol, the 1st Ranger Company (along with B Company of the 23rd Infantry Regiment) formed the regimental combat team reserve. The reserve positions were under frequent 82mm and 120mm mortar fire. Several Rangers were inside a hut making oatmeal for breakfast when a mortar round exploded outside the door. Ranger George Early, who had been sitting with his back toward the doorway, was killed by shrapnel from the exploding round.

The positions of the 23rd RCT and attached units at Chipyong-ni were arranged in clocklike fashion: the 1st Battalion (less Company B) covered the area from twelve to two o'clock, the 3rd Battalion from two to five o'clock, the 2nd Battalion from five to seven o'clock, and the French Battalion from seven to twelve o'clock. As the defenders prepared themselves, all signs pointed to an increased enemy buildup in preparation for an attack. On the night of February 13 the enemy struck.

First came the sound of bugles, their brazen call ringing from all points of the compass, then the sound of cymbals, followed by a pyrotechnic display that lit up the surrounding sky. Before midnight a strong artillery and mortar attack began to pound allied positions, followed by a powerful assault on the 1st Battalion. The attack quickly spread around the perimeter, beating like waves against an island shore. Heavy fighting lasted throughout the night. Just before daylight, the Chinese broke contact and withdrew to avoid exposure to air and observed artillery fire. The Americans and French spent the day in reorganization.

The Chinese resumed their assault early on the night of February 14, striking heavily at the 2nd and 3rd battalion positions. Chinese dead were being piled in windrows, yet still the attacks came on. The firing was continuous and, within the perimeter, ammunition stocks began to diminish. At several points the perimeter was penetrated, but counterattacks restored the position.

The worst was yet to come.

At 0315 hours on February 15 a furious Chinese assault shattered the defenses of G Company, 23rd Infantry. Suffering heavy casualties, the remnants of the company withdrew under command of Lt. Thomas Heath. The gap in the perimeter threatened to release a flood of the enemy into the heart of the defense.

A hastily organized composite counterattack force was formed under command of Lieutenant Curtis of the 23rd Infantry, to which the 1st Ranger Company was called upon to provide one platoon (approximately thirty-three men). An understrength rifle platoon with twenty-eight men came from F Company of the 23rd while sixteen survivors of G Company were included. Even the desperate nature of the situation could scarcely serve as justification for creating such a mix of strangers to make a hasty night counterattack.

Lieutenant Herman, the Ranger company commander accompanying the platoon, protested the piecemeal separation of his unit, arguing that the Rangers should be given the mission as a unit and that preparatory fire should be placed on the hill. The advantages of using a company accustomed to working together were obvious, but Lieutenant Herman was overruled. Preparatory fire was not available, as mortar and artillery ammunition was in short supply; scarcely a hundred rounds each of 81mm and 4.2-inch mortar ammunition remained for the whole force. Captain Remsburg, a 2nd Battalion (23rd Infantry) staff officer, was placed in command of the composite force. Lt. Mayo S. Heath and the 1st Ranger platoon were assigned the mission of recapturing the right portion of the hill; the men of F and G companies would be to their left.

The 1st platoon leader, Lieutenant Heath, was a daring, courageous officer. From Franklin, Indiana, Heath had served as an enlisted man with the 82nd Airborne Division during World War II. He earned the Bronze Star at Normandy, and in the Battle of the Bulge he won the Silver Star when he and another trooper made a two-man patrol behind German lines, stayed twenty-four hours to obtain information, captured a German prisoner, and returned. Heath had just recently been awarded an oak-leaf cluster to his Silver Star. His proven performance as a Ranger officer had earned the respect of his subordinates and peers. In the cold night he prepared his men for battle.

The counterattack began at 0615, and from the outset it was under heavy fire from Chinese machine guns, automatic weapons, and small arms. Sixty-millimeter mortars and two machine-gun teams from G Company supported the attack but were soon suppressed by Chinese counterfire. Men scarcely reached the base of the hill before they began to fall; Earl Baker was hit in the shoulder, and Mark Goyen went down, both legs penetrated by shrapnel.[2] Lew Villa felt a blow like being struck by a base-ball bat as he was hit by small-arms fire in the hip and leg. Robert Grubb died in the white phosphorous fire of an exploding mortar shell.

The Chinese had sited their machine guns well. Interlocking fire raked the men as they charged up the hill, shouting and firing as they moved. The hasty planning and lack of coordination now revealed itself, as machine guns believed to be located in the French position opened fire on the Rangers. An American tank crew that had been prewarned of the attack fired its .50-caliber machine gun into them.

Beset by friend and foe alike, the counterattack force was shattered. The few surviving Rangers were the only men to gain the crest of the hill. Lt. Mayo Heath was shot down, as was Lt. Thomas Heath from G Company of the 23rd. As was his custom, 1st Sgt. Romeo Castonguay had accompanied the attack force; he was mortally wounded, a portion of his face shot away. Rangers Dansberry, Nichols, Ed Meyers, Colbert, Layon, Trouche, and Simpson were hit. Gene Meyer and John Miess were also wounded.

Rangers Joseph Phillips and Robert Geer reached the top of the hill. "We've got the hill," they shouted. "Hold your fire and get some men up here." There were none immediately available to send. The two remaining Ranger platoons and B Company of the 23rd were still in reserve positions. The situation of the counterattack force was especially desperate, as earlier penetrations elsewhere had required counterforce moves. That, plus a mistaken report that the hill had been retaken, meant that no additional reserve forces were close enough to influence the action.

Wounded Rangers continued to crawl to the top of the hill. The Rangers there were giving a good account of themselves despite being mistakenly fired upon by G Company. Robert Geer saw his brother Richard crawling into the position, wounded in the left leg and below the knee. While they talked, a tracer came from the left (G Company position) and passed through Richard Geer's knee. Angrily, Robert Geer fired in the direction the round had come from. The fire ceased.

Among those to reach the top was Cpl. Glen Hall, who had covered the platoon attack by machine-gun fire, seized a carbine when the weapon malfunctioned, and fought his way up the hill. Hall was attempting to locate the platoon from F Company, unaware that it had been decimated and had not reached the crest. Under heavy fire, he moved to the flank where the platoon was supposed to be and found the position occupied by Chinese. Hall killed the enemy in one foxhole and occupied it. Though wounded, Hall kept up a withering fire on the enemy, preventing them from striking the flank of the Rangers who were fighting to hold the crest.

Robert Geer was in the act of reloading to engage a Chinese squad when one of the Chinese threw a stick grenade with such accuracy that it bounced off Geer's automatic rifle. Unable to locate the grenade in the darkness, Geer braced himself for the explosion. When it came, it lifted him from the ground, blinded him in the left eye, and bent his Browning Automatic Rifle. Unable to hold without additional support, Geer and Phillips covered the withdrawal of the wounded from the hill and broke free in hand-to-hand fighting. Armed only with a knife, Robert's brother Richard Geer fought a desperate battle against a bayonet-armed Chinese and won. Without additional support, Chinese pressure forced a withdrawal from the hill.

Though losing his sight, Robert carried his wounded brother down the slope, often depending on Richard's directions. Richard Geer was struck again during the trip down the hill. When they arrived at the base of the hill, a three-quarter-ton truck was being loaded with wounded. Despite having been hit at least three times, Richard Geer elected to sit in the front seat to allow those whose wounds were more serious to lie down. A short time later a bullet struck him above the heart. Richard Geer would die in a Korean hut while medics worked to save him. He died responding to a call from his brother Robert, who lay on a litter outside the door. Robert Geer would later regain partial sight in his right eye.

At 0800 hours the 2nd and 3rd Ranger platoons and B Company were ordered to attack to restore the lost G Company positions. On the hill, the Chinese were being prevented from following up their success. Captain Elledge, an artillery liaison officer, had put back in action a quad .50 Caliber half-track that had been abandoned by its crew. When assured that only the enemy and American dead remained on the hill, Elledge occupied the gunner's seat and placed a heavy fire on the hilltop. Three American tanks added the fire of their heavy machine guns.

Nearby were 155mm howitzers abandoned by their crews when brought under direct fire by the enemy. An artillery officer led a gun crew back into the position. Lowering a howitzer tube almost to the horizontal, they fired six rounds of white phosphorus at rifle range, the sound of the firing and resultant explosion coming almost as one.

Unable to hold the top of the hill, the Chinese fought a determined reverse-slope defense, controlling the crest and beating back counterattacks. American tanks could not move into position to provide support because the approaches were heavily mined.

Ammunition was in short supply. Air drops from C-119 aircraft were frequent, but initially overshot friendly positions. The Rangers were skilled in airdrop procedures and took over the task of ground control for the drop. Resupply began to fall within the narrow perimeter, but the men who secured the much-needed supplies paid a heavy price to Chinese mortars.

The M-1 rifle used an eight-round clip, and when the last round was fired, the clip ejected. Rangers Dahl and Lukasik recall that the air-dropped ammunition came in the five-round clips designed for the 1903 Springfield rifle of World War I. This required searching through the snow for empty M-1 clips and reloading them and Browning Automatic Rifle magazines by hand while under fire. The situation within the perimeter was desperate, but help was on the way. Task Force Crombez, built around the 5th Cavalry Regiment, was fighting its way toward the embattled defenders of Chipyong-ni.

The 1st Rangers' counterattack force had been under heavy fire throughout the morning. Sgt. Anthony Lukasik saw one of his automatic riflemen, PFC John Knigge, in textbook-perfect, prone firing position but not firing. Lukasik crawled close only to see that Knigge was dead, shot between the eyes. Moments later Lukasik himself was wounded, hit in the forehead and the arm. Evacuated to the aid station, Lukasik was placed on a stretcher close to Lew Villa and the mortally wounded First

Sergeant Castonguay. Grumbling that "The bastards shot my nose away," Castonguay died.

The counterattack by the remaining Rangers and B Company was now turning into a rout of the enemy. In a scene reminiscent of a Western movie, leading elements of the 5th Cavalry Task Force were now in sight. The Rangers launched a furious charge while French in nearby positions cheered, "Ah-Ranger! Ah-Ranger!" An exuberant report stated that hundreds of Chinese were fleeing, as the counterattack force was hitting the Chinese from one side while the 5th Cavalry hit them from the other.

Ranger Lt. Robert Fuller led the survivors of his platoon, four tanks, and a half-track mounted with a twin .40mm gun to make contact with the relief force. Ranger Robert Morgan found himself in a duel with a Chinese soldier armed with a Bren gun. Vastly overpowered, Morgan called on the nearby half-track. The advantage of firepower changed quickly, ending the Chinese soldier's ambitions.[3] Sgt. Andrew Adams distinguished himself in this action by leading his squad in suppressing Chinese antitank fire.

By 1720 hours on February 15 the commanding officer of the 5th Cavalry Regiment was at the 23rd Infantry Regiment command post. Artillery and aircraft continued to pound the fleeing Chinese while a light snowfall covered their dead.

On February 16 the wounded were taken out by convoy. The experienced Lukasik insisted on taking a bottom litter in the ambulance. Having someone over him was added insurance against shrapnel.

With their patrol action the 1st Ranger Company had opened the ball at Chipyong-ni. Their courageous performance contributed greatly to the successful defense; their casualties were eleven Rangers killed and thirty-one wounded. Given early losses, company strength was described as "less than a platoon." For these men there was joy and relief at having survived and defeated the enemy force. Over forty thousand Chinese had attacked the perimeter, which on February 14 and 15 had been completely surrounded. Chipyong-ni was the first defeat of Chinese forces in the Korean War. The American and French units who fought there were awarded the Distinguished Unit Citation.

The Rangers who died at Chipyong-ni were: Cpl. James O. Dance, Jr., 1st Lt. Mayo S. Heath, 1st Sgt. Romeo J. Castonguay, Cpl. Richard P. Geer, Cpl. Robert L. Byerly, Sgt. Robert

Grubb, PFC John H. Knigge, Jr., Sgt. Harold L. Rinard, Sgt. Edmund Mekhitarian, PFC George R. Early, and PFC William J. Graddy.

When the Rangers attacked at Chipyong-ni, they went into the assault yelling. The Ranger yell had roots in Indian war cries of the colonial period and the famed Rebel yell of the Civil War, but each man and each company sought to add their own flavor. The 3rd Ranger Company went into battle yelling "Die Bastard Die." The 2nd and 4th Rangers would shout "Buffalo." The "Devils" of the 8th Ranger Company (Airborne) had a perverse cry of "We'll All Be Killed," a sentiment that came from the involuntary cry of a company officer when a Chinese counterattack struck with fury.

In the U.S. the 2nd Rangers were front-page news. The Communist Chechon salient in central Korea was a threat that needed removal. On February 20 the 2nd Ranger Company captured Chuchon, eight miles to the northeast. The Rangers were reported by the International News Service as having carried out their own version of a "banzai" attack, racing through the town and raking the buildings with automatic weapons fire. With this victory, enemy resistance in the salient collapsed.

On February 22, while occupying a defense position along the Pyongong Ang River, Cpl. James S. Oakley was swept away by the raging current and drowned.

Relieved from attachment to the 17th RCT, the 2nd Rangers departed Chuchon at 0700 by motor convoy and traveled approximately two hundred miles to Taegu, where they arrived at 2000 hours and were attached to the 187th Airborne Regimental Combat Team. Two months of guarding logistical trains had the 4th Rangers in a savage mood. There had been one brief hope for action when the company was alerted to make a parachute assault on a guerrilla headquarters; the men had been chuted up and waiting by the aircraft when the mission was cancelled. Morale was getting low. But on February 28 fortune smiled on the 4th Ranger Company, in the form of news that the company was relieved from attachment to Eighth Army Special Troops and attached to the 187th. For the 2nd and the 4th Rangers the trip to meet the 187th was a joyous one. Like the scent of battle to the nostrils of a war-horse, the sense of an Airborne operation was in the air. It was the sweet and heady ambiance of adventure.

While the 2nd and 4th were en route, elements of the Eighth Army Rangers departed Polli, traveling by motor vehicle to Poonwon-ni, closing into an assembly area at 1530 hours. At 2200 hours Eighth Army Ranger patrols crossed the icy Han River in rubber boats to patrol the enemy shore.

At 0001, February 1, two additional Ranger companies were activated. The 12th Ranger Infantry Company (Airborne) was selected from five hundred volunteers from the 28th Infantry Division (Pennsylvania National Guard). This unit, commanded by Capt. Harold V. Kays, would consist of men reporting from Camp Atterbury, Indiana. The 13th Ranger Infantry Company (Airborne) would be comprised of volunteers from the 43rd Infantry Division (New England National Guard), and be commanded by Capt. Victor K. Harwood. Camp Pickett, Virginia, was the departure point for these future Rangers.

The Department of the Army was becoming concerned about the need for replacement volunteers for the Rangers; 245 volunteers were needed from men serving within the continental United States but by February only forty-one were received.

The next move was to turn again to the 82nd Airborne Division. The 82nd, however, was a strategic reserve unit required to be kept at a state of immediate operational readiness. Operations Division of G-3 requested that machinery be set up to provide the required volunteers rather then continue to draw from the strategic reserve.

Colonel Walker of Ranger Training Center called the Department of the Army to learn the status of incoming volunteers. When informed that this was the last call G-3 intended to make on the 82nd for volunteers, Walker suggested that in view of the need for replacements, the companies beginning training in February (7th and 9th companies) be used as replacements. Walker also suggested that the Ranger company for the 4th Infantry Division be organized from volunteers within the division in the same manner as was to be done with the National Guard divisions.

At Fort Benning, Georgia, training continued—to the great interest of the press. On February 5 a team arrived at the Ranger

Training Center from *Life* magazine to obtain material for an article about the Rangers.

On February 6 Colonel Van Houten completed his Airborne qualification. Major Zimmerman departed for Camp Atterbury to visit the 28th Infantry Division to discuss screening of volunteers for that division's Ranger company (12th Ranger Company). In a speech before the Columbus Kiwanis Club, Colonel Van Houten said, "I like to think of the Rangers as young men in the best American tradition of our pioneer heroes. They accomplish things we'd consider almost impossible."

One hundred ninety-six volunteers were obtained at the 82nd Airborne Division. These would be divided between the 7th and 9th Ranger companies. Capt. Robert Eikenberry would again command the 7th Ranger Company, while the 9th would be commanded by Capt. Theodore C. Thomas. Officers were arriving from across the country. Reporting for duty with the 9th, Lt. Robert Bodroghy was coming from Camp Gordon, Lt. Edward Roderick from Camp Carson, Lt. Edward Hilpert from Fort Ord.[4]

On February 7 the 6th Ranger Company boarded the nine-thousand-ton USNS *George W. Goethals* and sailed from the Brooklyn Navy Yard en route to Germany. Though they devoutly wished they were leaving San Francisco for Korea, the men of the 6th Rangers were trying to keep their spirits up; some felt they would be at war with Russia within a month of their arrival in Europe.

At the time there was a genuine belief among many Americans that war with Russia was imminent. The North Atlantic Treaty Organization had not been formed until 1949 and was not prepared to meet a massive Soviet Army that dwarfed American and European forces. It seemed that only the American superiority in atomic weapons held the Russians at bay. The Europeans, however, did not consider the possibility of their homelands becoming a nuclear battlefield a viable option. The Communist leadership played skillfully on this fear.

On February 10 at an officer's gathering, Colonel Van Houten presented a baby cup to Mrs. John Singlaub. Engraved on the cup was the Ranger patch and the birthdate of John Singlaub, Jr. Two days later, Colonel Van Houten led a night parachute jump, and men of the third Ranger training cycle began to arrive, be processed, and begin training. The third training cycle would consist of the 7th, 9th, 10th, and 11th Ranger companies.

February 17 found the 6th Ranger Company arriving in Bremerhaven, Germany. From there the company traveled by train to Kitzingen, where it began service with the 1st Infantry Division. The Rangers were told their move to Germany was classified information, and the move had been conducted under tight security. There was considerable surprise when they arrived in Kitzingen to find a banner that proclaimed, WELCOME RANGERS.

As every man in the company wanted to be fighting in Korea, morale was initially a considerable problem in the 6th. While reading the many requests for transfer to the battlefront, the officers of the 6th prepared a training program that would keep the company a model for other units in Germany.

Replacements were still a constant source of concern. On February 20 the Department of the Army, representatives of G-1 (personnel) and G-3 (operations and training) met in a preliminary session to prepare for a future discussion of the problem with Colonel Van Houten. As of the meeting date there were eleven Ranger companies on hand: three in Far East Command, three en route to Far East Command, one en route to European Command, and four in training. Nine more companies were planned: one each for the 28th, 31st, 43rd, and 47th divisions, three nondivisional companies for the Caribbean, one for Alaska, and one company to provide replacements for Far East Command.

The meeting report stated:

> It is estimated that approximately 30% of those who begin Ranger training fail to qualify. An additional 20% of those now in training are required at present as replacements for units in the Far East. From this, 200 men are required for training in order to obtain a 100 strength company. It is estimated, therefore, that to provide the 9–11 additional Ranger companies required, approximately 2,000 to 2,200 trainees must be trained during the next six months.

The conferees agreed that the best way to obtain personnel was as follows:

 a. To form the initial company from personnel within the division concerned.

 b. Obtain required replacements by implementing an intensive recruiting program similar to the one used by Airborne units.

Van Houten was deeply concerned about the replacement problem, and it would be necessary to use companies now in training to meet this need. Two hundred seventy-eight white replacements were scheduled to come from the third training cycle; from the fourth there would be eighty black and eighty white replacements. Ranger casualties were high.

On February 21 the 10th and 11th Ranger companies performed a night parachute jump; 9th Company jumped at midnight on the twenty-second. Difficulties were being experienced by the Ranger Training Center in getting aircraft for training. Complaints were rapid and continuous from Ranger Headquarters, but the Air Force seemed inclined to sigh and say, "Don't you know there's a war on?"

February 26 saw the beginning of the third week of training for the third cycle. Two companies spent the day firing Browning Automatic Rifles, while the other two practiced first aid, scouting and patrolling, intelligence work, and combat formations.

At 0001 hours on February 27 the 14th and 15th Ranger infantry companies (Airborne) were activated. The 14th Ranger Company was selected from volunteers within the 4th Infantry Division, a regular Army division stationed at Camp Carson, Colorado. Capt. Sam L. Amato, who, coming from the "Ivy" Division, soon gained the nickname "Poison Ivy," would command the 14th Rangers.[5] The 15th Ranger Company would be commanded by Capt. Paul W. Kopitzke. The company was made up of volunteers from the 47th Infantry "Viking" Division (Minnesota and North Dakota National Guard).

Chapter 10

Company (Airborne) at Fort Benning. On arrival in Korea he had
for a time period been attached to the Eighth Army Ranger Company.

The U.N. forces were on the move in March, continuing their
northward pressure. At 0700 hours, March 7, General Ridgeway launched Operation RIPPER, crossing the Han River east of
Seoul. Within a week the Communists were withdrawing across
the front. On March 15 Seoul was recaptured, and on the twenty-
eighth the 38th parallel was reached.

March also brought winds of change for the Eighth Army
Ranger Company. Captain Vann completed his tour of duty and
returned to the United States, reporting for duty with the Ranger
Training Center. On March 1 Capt. Charles G. Ross, the company executive officer, assumed command.[1] Lt. Glen W. Metcalf assumed the duties of executive officer.

At Taegu the 2nd and 4th Ranger companies joined the 187th
Airborne Regimental Combat Team in practice parachute jumps
followed by tactical problems. Weapons were checked by ordnance and test-fired. Intense training would continue through
the first three weeks of March.

At 1300 hours on March 2 elements of the Eighth Army
Rangers moved from their camp at Polli to an assembly area at
Songnim-dong. As darkness fell, Ranger patrols attempted to
cross the Han River in rubber boats, but thick ice frustrated the
crossing. The same day a 1st Ranger patrol captured two guerrillas along the 2nd Division's main supply route. Sixteen much-
needed replacements joined the unit on March 3.

Also on March 3, four men from the 4th Ranger Company
were selected from some 115 volunteers for a secret mission; no

one knew what they were volunteering for, but it was obvious it would be dangerous. The words of the campfire song—"I want to be an Airborne Ranger, I want to lead a life of danger"— were about to become real. Cpl. Edward Pucel, Cpl. Martin L. Watson, Cpl. William T. Miles, Jr., and PFC Raymond E. Baker hastily packed their gear and departed the company area for detached service with G-3 Eighth Army.

While the 1st Rangers were near Chechon on March 5, Capt. Charles L. Carrier joined the company and assumed command. Captain Carrier had been a member of the 7th Ranger Infantry Company (Airborne) at Fort Benning. On arrival in Korea he had for a brief period been assigned to the Eighth Army Ranger Company.

On March 9 eleven Rangers from the 4th Ranger Company under MSgt. Allen Lang were assigned and joined the 1st Rangers.

In the clear, cold night air of 15 March 1951 a C-47 aircraft made its way over North Korea. On board were 4th Rangers Pucel, Miles, Baker, and Watson; nineteen South Koreans dressed in North Korean uniforms; and three hundred pounds of C3 explosive. Pucel, Baker, and Watson were armed with .45-caliber pistols and six clips of ammunition. Miles would not travel without his M-1 rifle, and carried two bandoliers of ammunition. There were three days' rations, but the men also carried chocolate and bullion cubes.

The mission of this small band was to jump inland from the port of Wonsan and blow up a critical railroad tunnel. The South Koreans had been briefed that if the force was located, the cover would be that the Americans were prisoners of the Koreans. If that failed, first priority would go to rescuing the Americans. The South Koreans had more chance to blend into the landscape.

The mission, however, was in trouble from the moment the men stepped into space. They were dropped in the wrong place. Pucel, Baker, and Miles landed on the outside of a Korean village, and Marty Watson landed on the roof of a Korean hut. The redoubtable Watson joined his comrades in a few minutes, his .45 in one hand, and a well-honed knife in the other.

Several days were lost in locating and consolidating the Korean members of the force. The objective was some distance away, with steep mountains in between. They were astounded at the number of Chinese in the area; Pucel compared it to an anthill. Possibly because of Watson's rooftop landing, the Chinese were aware of the presence of the team and a massive search was under way.

For ten days the Rangers and Koreans moved cross-country through deep snow and intense cold. They did not have snowshoes, and wearied from struggling through snowdrifts, began to take chances by attempting to move by road at night. It was their misfortune to encounter a Chinese patrol resting by the roadside, an alert patrol that promptly challenged them. The Koreans managed to convince the Chinese that they were North Koreans and had lost their way. When clear of the danger, the tired men turned once again to the deep drifts and cross-country movement. The rations exhausted, they burned small amounts of C3 to melt snow and used the bullion cubes with that. Spirits were good until the cigarettes were gone.

The Rangers carried a SCR 300 radio, but it had not worked since landing. Each night they would hear the C-47 flying about; Colonel McGee was overhead trying to contact them. Many times they were tempted to destroy the radio and rid themselves of the dead weight, but they carried it with them in hopes of a miracle.

By March 30 they had reached the top of a mountain near Wonsan. Around the base of the mountain they could see Chinese forces in large numbers. Corporal Miles tried once more to make the radio work and by a freak of communications picked up the conversation of a Marine Corps forward observer later calculated to be some eighty miles distant. The Marines' initial assumption was that Chinese were attempting to deceive them. Ranger Miles pleaded with them to send a message to Colonel McGee at Eighth Army. The message was sent, and the next day a C-47 appeared escorted by three Navy Corsair fighters. The C-47 stayed close enough to establish communication but far enough away to not reveal the Rangers' location. It was too late. Chinese troops were moving up the mountainside.

The Corsairs went into action and were followed by Air Force jets using napalm, bombs, and machine guns on the Chinese located on the slopes and in the valley. The weather was settling in, a snow storm developing, and a hard, freezing wind howled about the top of the mountain. Visibility was dropping fast. If the fighter aircraft could not come, the end would be at hand.

From U.S. Navy ships in Wonsan Bay came three HO3S helicopters, one from the cruiser USS *St. Paul* and two from LST (Landing Ship Tank) 799. Radio communication was hampered, and the wind and snow made landing difficult. The first helicopter, piloted by Navy Lt. John Thornton, was hit by enemy gunfire and crashed, but Thornton was unhurt. A courageous man, Thornton's first thought was to continue the rescue mission. He directed the second helicopter, piloted by Navy Lt. Bob Felton, of Rochester, New York, into position to lower its sling, then signaled Corporal Baker to put the sling under his armpits. Felton engaged the winch, and Baker began to rise through a curtain of Chinese fire. Suddenly the winch jammed. To remain meant certain death, so Felton turned the helicopter away from the mountain and headed out over the valley floor five thousand feet below. Baker swung in circles beneath the chopper, pressing his arms against his sides to hold the sling against him.

Realizing that Baker could not hold on indefinitely and that he might have been wounded, Felton flew for about fifteen minutes, until he saw a stretch of sandy beach near a Korean village. Bringing the helicopter down, Felton lowered Baker to earth then brought the machine low enough to allow Baker to scramble on board. The two men then headed for Felton's ship.

On the mountaintop, Lieutenant Thornton signaled for the helicopter from the cruiser *St. Paul* to lower its sling. Pucel yelled at Thornton to head for safety, but the naval officer declined and told Pucel to take off. Giving Thornton a thermite grenade to destroy the downed helicopter, Pucel wrapped the sling about him and was lifted skyward. As soon as he was on board, the pilot again lowered the sling, and Miles was lifted off the mountaintop. The Chinese continued to pour a heavy volume of fire at the aircraft, and a bullet grazed Miles's face, causing profuse bleeding. The cold, though, was so intense that the blood rapidly froze. In a few moments Pucel pulled Miles on board, but the helicopter had sustained hits from enemy fire and was developing engine trouble. The pilot had no choice but to head for the *St. Paul* immediately. They barely made it, even with the *St. Paul*'s captain assisting by bringing the cruiser closer toward the coast.

With one helicopter down, one disabled, and another with an inoperable winch, the men on the hilltop waited in vain for rescue. Finally, with Chinese closing in, Thornton, Watson, and several South Koreans used the heavily falling snow to make their way through the encircling enemy. For over a week they evaded capture. Finally the two Americans, disagreeing on escape tactics, separated, each traveling with several Koreans. Within ten days both groups had been captured and had begun the long march into captivity.[2]

Martin "Marty" Watson was a man cut from the mold of Arthurian legend. He had served with the 1st Ranger Battalion in World War II and been captured at Cisterna when the 1st and 3rd battalions were trapped behind German lines. Now he would endure imprisonment under the Chinese. Watson was anything but a model prisoner. Dubbed a "reactionary" by the enemy, Watson underwent torture and frequent beatings, but continued to resist. He was one of the last American prisoners to be returned at the war's end.[3]

On March 12 the Eighth Army Ranger Company moved from Polli to Chinjung-ni, and on the seventeenth, a Ranger patrol captured two North Koreans. On March 20 the Eighth Army Ranger Company moved to Sansong-ni.

By mid-March the 1st Ranger Company was regaining its strength, but it would continue division security patrols until March 22. On the nineteenth six of the enemy were captured, and four more on the twentieth.

To be taken prisoner in any war is a dangerous business. Those Communists who survived surrendered early and in large groups. Those who fought till the last second could hardly be expected to surrender, and some men felt one or two prisoners were too much of a nuisance to escort to the rear.

The vicious treatment of American prisoners by the enemy, especially by the North Koreans, earned the undying hatred of most American soldiers. The sight of Americans laying dead in a ditch with their hands bound behind their backs and the evidence of mutilation of our dead cost many a surrendering Communist his life. Though there were times that Chinese and American units displayed chivalry to each other, it was best for a soldier not to bet his life on the enemy being a gentleman.

In the early stages of the war, the Chinese would occasionally release American prisoners, to make Americans believe that lenient treatment awaited a man who surrendered. A 24th Division soldier told of a man who was released to the catcalls of the Chinese soldiers, many of whom spoke English. "What do you think of the Chinese now?" they asked laughingly. As the unarmed American entered a village, he came face to face with a North Korean soldier. Both men immediately put their hands in the air, surrendering to each other. After a brief period of mutual embarrassment they put their hands down, sidled around each other, and went on their way.

As Rangers, we often spoke with or shared rations with the line infantrymen. Some Rangers had a low opinion of the line soldiers' fighting prowess, but most of us had a deep and abiding respect for our fellow Americans in the infantry divisions. Rangers were nomadic warriors constantly on the move, but the line infantry slugged it out day after day, night after night. Often on our nighttime missions we would see them locked in ferocious battle with the enemy.

The infantry soldier was kind, often sharing what little he had, and was often deeply affected by the senseless horror he saw. One weary-looking man with eyes peering out of blackened sockets—a man in his early twenties with six months on the line—told me sadly of a patrol during which they had picked up a young Korean male of military age and were bringing him in for questioning. The young man's aged father wept and screamed with rage at the patrol. He followed at a distance, shouting at them, then he suddenly had something in his hand, preparing to throw. A rifleman, thinking it was a grenade, shot and killed the old man. In his despair and anger the father had been trying to throw a stone.

Tension and fear were the soldier's constant companion. One great fear was being caught unarmed in a sleeping bag and being bayoneted while trying to get free. True or not, men believed the Chinese had caught the Dutch like that, and every precaution was taken. When a soldier slept in a sleeping bag, his bed partner was his favorite sidearm, although sleeping with a .45-caliber pistol provided little comfort, especially if he tossed and turned in his sleep.

On March 22 the 1st Rangers once again began penetrations of the enemy line. The following night a 1st Ranger patrol ghosted through enemy lines, established ambush positions, and identified enemy routes of travel. The next night, while part of the force provided security, others laid mines along the Chinese trails. En route home, the patrol killed two enemy soldiers without Ranger loss.

This operation was an example of many successful forays the
Rangers made through the Communist lines. The missions required skilled leadership and patience. The enemy frequently
employed defense in depth, and one line after another would be
penetrated by Rangers with blackened faces and soft caps, slings
and dog tags taped for silent movement. Covered by the black
cloak of night and moving in single file, a patrol would make
its way into enemy territory, freezing in position at the pop of
a flare. Often the Rangers formed a daisy chain, with a man
holding on to the cartridge belt of the man in front of him.
Passing through an enemy line or approaching an enemy position sometimes called for crawling for hours. If the men did
their jobs well and they were lucky, the mission went well.

These were nights when men remembered their God, nights
when a man had only the dark form of another Ranger to his
front to share his loneliness. There were hours of moving through
the blackness, tense hours when a Ranger's every sense and
nerve strained to locate the enemy before being discovered himself. Each sound in the night was magnified by the imagination.
Men listened . . . and listening . . . then whispered inwardly,
*Yea, though I walk through the valley of the shadow of death, I
will fear no evil*, and continued on.

Things did go wrong, however. A man would slip and lose his
grip on the belt of the man in front of him, and in moments the
column would split asunder, perhaps irretrievably. Hours would
be spent in silent movement, only to have the leader fall off a high
bank or someone slip from a wet paddy dike and land with a loud
splash. On occasion the head of the column would mistakenly
make a U turn; on one patrol that mistake resulted in the tail of
the column firing on the men at the head, wounding them.

When everything else went well, there was always the chance
of finding that the Communist sentries in the rear areas were
exceptionally alert. The Rangers would endure seven hours of
silent movement and gut crawl, only to have the alarm raised
short of the objective. Many of these nights ended like chase
scenes from Western movies, with the Rangers heading for
friendly lines at a fast pace, three or four Browning Automatic
Rifles covering the rear of the column and keeping the enemy
at bay. On some nights there were wounded to be carried home,
backpacked over long distances.

One clearly demonstrable fact remained: the Rangers could

infiltrate the Chinese lines. What was needed was worthwhile
objectives for them to attack. There was a lack of intelligence
effort on the part of the divisions and higher headquarters to
determine Ranger targets, and some divisions objected to having
Rangers operate behind enemy lines, as it interfered with the
division's harassment and interdiction fires. One unit even objected to the temporary loss of its Korean bearers while they
were bringing ammunition to the Rangers.

IX Corps was scheduled to attack at 0800 hours on March
22. This attack would be assisted by an Airborne assault to seize
objectives in the northern part of the Chunchon Basin and to
block enemy movement north through the Chunchon corridor.
The Airborne assault was canceled on March 21, but immediate
planning began on a secondary Airborne mission.

Operation RIPPER was moving well. To support the operation
and cut off Communist forces withdrawing north from Seoul,
Eighth Army directed the execution of an Airborne envelopment, to be named Operation TOMAHAWK. The jump would take
place at Munsan-ni, some twenty-four air miles northwest of
Seoul. The 187th Airborne Regimental Combat Team would be
employed, with the 2nd and 4th Ranger companies attached.
Ground linkup would be with Task Force Growden, which included the 6th Medium Tank Battalion, infantry, and artillery.
This force would attack from Seoul to Munsan-ni.

The 2nd and 4th Ranger companies would be part of the
second serial to jump on Drop Zone (DZ) North, preceeded by
the 3rd Battalion of the 187th. Each company would require four
C-46 aircraft. Planned drop time was H-hour plus five minutes.

The basic uniform and equipment of the individual soldier
included trousers and jacket—some wore the M1943 field
jacket—jump or combat boots, steel helmet, individual weapon,
.45-caliber automatic pistol, cartridge or pistol belt, and ammunition. The combat pack included extra socks, two days assault rations, toilet articles, and gloves. A horseshoe roll
consisting of a blanket wrapped in a poncho was fastened on
the pack, as was an entrenching tool.

H-hour was 0900, 23 March 1951. At 0730, with engines
roaring, the lead troop-carrier aircraft headed down the runway
at K2 airfield, Taegu. The aircraft allocation table for the 187th
called for the unit to be moved in five serials, with drop time

extending from H-hour to H plus fifty. One hundred forty troop-carrier aircraft were allocated, ninety C-119 and fifty C-46 air-craft. Approximately 3,500 parachutists would jump, and air-delivered support would include twelve 105mm howitzers.

The procession of aircraft flew out over the Yellow Sea to avoid ground detection, then headed inland north of Seoul. Nearing the drop zone, the jumpmasters could see the bend of the Imjin River. At 0915 hours the men of the 2nd and 4th Ranger companies exited their aircraft over the Munsan-ni drop zone. In over three centuries of American Ranger history, this was the first combat jump by Ranger units. The men had no time to ponder the history they were making, however—the work was at hand.

The 2nd Rangers had the mission of seizing Hill 151, a key piece of terrain in the zone of the 2nd Battalion, 187th RCT, the unit to which the 2nd Rangers were attached (4th Rangers were attached for operational control to the 3rd Battalion on landing). The drop zone had to be cleared fast, because the 2nd Battalion was jumping right after the Rangers. The jump went well, with only two of the 2nd Rangers injured; the 4th also had men in-jured on the drop, who were promptly treated by a medical de-tachment of Indian soldiers, who did yeoman service on the drop zone. These were the men of the 60th Indian Field Ambulance Unit under the command of Colonel Rangarj who jumped at Munsan-ni with the Rangers and the 187th Airborne Regimental Combat Team. The Indian doctors treated 102 jump casualties and evacuated ten of the seriously injured paratroopers.

There are so many variables in war, it is unlikely that any combat operation goes exactly as planned. Airborne operations are particularly susceptible to error, and Munsan-ni was no ex-ception. The 1st Battalion, which was supposed to be dropped on another drop zone, came in on the primary drop zone, minus the battalion commander and staff who were dropped in the correct, though lonely, place. Accustomed to these incidents, the men continued the mission. The incorrect drop did not even rate a comment in the S-3 journal of the 187th.

The 2nd Ranger Company assembly area was near an orchard at the east end of the DZ. First Sergeant West was an early arrival and from his location he could see two enemy machine guns in position to fire into the company. Taking those few men who had reached the assembly area, West charged the guns, capturing them before the startled enemy could react. The S-2 journal of the 187 Airborne RCT for the Munsan-ni operation shows that the 2nd Rangers turned in the first prisoners taken and the first captured weapon. The prisoners were from the 36th Regiment, 19th North Korean Division, the weapon was a water-cooled Russian Maxim, a .31-caliber heavy machine gun.

At approximately 1030 hours, the 2nd Rangers attacked and cleared the village of Sangdokso-ri, capturing approximately twenty enemy soldiers and killing six. After a quick reorganization, the company began its assault on Hill 151. The attack was supported by F-51 fighters and 81mm mortar fire directed by the company's executive officer, Lt. James Queen. The assault took the objective at the loss of PFC William Van Dunk; Sergeant First Class Boatwright and Sergeant Robertson were wounded. The company established a defense on position, and at 1800 hours they reported the linkup column in sight.

The 4th Rangers had the mission of seizing Hill 205, an objective best described as a hill upon a hill. The enemy defense was stubborn, and two attacks on March 23 were unsuccessful. After using air fire to soften the resistance, the 4th Rangers took the hill on March 24. Cpl. Frederick Manship was killed in action. Sgt. John Critchley, SFC. Earl Higgins, Cpl. Fred Hamlin, Sgt. Raymond Oliveri, Sgt. Frank Andrczeyck, Sgt. William Johnson, Cpl. Thomas McGuines, Cpl. Thomas Patterson, and PFC Roy Riggs were wounded.

From March 24 through 28 the Airborne forces pursued the enemy. *Life* magazine reported that tanks followed Ranger patrols toward the 38th parallel. On March 28 two platoons of the 4th Rangers attacked and seized Hill 279, securing the left flank of the Regimental Combat Team. Lt. Joseph Waterbury, SFC William Putnam, and Sgt. Pedro Alvarado were wounded in the action. Late on the twenty-eighth the 4th Rangers thwarted an enemy effort to strike the 187th RCT on the left flank. The 4th Ranger records list twenty-two casualties for the Munsan-ni operation.

Relieved by troops of the 3rd Infantry Division, the 187th Airborne and attached units began moving from Suwon to Taegu. The 4th Rangers reached Taegu at 2230 hours on March 30; the 2d Rangers arrived at 0530 on March 31.

On March 26 the 1st Rangers began a series of foot marches. As enemy forces withdrew, the Rangers sought to maintain contact, moving forward by day, digging in at dusk, and sending patrols forward at night.

On March 24, the Eighth Army Ranger Company moved into the vicinity of Ungdal-li and at 2400 hours went into a blocking position on Hill 149. On the night of the twenty-sixth an Eighth Army Ranger patrol drove in on a Chinese outpost and knocked out an enemy machine-gun nest, killing its crew. There were no Ranger casualties. This was the final combat action of the Eighth Army Ranger Company (8213 Army unit). On March 28 the unit was disbanded and its men were assigned to a wide variety of units within the 25th Infantry Division—many to the famed 27th Infantry (the Wolfhounds). Most of the parachute-qualified personnel were assigned to the 187th Airborne Regimental Combat Team.

Debate raged within the Army as to whether select men—those who were volunteers, highly motivated *and* well-trained men with leadership capabilities—should be in separate units or scattered among the regular infantry divisions to set an example for the rest of the men. The Ranger Training Center was opposed to piecemeal assignment of men from the companies, and raised the following objections:

1. Rangers were quality rather then quantity soldiers.
2. The Rangers would initially be strangers in the unit, separated from those they trusted.
3. Rangers would not necessarily hold rank commensurate with their leadership responsibilities.
4. Rangers would probably be goaded psychologically into rash actions to justify their special status. (This appears to be true of those Rangers who served with line infantry units after the Rangers were deactivated. "Tex" Kimmel, a member of the 6th Rangers, claims that men of that unit who later served with line infantry units earned eighteen Silver Stars. A 6th Ranger, Eugene Kuta, volunteered repeatedly until he made it into combat; constantly setting the example of courage, he was badly wounded.[4] Donn Porter of the 9th Rangers was posthumously awarded the Medal of Honor for his service with a line unit.[5])
5. These small teams of Rangers might lead the unit into situations it was not prepared to handle.

The Ranger Training Center recognized that Ranger units should serve as an example and set a higher standard for the rest of the Army to emulate. They proposed to do this by producing successful Ranger units. If line units chose to, they could send small numbers of men to these Ranger companies for training. These men would receive quality training and example, then return to their own units and raise the standard.

On Monday, March 5, the 3rd, 5th, and 8th Ranger companies took the ferryboat *Sacramento* to the port of San Francisco, where they boarded the 17,250-ton troopship *General William F. Hase*. The companions of the Rangers on the voyage included large Air Force and Marine contingents.

The gray ship on a gray ocean sailed into fog and mist. It is said the swells off of San Francisco are among the roughest in the world; true or not, the yaw and pitch soon had Ranger, Marine, and airman shoulder to shoulder at the rail. Below decks in the ship's heads, men who thought death preferable to the wretchedness of seasickness lay facedown in commodes and urinals. Periodically, a pasty-faced man would appear at the hatch, hands pressed over his face, glance wildly about, then charge to the nearest receptacle.

As a young Ranger I was initially unaffected, and to prove my mental control, took an orange to the ship's head and proceeded to eat it in front of my sick brethren. After the second bite, I began to be overwhelmed by the sights and smells of a Hell worthy of Dante. For three days and nights my body sought to turn itself inside out.

Meanwhile, on the same day the 3rd, 5th and 8th Rangers embarked for Korea, back at Fort Benning the fourth week of training began for the third Ranger training cycle. Small-unit tactics, rocket launchers, mines and demolitions were featured.

On March 6 plans were completed for moving the Ranger Training Center to the F5 Harmony Church area of Fort Benning, an area that consisted of twenty forty-man barracks and attached kitchens and accessory buildings. The plans called for the move to take place from March 10 to 20. An Associated Press team arrived to do a story for worldwide publication.

Arrangements were also made to receive 197 Ranger volunteers from the 43rd Infantry Division for Airborne and subse-

quent Ranger training. On March 12 designations were made
and reserved for companies that would be filled. These were:

12th Ranger Infantry Company (Airborne) . . . .
    28th Infantry Division
13th Ranger Infantry Company (Airborne) . . . .
    43rd Infantry Division
14th Ranger Infantry Company (Airborne) . . . .
    4th Infantry Division

These units would be attached to the Airborne Battalion of the 1st
Student Regiment until Airborne training was completed.

The fifth week of training for the third training cycle began,
and weapons and range firing were the main training subjects.
At 2305 hours on March 12 an explosion, later estimated to have
been a one-pound block of TNT, was heard near the 7th Ranger
Company area. It was the second such explosion in two days
and was viewed as a request from the 7th Rangers that they be
sent to Korea. Major Heard was appointed to investigate and
recommend corrective action.

At the same time, somewhere in the middle of the Pacific
Ocean, the men of the 3rd, 5th, and 8th Ranger companies had
found their sea legs and were occupied with physical training
and weapons practice. Long lines of people waiting for chow
were normal. Ranger Chester A. Wolfe used his time in line by
teasing Marines with stories that habitually ended with the line,
"One riot, one Ranger."

As was inevitable when two proud organizations of American
fighting men got together, there were brief scuffles. A group of
Rangers who desired to see the evening movie had followed
instructions and gone below decks. Standing in line outside the
compartment designated as the ship's theater, they waited for
the hatch to be opened. After an hour the lowing and stamping
of feet began. Soon the hatch was swung wide, but as the Rangers moved forward, they were halted by a Marine guard who
announced the theater was full and the movie was in progress.
While the Rangers had waited in line, the Marines had been
allowed to pass through another hatch and occupy the theater.

A large Ranger from 5th Company stepped forward, took the
Marine guard by the throat, and began to reason with him. Other
men from the Ranger companies surged past and began to rea-

son with the Marines inside. After considerable reasoning, the Rangers took their seats and the movie was restarted. Both sides took this event as a welcome break from the everlasting boredom of shipboard life. Skinned knuckles, shiners, and bite marks were worn like medals for several days.

One of the anomalies of the war was that Air Force units bound for service in Japan were equipped with the M-2 carbine, giving them a selector switch that allowed for automatic fire. The Rangers who were destined to close with the enemy had only the M-1 carbine, a semiautomatic weapon. Some Air Force men swapped willingly, others demanded money. Those Rangers who could afford the cost, paid. The increased firepower was worth the price. Some men favored the automatic carbine over the M-1 rifle because of its relatively light weight—at 6.10 pounds with a fifteen-round magazine, loaded, as opposed to the 9.5 pounds of the rifle. In place of the fifteen-round magazines, most men used the thirty-round "banana" magazines. These in turn were taped together with one up into the weapon, the other two pointing down. This allowed for ninety rounds of readily available ammunition, as a magazine could be changed with the flick of the wrist. One had to be careful, though: the weight of the three loaded magazines could unseat the one being chambered, resulting in failure to fire.

In Germany the 6th Rangers were involved in practicing all the skills they had learned at Fort Benning. The Rangers made an ideal aggressor force in war games, posing as the enemy in the training of American units. In addition to weapons, demolitions, land navigation, and patrolling skills, the 6th practiced tactics that would test the security of American units.

On March 13 the 13th Ranger Company arrived from Camp Pickett, Virginia, to begin training at Fort Benning. On March 15 and 16 a party of general officers, headed by Gen. Mark Clark, visited the Ranger Training Center and inspected its operation. NBC Radio also visited, to gather material for a program featuring Rangers. On March 17 and 18 the move from area H1 to area F5 Harmony Church was completed. One of the benefits of the move was that new doors were acquired. The old ones in H1 were scarred and splintered from the Ranger practice of hurling his knife at the nearest door.[6]

On March 18, 173 Ranger volunteers were received from throughout the continental army; 246 had been hoped for. The same date, 197 volunteers from the 28th Infantry Division (12th Ranger Company) arrived to begin training.

On March 19, the seventh week of the third training cycle began stressing small-unit tactical training, including night operations.

On March 22 men began to arrive from the 4th Infantry Division to begin Airborne training. On the thirtieth, sixteen F-84 aircraft participated in realistic tactical training in air support.

March 26 saw the 12th, 13th, and 14th Ranger companies begin Basic Airborne Training. The 250-foot tower proved particularly exciting when Ranger Chaplain Charles A. Meek, who was taking training with the companies, found his chute entangled with the tower, high above the earth. Meek had been a Marine captain during World War II, and as a Marine raider, he participated in campaigns in New Georgia and Guam before leaving the Marines to become, in time, the Ranger chaplain. Meek's coolness, faith, and the fast action of the instructors, corrected a dangerous situation. He was brought to earth safely.

Herman "Herm" Boldt of the 13th Rangers dislocated his back, but needed to make an additional qualifying jump to stay in the program. Another Ranger grabbed him under the armpits and jerked upward, and despite excruciating pain, Boldt hobbled back to the harness, was towed aloft, and made a successful jump.[7]

On March 28 the men of 7th and 9th companies received the bad news that their units would be used as cadre for new companies to be formed or sent as replacements. To work off their anger, the 9th Rangers went on a speed march, doing fifteen miles in three hours and fifteen minutes. The 9th Ranger Company had a high percentage of veteran paratroopers and claimed an average of between twenty and thirty jumps per man. Both companies were filled with new personnel in later cycles.

At sea, the men of the 3rd, 5th, and 8th Ranger companies, like the men who had proceeded them, had plenty of time for reflection on what the future might bring. In an article about the Rangers, Drew Pearson had said that, "If captured, the Rangers knew they would be killed." Few men accepted the possibility of their own capture or death, though they sang about it:

Take down your service flag, Mother
Replace the blue with the gold
Your son is an Airborne Ranger
He'll die 'fore he's twenty years old

Few men pictured themselves as killers. When they said they wanted to "kill a Commie," they were classifying the foe as something subhuman, a "damn varmint" that deserved obliteration for the benefit of mankind. Some of those they met on the battlefield, particularly the North Korean soldiers, gave them no reason to change their view.

The thing that stayed rooted in the hearts and minds of most men was the challenge. It was important for them to know for themselves if they were "men enough" for the task. The closer they got to Korea, the more the bravado faded away. The greatest concern was to not embarrass themselves by failing their friends.

Despite the weapons practice, calisthenics, and shipboard classes, there was time to get to know other men in ways they never did during barracks life or training. Standing by the rail as the ship pitched its way across the Pacific, men opened their souls and talked of their hopes and their dreams for after the war. They were thoughts of peace: to start a business, to marry, to raise a family.

Antonio Velo, 8th Airborne Ranger, was a man who could wear clothes with the grace of a fashion model. I remember talking with him of his plans to marry his girl and open a fashionable men's clothing store in California. My friend Ranger Jimmie White and I were less definite; we thought we might get jobs as executives and draw big salaries.

It was a time of reflection and big dreams, but our young hearts felt the surge of high adventure with every throb of the ship's engines. To be young and standing in the bow of a ship steaming into Yokohama harbor at night, with the salt spray in your face and a thirst for excitement in your heart, is the stuff that stays with a man. It anchors itself in the marrow of his bones, bringing warmth to the chill night of later life.

The *Hase* touched at Yokohama to offload some of the other men on board, then sailed for the port of Kobe. Word flashed around the ship that before the *Hase* continued to Korea, men would be allowed a few hours on shore. The joy of this announcement was dampened by the fact that few men had money. Ranger ingenuity overcame this obstacle.

Soon after the pass list was announced, men emerged from below decks. It was a pleasant day, yet most men wore overcoats. Standing by the gangway, the officers struggled to keep from laughing while letting the men know they were not fooled. As each man waddled toward shore, he would pass through a gauntlet of officers' comments like, "Getting a little fat, aren't you?" and, "A good five-mile run might take off some of that excess weight." If Kobe had any scenic beauty, few Rangers noticed it. Within a short time the men were indoors swapping overcoats, blankets, sheets, and pillowcases they had wrapped around themselves for a variety of entertainments. Sake and Suntory whiskey flowed in copious quantities.

Young men in fine physical condition have an ever-ready need for the opposite sex. When that sex drive is matched with the knowledge that you are going to war, it becomes an irresistable force. It seems of vital importance to mate, to empty your compounded tensions and fears into any feminine vessel, to do an act of life that laughs at death and makes man immortal. There were plenty of black-haired, rose-cheeked, Japanese girls to satisfy the pre-battle libido of the Rangers.

That evening the Kobe dock resounded to the boisterous sound of returning Rangers. Sobriety was an orphan as men returned in all manners of undress, some even having swapped their shorts and socks. Most Rangers came back by foot, though there were those who had saved enough for a pedicab or a rickshaw, and a few managed taxis. The most startling apparition was a very large Ranger who returned wearing nothing but pedicab driver's pants with the seat and legs split open and a pair of shower slippers.

Entertainment was so good in Kobe that men returned to the *Hase* in an attempt to secure more trading material. Once on board, they found the gangway barred to exit. Frustrated, some Rangers waited till after dark, then went down the mooring hawsers, hand over hand. The trip back up the hawser and around the rat guard was far more difficult, and occasionally an inebriated cry was followed by a loud *splash*!

At 1500 hours on March 24, the 3rd, 5th, and 8th companies debarked at Pusan and moved to the Pusan assembly area. This place was aptly described by one Ranger as "a mud pile surrounded by anti-aircraft guns."

For most young Rangers there was nothing in their experience to prepare them for the sights and sounds of Korea. Every truck and train swarmed with refugees; all was filth, mud, and stink. For excitement one could watch Korean townsfolk urinating in the street. One day, when there was a large explosion, one waggish Army engineer quipped that it was caused by the gas from two thousand years of accumulated feces.

After several days of processing, the 3rd, 5th, and 8th Ranger companies embarked at 1830 hours on March 28 on the 1,600-ton LST Q018, weighed anchor, and proceeded into the Yellow Sea en route to Pusan. The ship phonograph had one record, a Japanese song called *"Sina-no Yoru,"* or "China Nights." The song played endlessly, embedding itself in memory, while men checked and test-fired weapons.

Dawn on March 31 revealed the port of Inchon across the oily-surfaced water. By afternoon, unloading had begun. The men of the 3rd, 5th, and 8th companies said farewell to friends and separated to join their separate divisions. The 3rd Ranger Company was going to the 3rd Infantry Division, the 5th to the 25th, and the 8th to the 24th Infantry Division.

Back at Fort Benning, the night of March 31 saw the first Ranger courtesy patrol (under the command of Captain Kelso) patrolling the streets and bars of Columbus, Georgia, and Phenix City, Alabama. It was a payday night, which the patrol report, in a masterpiece of understatement, said was "relatively quiet." In 1951 Phenix City, Alabama, had a well-deserved reputation as a haven for vice and crime. Its night spots preyed on the soldier, and in the early months of the year a group of Rangers had planned to put the infamous Beachie's Swing Club out of business. On the night of Saturday, March 3, a group of 200 to 250 service men, mostly Rangers, had gathered at the club, primed to demolish the establishment on signal. Regrettably, security was bad; the civilian and military police had been forewarned and were present in force. Frustrated, the men left the club gathered in formation and marched out Opelika Road, taking their business elsewhere.

Chapter 11

As April opened, the bloody game of give-and-take found the U.S. Eighth Army once more on the attack. Driving beyond the 38th parallel, the U.N. forces advanced twenty kilometers northward. Mid-month, there was a major and controversial change in American command, and on April 22 the Chinese began a massive attack they called "The Fifth Phase Offensive."

On April 3 the 5th Ranger Company was given the mission of checking out a town near the Yong-Pyong River and establishing ambush positions. After crossing the river, the company moved a thousand yards behind enemy lines, giving them the distinction of being the first unit in the eastern sector to cross the 38th parallel on the U.N. return north.

At dawn a Chinese force was engaged. The Rangers were fighting hungry, as there had been no opportunity to open rations. After a brief firefight, several enemy machine guns were silenced and the Chinese withdrew. The Rangers consolidated their position and were having breakfast when the lead elements of the 25th Division moved forward to assume control of the area.

April 4 found the 2nd and 4th Rangers on the way to new assignments. The 4th found itself in line for a new operation. The 2nd was about to become a training base for black soldiers assigned to the 7th Infantry Division. The initial mission was to give fifty-two replacements two weeks of training for possible formation of a provisional Ranger company, but soon another seventy-eight were added, then eleven more. The roll call continued to swell, and by April 30 the 2nd Rangers had 125 men assigned and 282 attached. Integration was coming; the 2nd Rangers had the patience to await its arrival.

While this training mission was in progress, the 2nd Rangers were also performing combat patrols with the 3rd Regiment, 7th ROK Division. Though the training mission was lifted on April 24, it would be early May before the last of the attached soldiers were gone. While present with the 2nd Rangers, they had an ample introduction to combat. Besides patrols, the 2nd Rangers were used in their "fireman" role to plug gaps in the 17th and 31st regiment zones.

On April 8 PFC John Pointeck, Jr. was released from attachment to the 4th Rangers and reassigned to the 1st Rangers. Pointeck was a man out of his century: he seemed to be born to the role of the Western gunslinger. He constantly practiced the fast draw, was quick to challenge, and went by the nickname of "Johnny Montana." This was a man ready to demonstrate that he was a top gun, and on one occasion he outdrew and shot another Ranger in the stomach.

On the night of April 8–9 the 5th Rangers provided security for a battery of 155mm self-propelled howitzers from the 927th Field Artillery Battalion. Under cover of night the battery moved to forward positions and fired 120 rounds of high explosive into Chorwon. The following night the 5th Rangers were back in action. The objective was a hill of tactical importance located behind enemy lines. Hill 383 was to be occupied, then used as an observation point and a patrol base from which to capture prisoners. The original plan called for the Rangers to return to friendly lines by 0200 hours on April 11. The plan was revised; the 5th Rangers would secure the hill and hold it pending an attack by the 24th Infantry Regiment. The 24th was to attack on the eleventh and relieve the 5th Rangers in position. Recognizing the hazards of the mission, 25th Division authorized Captain Scagnelli to withdraw the 5th Rangers if necessary.

The route required a 7½-hour night march that included crossing the Hantan River. Radio communications were maintained with the 24th Infantry Regiment, and the 25th

Division artillery continued normal harassing and interdictory fire, while suspending fire along the Rangers' route of march. At 0435 hours on April 10 the 5th Rangers arrived at an assembly area near Hill 383. Staying unobserved, the Rangers prepared for the attack while the hill was pounded by artillery.

At 1000 hours on the eleventh, with Lt. Mack McGinnis's platoon in the lead, the 5th Rangers attacked. The first assault was beaten off by a tenacious Chinese defense, so the Rangers withdrew, softened up the hill with air strikes, then attacked again. The Chinese again put up a determined resistance, and grenades soared back and forth. One Chinese grenade landed between Lieutenant McGinnis and Sgt. Robert "Duke" Dulaney, but fortunately for both, the Chinese grenadier had failed to pull the ring. The Rangers pressed steadily upward, but it would be 1630 hours before the hill was secured. Eighteen of the enemy were killed and a prisoner taken. Ranger John "Red" Eisman found a badly wounded Chinese soldier, a boy scarcely into his teens. Eisman carried the youth to the bottom of the hill, propped him against a tree and looked for aid, but the wounds were too grievous. The boy died.

The Rangers waited in vain for the 24th Infantry to fight their way to the hill. The Chinese were greatly disturbed that a hill behind their front had been taken, and wasted no time in assembling a sizable counterattack force. As darkness fell, the voices of Chinese commanders could be heard at the base of the hill. The enemy officers were exhorting their men for the attack. It came at 2000 hours, opening with a stunningly heavy barrage of mortar fire. Twenty minutes later two red flares and the sound of bugles heralded the Chinese counterattack.

From his outpost, Sgt. William Kirshfield yelled to his platoon leader, "Hey, Jack, here they come!" Moments later everyone was firing and throwing grenades. It was close fighting. Ranger Ronald Mott remembered that the enemy was so near he could smell the garlic they frequently ate. The battle raged for forty minutes, with the Rangers taking a heavy toll on the attackers. It was clear, however, that because the battle was being fought behind enemy lines, continued Chinese reinforcements must in the end overwhelm the small Ranger force. The Chinese were following close behind their mortar fire attacking the hill on three sides. The fourth side was so steep that it was really a cliff.

At 2100 hours the Rangers began to withdraw toward friendly lines. Two Rangers badly wounded by mortar fire refused to burden their comrades and volunteered to remain behind and provide covering fire for the withdrawal. Sergeant Kirshfield and Cpl. Walter J. Maziarz, Jr. both gave their lives. When last seen, Kirshfield was still firing a Browning Automatic Rifle.

The three-sided Chinese attack left only the steep face as a route of withdrawal. Individually and in groups, men jumped or clawed their way down the face. Rangers Whitehead, Brutsche, Teel, Emerson, Moore, Shemits, Westmoreland, and Stankich were wounded by enemy fire; others were injured in the jump.[1]

Several men, including Rangers Mott, Mailhot, Eisman, and Goldbaum, became separated from the main body. The following day this group would successfully evade enemy forces, cross the river under enemy and friendly fire, and return to friendly lines.

Approximately three miles behind enemy lines, in the 24th Division sector, was the hamlet of Topyong-ni, a small grouping of five to seven houses that intelligence reported was a feeding station for Chinese troops. The terrain was flat to the front of the hamlet, with high ground to each side and a ridgeline to the rear. Intelligence was vague on the Chinese feeding schedule, but here was a mission for which the 8th Airborne Rangers were designed. The plan was to attack with the 2nd platoon while 1st and 3rd platoons blocked on the flanks. Artillery would be called in on the high ground surrounding the hamlet, to pin any enemy in position there.

The first three rounds of artillery fell short, concussing some of the Rangers. A Chinese outpost opened fire but was speedily silenced by squad leader Park Hodak and BAR man James Reynolds. The Rangers then swept forward, shooting up the houses and setting them ablaze. The action was brief and violent, and within moments the Rangers had destroyed the station, killed the enemy inside, and were on their way back. Ranger James Teague recalls that as the 2nd platoon slipped away, all that could be heard was "the crackling of fires."

The 3rd was the only Ranger company to share the designation of the division to which it was attached. The 3rd Infantry Division was commanded by Maj. Gen. Robert H. Soule, and included the 7th, 15th, and 65th infantry regiments, the British 29th Infantry Brigade, The Belgian United Nations Battalion, and the 10th Battalion Combat Team, Philippine Expeditionary Force. At the beginning of April the 3rd Division and attached elements were attacking north along the Seoul–Uijongbu axis in the vicinity of the Imjin River. The division was conducting a series of limited-objective attacks intended to keep the enemy off balance and harass him into launching a premature counteroffensive.

The Imjim River was crossed and the advance continued on the road to Chorwon. The 65th Infantry Regiment was attacking.

It was cold and cloudy when, at 0700 hours on April 11, the 3rd Ranger Company fixed their bayonets, mounted tanks, and crossed the line of departure. The Rangers, along with F Company, 65th Infantry, were attached to the 64th Heavy Tank Battalion. The 3rd Ranger Company was further attached to Company C of the 64th HTB, a unit comprised of black enlisted men and white officers. The commanding officer of Company C and the man in charge of the operation was a Capt. Daniel Boone of Kentucky.

The mission of this task force was to penetrate the enemy line and disrupt his defenses and supply routes.

Capt. Jesse Tidwell, the 3rd Ranger Company commander, rode Captain Boone's tank. It was intended that the tanks and infantry would stay together. No one remembers an artillery forward observer being present. Indirect fire support would be handled by the command group of Boone and Tidwell. The Rangers' 57mm recoilless rifles were being carried on the tanks.

As the task force reached the village of Kantongyon, they came under light fire from rifles and automatic weapons. Leaving their recoilless rifles on the tanks, the 1st and 2nd platoons of Rangers dismounted. Tidwell held the 3rd platoon in reserve on the tanks. Capt. Robert Channon, the Ranger company executive officer, and now the senior man, dismounted.[2] Channon had a radio, but did not have the frequencies of the artillery.

Supported by point-blank tank fire, the Rangers cleared the village. Ranger James Stamper killed a Chinese soldier as the man was coming out of a doorway. When a second enemy soldier appeared, Stamper was astounded to learn the short burst he thought he had used on the first of the enemy had actually been a full twenty-round magazine. The second Chinese soldier was dispatched with grenades.

The Rangers passed through the village and moved up the hill behind the town. Reaching the crest, they could see the valley stretching before them. At the base of their hill was a broad, terraced rice paddy that stretched away for some seven hundred yards. At the far end of the paddy was a ridgeline that extended from the Rangers' east, looking like a nose thrusting itself inquisitively into the valley floor. Although this intersecting ridge blocked movement on the right, the valley was broad and the ridge could be bypassed on the left—provided the Rangers could suppress the enemy fire that would be brought from the ridge. Though enemy emplacements were not visable from the hill above the town, the ridge was fortified with numerous bunkers at its base. Connecting trenches from the lower-level bunkers coursed up the slopes to connect with a large bunker that surmounted the ridge. The ground sloped away behind the ridge, providing an excellent position for mortar emplacements. The ground then rose again to a main ridge pointed north, which provided higher elevation and excellent observation for the enemy. As the dismounted Rangers moved down the slope toward the rice paddy, mortar rounds began to explode among them. Captain Channon's radio operator Carl Walker was struck and unable to continue, and Channon received fragments in his legs and face. Channon put the radio on a protesting Korean soldier and continued on.

Unknown to Boone, Tidwell, or Channon, the task force had split. The majority of the tanks and the 3rd Ranger platoon had passed to the left of the hill and were advancing up the center of the valley, taking the 57mm recoilless rifles with them. Remaining with Channon and the dismounted 1st and 2nd platoons were two tanks.

Channon called Tidwell for instructions. Tidwell, believing the tank and Ranger companies were together, radioed back: "Move out when the tanks move out." Shortly after these instructions were received, the two tanks with the 1st and 2nd platoons moved off at high speed to rejoin the tank company. The 1st and 2nd Ranger platoons were left dismounted, separated from the rest of the task force, and without tank support—they began to come under increased mortar fire and direct fire from the ridge.

Boone and Tidwell's element also came under fire. Tidwell recalls that as the firing became heavier, Boone, apparently under the belief that the task force was still together, directed the Rangers to withdraw under covering fire of the tanks. This message was sent to Channon. Possibly as a result of the wounding of his radio operator, Channon did not receive this message and continued forward. In any event, the tanks were not in view of the 1st and 2nd Ranger platoons and could not have supported their withdrawal. The two platoons were in the open under accurate mortar fire. They could not remain where they were. The choices were limited, either move forward or move back.

Using fire and movement and individual initiative, the 1st and 2nd Ranger platoons swept forward, taking maximum advantage of the limited protection of paddy dikes and the terraced effect of the land. Several men recall at least two machine guns firing on the Rangers from the lower bunkers and a third operating from higher up the slope. Ranger Jack Shafer was gaining a new respect for his supposedly short-range carbine. Firing at six hundred yards, Shafer could see the strike of his bullets around the firing ports of enemy bunkers.

Halfway to the base of the ridge the Rangers came under a particularly vicious and accurate mortar barrage. Committed to the attack across the open ground, there was no going back. Bending into the shrapnel storm, the Rangers continued on. The list of casualties was climbing. Rangers Aldridge, Knoebel, McCormick, Herholz, Walker, Drost, Pike, Adamaitis, Rhyne, and Akins had already been hit. Captain Channon received more mortar fragments in the legs and two rounds of automatic-rifle fire in the calf of his left leg; one passed through, the other lodged in the muscle.

Channon's second radio operator had also been wounded. When Ranger Bob Scully's weapon had been damaged, he picked up the radio and followed Channon up the hill, unarmed until he found a pistol. The Rangers were also under fire from Chinese snipers. As one Ranger raised to fire, the Chinese sniper creased one side of the Ranger's helmet, then the other side. The Ranger laughed and again raised to fire. This time the Chinese sharpshooter hit the center of the helmet, killing the American.

About the time that Channon radioed for support, two tanks arrived and took up station to the rear right and left of the 1st Ranger platoon. Channon crawled up on the back of one tank, Lt. Pete Hamilton on the other. The tanks began to systematically destroy the lower bunkers, and knocked out the two lower machine guns. Sharpshooters of the 2nd Ranger platoon eliminated the machine gun at the higher elevation.

Lieutenant Hamilton, platoon leader of the 1st platoon, was an inspiration to his men. Despite multiple wounds, he encouraged them forward. According to the citation of the Bronze Star he was later awarded, Hamilton encouraged his men by shouting. "I've got a cluster to my Purple Heart. They can't hurt you."

When Hamilton's wounds prevented him from continuing, Sgt. Harold L. Barber took command of the platoon and led them in a bayonet charge against the enemy entrenchments. The attack was supported by fire from the 2nd platoon.

Flights of concussion grenades came sailing down from the enemy trenches. Rangers Jack Shafer and Arthur Cisneros were moving up the slope when the explosions of concussion grenades knocked them flat and rolled them down the hill, bumping and jostling each other. Half stunned, the two Rangers struggled to their feet, said "Excuse me" to each other, and went back to the attack.

Sgt. Mas Najako caught a Chinese grenade and threw it back. The Rangers replied to the enemy bombardment with fragmentation grenades and closed into the trenches with rifle and bayonet. Cpl. William Osbourne bayoneted two Chinese in rapid succession. Men later reported that the enemy cringed before the cold steel. Going from bunker to bunker, the Rangers cleared the nose of the ridge. In addition to those

killed in the assault, eleven Chinese were killed clearing the
position and one captured. The remainder fled.

Cpl. Wesley Mohagen, Cpl. Franciso Misseri, and Cpl.
Franklin A. Nicholson were killed. Ranger James E. Jones
would later die of wounds. Lieutenant Hamilton, Sergeant 1st
Class Davis, and Rangers Campbell, Lee, Miller, Georgiou,
Edwards, Gaither, Tanona, and Pellon were wounded. Sgt.
Raymond Pierce, who had constantly risked his life to help
the wounded, was himself struck by enemy fire.

Of the thirty-two men of the 1st platoon who had started
across the paddy, eight reached the top of the ridge, and only
three of these remained unhurt. While the Rangers reorganized on terrain that they would later name "Bloody-Nose
Ridge," Channon reported the situation to Tidwell. The tanks
and 3rd platoon were farther north and in the center of the
valley. Channon's force was instructed to move northwest and
join them. The trip was made under sniper and mortar fire.

Lt. William Hutcheson, the platoon leader of 3rd platoon,
had been wounded, and MSgt. Fred Davis took over command of the platoon. With the surviving members of the task
force reunited, the final objective was attacked. Minimal resistance was encountered; the enemy continued to use mortar
and sniper fire, but could not sustain their positions.

The attack of the 1st and 2nd platoons across seven hundred yards of open terrain against an entrenched enemy was
the equivalent of a small-unit "Charge of the Light Brigade."
The 3rd Infantry Division G-3 reported, "Mission accomplished."

On April 11 a shock rolled along the front. President Truman had relieved General MacArthur, and General Ridgeway
would be the new commander of United Nations forces, with
Gen. James A. Van Fleet assuming command of the Eighth
Army.

Indications of an enemy buildup continued. Concerned
about the vulnerability of the main U.S. supply route where
it crossed the Hantan River, the 3rd Division dispatched the
3rd Ranger Company to guard the vital bridge.

On April 14 the 3rd Rangers and 3rd Division Reconnaissance Company, along with air control and forward observer
parties and engineers, formed Task Force Rogers. They

ranged north, along with other 3rd Division task forces. Fire-fights were encountered, but no determined resistance.

On April 17 the 5th Rangers and the 25th Division Reconnaissance Company secured a bridge site to the front of the 27th Infantry's positions. This was to allow engineers to make repairs that would assist the advance.

On April 18 the 5th Rangers occupied positions between the 24th and 27th regiments, to facilitate the coordination of these to units. The next day the Rangers were attached to the 27th Infantry Regiment for operational control.

General Van Fleet's welcome to command of the Eighth Army was rude. On April 22 the Communist forces began what would be the first wave of their Fifth Phase offensive. The Chinese made careful preparations. As early as a month before attacking, they had cleared all civilians from the area. Movement of troops was done under cover of darkness; during daylight men were concealed in woods and valleys. Forest fires would be started to generate a smoky haze that reduced visibility for United Nations pilots. Aggressive reconnaissance was the rule, and North Koreans dressed in civilian clothes or posing as refugees would cross over into U.N. territory to either return with information or reassemble as units behind U.N. lines.

The Chinese endeavored to thwart American airpower by attacking early in the evening, fighting until three or four o'clock in the morning, then taking cover before dawn brought U.N. fighter-bombers. The enemy also favored attacking on unit boundaries and sought to exploit the often poor level of preparedness of ROK units. Many Chinese spoke English, and their troops were taught sufficient Korean to confuse an unwary guard.

Five U.S. tanks had been disabled behind Chinese lines in the 3rd Division sector. On April 20 the 3rd Rangers and 3rd Division reconnaissance companies—with tank retrievers, quad-.50-caliber and twin-40mm-armed half-tracked vehicles—and engineers, set forth to bring the tanks back. Passing through 15th Infantry positions, the column headed north on a dirt road. The terrain was mountainous, with steep grades and drop-offs beside the road. Firing erupted about two miles into enemy territory, but it was only a tanker shooting a pheasant for dinner.

After a few more miles the column came upon Chinese tank traps dug across the road. The Rangers were called forward, crossed the deep ditch, and began to attack up the far slope. The Chinese had sited their fields of fire well. MSgt. John Jenkins was struck in the head and face by machine-gun fire.[3] A quad-.50 worked its way toward the head of the column and began to place suppressive fire on the hill. Some men of the Rangers' 2nd platoon were higher on the slope and came under the quad-.50 fire, but, fortunately, MSgt. Fred Davis and Ranger Bob Exley, who was serving as radio operator, got the fire lifted to the proper location.[4]

Engineers and a tank with a bulldozer blade managed to fill the tank traps and widen the road in spots so the task force could bring its firepower to bear on the Chinese position, but now the quads fired on the 3rd Ranger platoon. Some flares fired by Master Sergeant Davis identified the Rangers, and the task force began a heavy working-over of the Chinese positions. Under heavy Chinese mortar fire, the Rangers held the crest of an intermediate hill until the disabled tanks were recovered. The task force returned to friendly lines, reaching them after dark.

Two days later, on April 22, the 3rd Rangers were back in action. The Rangers and the 3rd Reconnaissance Company located an enemy force dug in on a hillside. The Recon tanks and 1st and 2nd Ranger platoons acted as a base of fire while the 3rd platoon maneuvered to the assault. Upon reaching the enemy position, the Rangers went on line, laying down a heavy volume of fire. The Chinese were initially surprised, but responded quickly. U.S. and Chinese grenades sailed back and forth, wounding Rangers Andrews, Richards, and Saylor, but the attack pressed on.

Sgt. Homer Simpson, from Havre, Montana, was small in stature but large in courage. Simpson had earned a Bronze Star with the 96th Division while serving in the Pacific during WWII. His warm-hearted good humor made him one of the most popular men in the company. When, on April 22, an enemy automatic-weapons position was slowing the Ranger attack, Simpson charged the position armed with only a rifle and a white phosphorous grenade. Other 3rd Rangers were close behind. Suddenly the enemy began to stand up in position, firing automatic weapons directly into the Rangers. An enemy soldier emptied a drum magazine, and Sergeant Simpson was struck in the eye. His death was instantaneous. PFC Taylor was knocked backward from a head shot; his scalp was split, but he survived. Ranger Bob Exley took seven bullets through the sleeve and side of his jacket but was unharmed.

Sgt. James Stamper leveled his Browning Automatic Rifle and killed the man who had killed Sergeant Simpson.

The death of Homer Simpson fired a blood lust in the Rangers. They stormed into the position, shooting and grenading the enemy. A light aircraft dropped a message to bring back a Chinese prisoner. This order came barely in time, but one of the enemy was saved—a man who provided valuable information to the 3rd Division about enemy intentions.

During the afternoon of April 22 Chinese preparatory artillery and mortar fire began. With darkness came furious Chinese attacks. In the I Corps sector the British 29th Brigade was to the left of the U.S. 3rd Infantry Division. To the left (west) of the British was the ROK 1st Division. This unit abruptly withdrew from position on April 23, leaving the 1st Battalion of the Gloucestershire Regiment isolated. Few of the Gloucesters survived. Elements of the 3rd Division were heavily involved in blocking the enemy penetration.

On April 23 the 3rd Rangers, with approximately two platoons of effective soldiers remaining, moved to the Han Tan branch of the Imjin River to make contact with the 29th British Brigade; 3rd Division was concerned about the status of the 1st Battalion of the Gloucesters.

The Rangers moved on foot, paralleling and sometimes wading in the river, and passing to the west around a long north–south ridge. In the next valley they turned south, expecting to find the Gloucesters.

It was quiet—a peaceful, bucolic scene with only an old peasant in sight, busily working in his rice paddy. Captain Tidwell and the newly joined Lt. Richard Eaton went forward to reconnoiter.[5] Some thirty yards in front of the platoon the two officers came under heavy small-arms fire. Diving behind a boulder, the two discussed the situation and saw only two options, run and pray.

Under heavy fire, they hastily returned to the company.

The Chinese had all the advantages. They held the high ground and were peppering the pinned-down Rangers with small arms. With bullets kicking dust around him, Lieutenant Eaton rose to his feet and moved among the Rangers. Under his instructions they moved out by squads, breaking contact by disciplined movement and heavy fire on the enemy. There were numerous close calls. Master Sergeant Ballou had the toes of his boots shot off, while Sergeant First Class Trojchak had the heel shot off his boot. Corporal Ross felt a bullet pass through his ammunition belt. The open ground and heavy enemy fire made it necessary for him to play dead until the enemy fire had lifted. Another Ranger had bullets pass through his pack, destroying his canned fruit. The juice running down his body caused considerable concern.

In fighting later that day, SFC Roy Clifton was killed and Rangers Grossman, Deluca, Shafer, and Cisneros were wounded. During the night Tidwell sent Eaton with a platoon to occupy a high point of terrain. When dawn came, the Rangers found they had a far-ranging view of the battlefield. They improved positions in the morning, and by afternoon could see 3rd Division units withdrawing and the final futile effort to break through to the Gloucesters.

A tank/infantry team moved west, about two thousand meters from Lieutenant Eaton's platoon, to come to the aid of the trapped Gloucesters. The Chinese quickly broke the attack, knocking out tanks, then climbing over them to kill the crews. They then began a fast-developing attack south, directly at the small force of Rangers. Eaton called artillery fire down on the Chinese, but their attack was determined. The 3rd Division was withdrawing units, and G-3 told the Rangers to pull out. The action was accomplished under a time-on-target salvo of artillery called by Lieutenant Eaton.

The 3rd Battalion (27th Infantry) and 5th Rangers maintained a blocking position. The Chinese Fifth Phase Offensive was hitting on a broad front. The 6th ROK Division retreat was being halted behind a screen of the British 27th Brigade and U.S. 5th Cavalry Regiment.* When the 6th tried

---

*The United Kingdom maintained two brigades and support forces totalling about forty thousand men in Korea. The 27th Brigade began arriving on August 28, 1950, and with the addition of Austrailian forces

to reorganize, the Chinese attacked and dispersed the 35th Regiment. The 2nd Ranger Company, reinforced, moved in and held the position while the 35th Regiment reorganized.

The U.S. 25th Division's 35th and 24th regiments were attacked by the enemy at 0100 hours on April 25. Enemy pressure continued as the division withdrew to new defensive positions. By evening the front of the 2nd division consisted of the 27th Infantry on the left and 35th on the right.

On April 27 the 5th Rangers were assisting the 2nd Battalion, 27th Infantry. Company G was driven out of position. The Rangers counterattacked into the gap and held the position, fighting furiously while the Wolfhound soldiers regrouped. During this action, Ranger sergeants assumed command of line-infantry units.

In late April Lt. Fred Lang's platoon of the 5th Rangers were forward of friendly lines when they found themselves in front of a large enemy force bent on attacking the main line of resistance. Lang and his men engaged the enemy, breaking the momentum of the attack. The Rangers began to execute a fighting withdrawal before the full wrath of the enemy attack. The enemy was in hot pursuit when Fred Lang was struck by enemy fire. Lang's men tried to drag him to safety, but the enemy was close behind. The young lieutenant knew that in trying to rescue him, the lives of his men would be jeopardized. The gallant officer ordered his men to leave him behind. He was killed by the oncoming Communists.

Back at Fort Benning on April 2 the eighth and final week (Hell Week) commenced for the third training cycle. All units were in the field for four days of round-the-clock operations.

The fourth cycle had meanwhile concluded its first week of Airborne training. Twenty-eight men were disqualified for physical reasons while ninety-two were disqualified for other reasons, including refusing to jump from the thirty-four-foot-tower. There were eighteen temporary disqualifications and fifty probations.

on September 28, 1950, it was renamed the 27th British Commonwealth Brigade. The British 29th Brigade arrived at Pusan from November 3 through November 18, 1950. In July of 1951 the two brigades were united into the 1st Commonwealth Division.

Some men defied fate. Cpl. Phillip Hanes of the 10th
Rangers had trouble on six parachute jumps in a row: on the
first jump it was a "Mae West," the second it was a "cigarette roll," on jumps three and four there were blown panels,
number five was another Mae West, and on a night jump the
suspension lines wrapped around his feet.[6]

PFC Alfred Ball and Cpl. Calvin P. Jones of the 10th
Rangers both fractured their legs on early jumps but hid the
fact from instructors and continued to make their jumps. On
the final training jump Jones broke his fractured leg.

Some men had multiple duties. PFC Leslie Hunyada of the
11th Rangers served as radio operator, company clerk, mail
clerk, jeep and truck driver, and company runner.

The 7th Rangers were justly proud of the Doberman pin-
scher who jumped with them. The hound loved parachuting.
The 7th were also working on a private insignia for themselves, a skull and crossbones with parachute wings and a
pair of dice showing a five and two. For field duty the Rangers wore the field cap with the black and gold RANGER tab
sewed in the center above the brim. This was the favorite cap
of the Rangers and was used most of the time by the units in
combat. In most cases when the Rangers wore "Steel," it
was by division order, another example of how little understood Ranger procedure was. When the divisions did appre-
ciate the Ranger stress on stealth, orders to capitalize on this
quality were rescinded and if not, they were ignored.

In garrison the Rangers wore the jaunty "overseas" cap
with the red, white, and blue parachute patch, with infantry-
blue piping for enlisted men. It was a good piece of headgear,
lightweight and easily foldable for tucking under the belt or
the shoulder epaulet. The problem was that it was worn by
all soldiers, and all Airborne personnel wore the Parachute
patch. Some Rangers took exception to being mistaken for a
CAP ("common-assed Paratrooper").

From the beginning of the Ranger Training Center, there
had been a search for distinctive items that would reflect the
extra effort it took to be a Ranger. During the second cycle
there was a rumor that a black beret was coming. It was
eagerly awaited but did not come into being until the third
cycle, when the 7th, 10th, 11th, and 12th companies began
to wear them. The 10th, 11th, and 13th companies had pho-

tographs taken at Camp Carson showing them in the black beret, but a close examination of the pictures shows the overseas cap tucked in the belt. The beret was not authorized.

Colonel Van Houten supported the project, and Lt. Col. Wilbur "Coal-Bin Willie" Wilson was the project officer. Sgt. John Roy of the 7th Rangers modeled the uniform the Rangers sought. Black beret and black boots (the Army was wearing brown). Ranger Roy went about Fort Benning armed with an authorization slip to test the new uniform, which was anathema to the traditionalists. It was unthinkable that the Rangers should appear different than other soldiers!

Company commanders issued slips to their men that read,

I HEREBY CERTIFY THAT_____IS A MEMBER OF THE____ RANGER INFANTRY COMPANY (AIRBORNE) AND IS ENTITLED TO WEAR THE BERET, WHICH IS PART OF THE RANGER UNIFORM.

This certification carried all the validity of Confederate money after the Civil War. Many senior officers of the army viewed these efforts to be "different" as nothing short of heresy. Harry Truman was still in the White House, and it would be some years before President John Kennedy would favor Special Forces with a green beret and the beret would become common headgear in the United States Army.

In 1951 the black beret, black boots, tailored khaki uniform with parachute wings and Ranger insignia, all supported by a magnificently conditioned young body, was an irresistible pass/leave combination that won many girls' hearts. All one had to do was avoid the military police.

On April 5 the term "Ranger Training Command" replaced "Ranger Training Center."

On April 6 General Collins, Army chief of staff, visited the command and inspected training. This was the final day of training for the third training cycle.

A check of Rangers in training revealed that their average age was 21.8 years. Scores on the Army General Classification were high, and 10th and 11th company scores averaged higher than the requirements for admission to officer candidate school.

The Army was greatly concerned about raising the stan-

dards of American infantry, and the chief of Army field forces
turned to the Ranger Training Command for views on how
this might be achieved. Colonel Van Houten and his staff felt
that Army training was designed for the poorest recruit, the
weakest link in the chain, and therefore trained down to the
lowest capability rather than reaching up to its highest potential. The suggestions offered would result in a long-term benefit to the United States Army. The options presented were:

1. To bring volunteer officers and noncommissioned officer
   teams from within (or without) the divisions to the
   Ranger Training Center, train them, then send them to
   the divisions to train others
2. That a postgraduate course for infantry battalions be
   established by the Ranger Training Command to give the
   battalion three months of superior training in which the
   unfit would be eliminated
3. That an indoctrination course be set up for officers up
   to and including division commanders. The course
   would include practical experience. (It is possible that
   by this time Van Houten was looking for ways to torture
   some division commanders.)
4. That selected volunteers from each rifle company attend
   the Ranger Training Center for Airborne and Ranger
   training then be returned to their units to provide example and instruction

The proposals envisioned training under varied environ-
mental circumstances. Individuals or units would be rotated
through amphibious and rugged terrain sites, a desert site, a
winter snow site, and forest site. With this document the
seeds were sewn for a Ranger department that would one day
spread the Ranger philosophy throughout the Army.

General Collins returned to Fort Benning on April 11, observing a river crossing and rubber-boat training. The general
was overheard to say that every division should have Rangers.

On April 13 the graduation parade for the third training
cycle was held at French Field. General Church and Colonel
Van Houton were the reviewing officers. The 7th, 9th, 10th,
and 11th Ranger companies passed in review. These men were
justly proud of their accomplishment. From the select vol-

unteers that had begun training, each company had seen many men fall by the wayside. The 10th Ranger Company lost thirty-seven men, nineteen in Airborne training and eighteen in the Ranger training that followed. The 11th Rangers had two officers and forty-four enlisted men that dropped out along the way.

The graduation exercises proved that the spirit of company competition was still in effect. All the companies were standing tall, but Capt. Robert Eikenberry and the 7th Ranger Company surprised everyone by showing up in black scarves and white boot laces. To add to the chagrin of the other units, the 7th Rangers double-timed past the reviewing stand while others marched. Colonel Van Houten was so taken by the display that he directed the black scarves and white boot laces would be used by the command for future dress parades.

On April 14 the 7th, 10th, and 11th Ranger companies departed for Camp Carson and three weeks of mountain training. The strengths of the units were: 7th Company, three officers and ninety-six enlisted men; 10th Company, seven officers and 133 enlisted men; 11th Company, five officers and 141 enlisted men. The units arrived at Colorado Springs on 16 April 1951.

The 10th Rangers had assigned Lt. Drew Owens a special mission. Stopping off in Oklahoma City on his way to Camp Carson, Lieutenant Owens made a newspaper appeal to the citizen of Oklahoma for bagpipes and kilts for three pipers. According to the local newspapers, the reason was that World War II Rangers trained in Scotland, wanted to keep a tradition alive: the 10th wanted music on the long marches.

On April 16, 243 men completed Airborne training and reported to the Ranger Training Command. These men and an additional 200 that arrived on April 21 were for assignment to the 12th, 14th, and A and B Trainee Ranger companies.

On April 30 the first week of the fourth Ranger training cycle commenced, with weapons training concurrent with leadership, hand-to-hand combat, and compass instruction. The 12th, 13th, and 14th companies and training companies A and B were beginning their Ranger adventure.

Capt. Sam L. Amato had been a forward observer with the 7th Infantry Division in World War II and twice recommended for the Silver Star, although the executive officer of his battalion did not process the awards. At the war's end, Amato returned to his job at *The New York Times* and remained in the Army Reserve. Recalled for Korea, Amato was assigned to the 4th Infantry Division. He volunteered for the 14th Rangers but did not have high hopes. Over one hundred officers had asked for the assignment. Amato was surprised to find he had been selected to command the company. It turned out that the division G-1 was the man who had neglected to process Amato's awards, and had selected Amato for the post because his conscience bothered him. Years later Amato told his men that command of the company meant more than the awards.

The variety of ability in the Ranger Training Command covered all aspects of life. Capt. Charles E. Kuhn was an ex-big league umpire, 1st Lt. John Folks of the 14th Rangers had a masters degree in Agriculture and was aiming for a Ph.D. PFC Richard Anderson of the 10th Rangers had been everything from a band leader and TV actor to a professional wrestler.

Chapter 12

In the high mountains near the city of Hwachon is one of the largest reservoirs in Korea, extending over thirteen square miles, with an estimated capacity of 19,140,000,000 cubic feet of water. The dam is a straight-line overflow type, 275 feet high, with a spillway 826 feet long. There are eighteen spillway gates and an identical number of penstocks at the base to run the dynamos for electrical power. When the gates are closed, they contain up to thirty-two feet of water above the spillway.

There was more chill than warmth in the early April winds, but the melt of the winter snows would soon be at hand. The waters of an uncontrolled river would flow swift and deep, fords would become impassable, and bridges could be washed out. The Hwachon dam held at bay the Pukhan River—and the dam was in the hands of the Communists.

While the dam was a problem, it did not appear to be a 1st Cavalry Division problem. The division, attacking north, was scheduled to be relieved by the 1st Marine Division on April 10. Relief would be at phase-line "Kansas" about four thousand yards south of the Hwachon dam.

Intelligence reports on the dam were ominous. Aerial observers reported that the spillway gates were closed to their maximum extent and only a trickle of water was being released. Local civilians said the water level of the river below the dam was well below normal. If the enemy planned to bring the water behind the dam to its maximum height, then suddenly open the gates and release it, the effect could seriously hinder operations of IX Corps. A ten- to twelve-foot rise of water would occur in the Pukhan and Han rivers, bridges would be washed away, low areas flooded, and corps units separated from each other. Eighth Army Engineers doubted the Chinese capability to destroy the dam by demolitions, and it is likely that neither side wished to do this. The Hwachon reservoir and dam had been built to provide water and electric power to the city of Seoul; to the victor would go the prize.

Though the dam was too valuable to be destroyed, General Ridgeway and Maj. Gen. William Hoge, commanding general of IX Corps, felt that some action must be taken to eliminate the threat of flooding. General Hoge thought a raid was in order, an operation that would last but a few hours. After closing the floodgates, the machinery would be blasted. While leaving the dam intact, the threat would be removed.

General Hoge felt the 4th Ranger Company was the unit to perform the mission and ordered the 1st Cavalry Division to begin making plans. The 4th Rangers moved from Taegu on April 4 and reached 1st Cavalry Division headquarters the morning of April 6. At 1905 hours on April 8, Hoge informed General Ridgeway, who approved the Hwachon dam mission but ordered that it be done without a large number of casualties.

The Chinese had also reviewed their options. The night of April 8 two squads of Chinese soldiers and five Koreans who worked at the dam began to open the floodgates. A rush of water sped away. Between April 9 and 11 all of the five bridges that spanned the Pukhan and Han rivers were at one time disconnected and inoperable or washed out. Still, fortune smiled on the U.N. forces. The central power system was not operating, and only two of the eighteen gates were raised completely; two were raised three-quarters of the way and six opened only slightly. For some reason—perhaps because it took ten hours to raise one gate manually—the Chinese did not open the remaining gates.

The action of the Chinese demonstrated that they could turn the water on and off at will. Spurred by concern over this fact, General Hoge ordered the 1st Cavalry Division to move immediately against the dam. Caught up in preparation for the relief of his division, Maj. Gen. Charles Palmer, commanding general of the 1st Cavalry Division, gave vague instructions to the 7th Cavalry Regiment. The 7th felt Division wanted the dam seized because it "would be nice to do so," though preparations for relief were the highest priority.

Capt. Dorsey B. Anderson, company commander of the 4th Rangers, had been informed on April 7 by Lieutenant Colonel Carlson (G-3, 1st Cavalry Division) that the Rangers would be given the job of making the dam inoperative.

On April 8 Anderson had accompanied Major Wilson, commander of the 8th Engineer Combat Battalion, to the Chongpyong dam, as the machinery there was believed to be similar to that of the Hwachon dam. The officers decided the floodgates could be made inoperative by destroying the cogs on the powerwheel that controlled them.

On April 9 Captain Anderson made an aerial reconnaissance. Below the wing of the light aircraft, some six thousand meters west of the city of Hwachon, in terrain so steep the map contour lines crowded one upon the other, lay the reservoir that contained the waters of the Pukhan River. Before the river could pursue its meandering course southward, it was rudely thrust north then west by a thumblike projection of land some five thousand meters long. Thus the spillway of the dam faced north, with the dam laying on an east–west axis.

An attacking force moving north up the thumb to reach the west end of the dam would find their approach channeled into an inverted V, some six hundred meters wide at the base. The defense had reason to be inspired: with water at their back and flanks, they were hemmed in.

Anderson saw the difficulties in attacking up the thumb, but there was a daring alternative—one Anderson believed in. If assault boats were used, the Rangers could embark under cover of darkness from land at the eastern base of the thumb, cross 1100 meters of open water, and land on the Tongchon-ni peninsula about a thousand meters south of the east edge of the dam. Surprise was critical, and this route offered a chance of getting to the dam before the enemy was aware of the Ranger presence. Anderson's reconnaissance was interrupted by a message saying that an attack was under way to seize the dam and that the 4th Rangers were involved. He hurriedly rejoined the company.

The 2nd Battalion, 7th Cavalry, was in the attack, moving northward up the thumb of land, and the 4th Rangers followed, ready to pass through and close or destroy the floodgates. Rapid progress was made against light resistance until the battalion reached an east–west road at the narrow base of the thumb. Here they came under heavy fire from well-constructed and mutually supporting pillboxes. Simultaneously, enemy machine gun and mortar fire was received from the high ground west of the Pukhan River. The battalion attempted to maneuver to flank the enemy position but was unable to penetrate the defense.

Again there was uncertainty about the mission. The 2nd Battalion was told to prepare for relief at the same time it was told to advance—and to do so without getting cut up and without withdrawing unless necessary. Night was coming on, so the battalion requested permission to continue the attack in the morning. Permission was granted.

The attack kicked off at 0730 the morning of April 10. The weather was bad, so there was no air support. Once more enemy fire broke up the attack. Casualties in the battalion were six killed and twenty-seven wounded, most by mortar fire.

At 1000 hours that day General Hoge visited the 1st Cavalry Division and found units moving rearward to Army reserve. As Hoge reviewed the situation, his anger grew. In blunt and direct language he told General Palmer to make a "bona fide" attempt to take the dam. The mission would be completed before the 1st Cavalry Division was relieved.

With a clear sense of purpose, the 7th Cavalry Regiment discontinued relief planning and geared up to attack the dam. The plan was to have the 2nd Battalion continue its attack north on the thumb of land toward the west end of the dam. The attack would be made prior to dawn on April 11. The 1st Battalion would make a diversionary attack on the high ground to the west of the Pukhan River in order to draw off the heavy flanking fire the 2nd battalion had been receiving. The 4th Rangers would embark in assault boats under cover of darkness, cross the reservoir, and land on the peninsula east of the dam, as Captain Anderson had envisioned. The 3rd Battalion would meanwhile be prepared to assist either the 2nd Battalion or the Rangers.

American fighter-bombers had worked over Chinese positions with Napalm; these fires and a grass fire in the Greek Battalion area created a heavy smoke that obscured visibility.

By nightfall on April 10 the attack had encountered enormous problems. The terrain was so difficult that four-wheel-drive jeeps could not use their light trailers when bringing ammunition for-

ward. The engineers of the 1st Cav had already departed to go
into Army Reserve. The 105mm howitzers, the workhorse of
the artillery, could not be brought forward close enough to support the operation. Only the 155mm howitzers and 8-inch guns,
with their slower rate of fire, could provide support. There were
no assault boats or outboard motors or engineers to operate
them, yet the operation had to be done that night.

Frantic efforts were begun to improve trails and locate boats
and motors. Volunteers were summoned to operate boats; smoke
pots, generators, and life preservers were requested; air-sea aircraft were requested to drop power launches; artillery and air
priority were requested and air smoke missions planned for. The
effort by the division staff was Herculean, but division resources
were scattered, bad weather precluded air support, and time was
running out.

At 2200 hours Captain Anderson was summoned to a meeting of the regimental staff and battalion commanders. Anderson
knew he would be required to do something with the dam; just
what he was not yet clear. He had been told first to destroy the dam
machinery, then was told his mission would be to seize the dam.
The latest instruction was to destroy the dam mechanism if the
Rangers could not hold the high ground east of the dam. Anderson had briefed his officers on the courses of action.
Throughout the afternoon of April 10 the Rangers were preparing demolitions, organizing into teams, and rehearsing. They
were prepared to carry out any of the missions.

The regimental staff briefed the gathering. S-2 (Intelligence)
said that enemy forces were believed to be a regiment with one
battalion on the high ground west of the river, another on the
thumb of land, and a third on the peninsula east of the dam.
(Later information reported that the 115th Communist Chinese
Forces [CCF] Division was dug in throughout the zone.) The
S-3 said that the Ranger covering party would embark at 0230
hours to seize the landing site; the remainder of the company
would cross at 0330, and 2nd Battalion would begin its attack
at 0400, assisted by the 1st Battalion's diversion. Nine engineer
assault boats were available, as were six motors, of which only
two worked.

By 2300 hours the instructions were issued. Anderson still
had to move his company from their defensive positions in the
2nd Battalion area to the embarkation site. The move was begun

under the direction of the company executive officer Lt. John S.
Warren. Anderson briefed his leaders on his plan.

The assault boats could carry a maximum of twelve men. Lt.
Michael Healey, 3rd platoon leader, would lead his 1st squad as
a "killer" element armed with knives, hand axes, grenades,
pistols, and carbines.[1] This group would secure the landing site
while a team from another squad would carry and place demolitions. The remainder of the platoon would carry sniper and
automatic rifles and machine guns plus Ranger field-expedient
rifle grenades (60mm mortar shells rigged to fire from a grenade
launcher on M-1 rifles). This group would provide close support
to the killer and demolitions teams.

The 2nd platoon, company headquarters, and attachments
would follow the 3rd platoon to shore. A twenty-one-man
machine-gun section from Company M 7th Cav, 81mm and
heavy mortar forward observers and their radio operators, plus
an artillery forward observer party, were attached. Due to the
shortage of assault boats, the 1st platoon would have to be carried over in a second lift. Lieutenant Warren would come with
the last group and serve as beachmaster organizing the landing
site for resupply and evacuation.

The 410-pound boats would be paddled across; motors would
not be used until the enemy was aware of the landing force, or
until daylight—whichever came first.

The 2nd Battalion moved to attack at 0400 on April 11. Delayed by the need to move into position, the Rangers did not
embark until 0345 hours. The quiet blackness of night and soft
sound of water lapping at the shore were made eerie as a gray,
clammy fog mixed with smoke crept stealthily across the surface
of the water. Visibility was extremely limited, and navigation
would have to be by compass; a 28-degree azimuth had been
plotted for the voyage. The men entered the boats, unbuckling
web gear and slinging bandoliers on one shoulder so that equipment could be shed easily should the boat overturn. Assault-
boat crossing was a part of the Ranger training, and the men
adjusted to the paddles quickly.

The crossing and landing were successful, with Lieutenant
Healey and his men reaching shore at 0420 and securing the
landing site. Captain Anderson, the 2nd platoon, and attachments arrived, their boats grounding lightly on the rocky shore.
Sergeant Goolsby hung as a landing marker a purple light that

could only be seen from the water. Moving quickly, the Rangers began to climb through a cold, sleeting rain, toward a hill some five hundred meters north designated as Objective 79.

The hill was occupied by a squad of Chinese who, apparently mistaking the climbing Rangers for their own forces, stood in the first light of dawn and waved and shouted to the men. The Rangers waved back and continued climbing. The Rangers had closed to within a hundred meters when the enemy discovered their mistake and opened fire with a machine gun. The first burst of fire killed the radio man for the 81mm mortars forward observers and wounded Sergeant Williams of the Rangers four times in the leg. Sergeant Goolsby and the aid man immediately went to Williams's assistance.

The hill was barren, without trees or ditches, and the Rangers had to use fire and movement to close. Another enemy machine gun opened up from the right front and enemy snipers engaged from the left. The 3rd platoon's 57mm recoilless rifle knocked out the machine gun on the right but could not locate the one on the left. Lieutenant Healy and the two lead scouts flanked the gun position, assaulted with grenades and small arms, and killed the machine-gun crew. The rest of the enemy retreated. Around 0615 the Rangers were in possession of the hill, but their presence was known to the Chinese and they were some six hundred meters short of the east edge of the dam.

To the west the 2nd Battalion was stalled, unable to penetrate Chinese defenses that included reinforced concrete pillboxes. The 1st Battalion's diversionary attack was also unsuccessful. Anderson was now faced with a dilemma. His 1st platoon had not yet landed, and its boats were receiving heavy fire from machine guns and mortars. There was high ground to his immediate front (designated Objective 77), but to attack there would expose his force to a flank attack from a hill to his left (designated Objective 80). Anderson was convinced that if he moved forward, reinforcements would not be able to land and those on shore would be cut off from the beach. He sent a patrol to keep watch on Objective 80.

On the other side of the reservoir twenty additional boats were now available with ten motors (none of which worked). One of the two working motors had expired; there were now twenty-nine boats and one motor. Four boats were disabled by enemy fire, which became increasingly heavy, forcing men to paddle in a roundabout manner to reach the beach.

Between 0600 and 0700 Lt. James L. Johnson's 1st platoon had paddled to reach the landing site. Sergeant Goolsby, who was waiting on shore with the wounded Sergeant Williams, guided them to land. Goolsby then placed Williams in a boat and joined the disembarking platoon to guide them to the remainder of the company.

The 1st platoon came up the hill about 0815 and was immediately dispatched by Anderson to seize Objective 80. The platoon came under heavy fire from its front, tried to flank the objective, and received fire from the front, right, and rear. The Chinese mortar fire was galling, and attempts to respond were not effective. The Greek Battalion was providing supporting 81mm mortar fire. In communication between them and the American forward observer, accuracy was lost. At about 1330, under heavy Chinese mortar fire, the 1st platoon was hit by an enemy counterattack of fifty to sixty men. Anderson sent two squads of the 3rd platoon to assist, and the attack was repelled. Sergeants Wilcoxson and Anglin and corporals Chada and Braxel distinguished themselves in this action, Chada cradling an A-6 machine gun in his arms and firing into the Chinese. The 1st platoon (reinforced) then returned to Objective 79 and tied in on the left flank of the company. The 2nd platoon was in the center, company headquarters and a 3rd platoon squad on the right.

The Chinese may have made this attack as a diversion to draw the Rangers off from the point of their main thrust. In any case, the Chinese were reinforcing—sending men across the dam to face the Rangers from the north and from the west.

Some men of the 1st Cavalry arrived with water-cooled machine guns which they set up to the left of the 2nd platoon. The Rangers were spread along the crest with a man about every twelve feet. Across the way the Chinese began bobbing up and down, trying to draw automatic weapons fire and pinpoint the positions of these weapons. The Rangers did not take the bait; instead, a Ranger rifleman promptly killed one of the Chinese and the rest decided to stay low.

In the afternoon firing picked up slowly, growing increasingly heavy, and at approximately 1415 hours three to four hundred Chinese launched a screaming, bugle-blowing charge on the positions of the company headquarters, the 2nd platoon, and the almost-vacated 3rd platoon area. Sergeant Goolsby, who had left the 1st platoon when there were no casualties to treat, saw the Chinese coming toward company headquarters and gave warning.

The Chinese made no attempt to use terrain or covering fire; theirs was a headlong banzai charge by a mass of men, terrifying in its ferocity. Due to depressed ground to their front, the Rangers had to stand up, exposed against the skyline, to pour fire into the close-packed advancing bodies. In the 2nd platoon area, BAR men Forbes and Sanchez moved across the crest and down the hill past a water drainage ditch to get better firing positions. Forbes had fired six magazines into the massed Chinese when he heard men screaming for him to get back on line. Stuffing empty magazines in his pockets, Forbes ran back up the hill. As he crossed the drainage ditch he felt two sharp blows in his lower body. He saw Ranger Cyril Tritz stand up and fire a carbine directly at him. The bullets were intended for, and killed, a Chinese soldier who had shot Forbes from a few feet behind— one of a number of Chinese coming up the ditch. Forbes made it over the crest, where his wounds were treated by aid-man Leonard Koops. Lieutenant Forney, the artillery F.O. from the 1st Cav, and the 4.2-inch mortar observer called down accurate fire to within seventy-five meters of the Rangers, but the Chinese came on into machine guns, rifles, and carbines until, finally, the Rangers were using pistols. Captain Anderson, Sergeant Schroeder (the communications sergeant), and the six men in the company headquarters position fired for fifteen minutes, stopping only to reload.

Elsewhere on the line, Corporal Angarano was hit, his arm almost severed. Goolsby pulled Angarano to cover, treated him for shock, and tried to inject albumen, but Angarano's veins had collapsed and he died from loss of blood. Private Young, a BAR man, was hit in the head, convulsed, and died. Ammunition was taken from the dead and redistributed. Squad leader Ken Robinson doled out five to six rounds per man, telling them, "Don't use it all on one man."

The number of wounded began to increase. Sergeant Carbonel and privates Sanchez and Bauer were seriously wounded; Rangers Blacketter, Takach, Williams, Gustafson, Capone, Ackley, Dillan, McClellan, Tritz, Bigelow, Gibson, Lopes, Anglin, Pinckney, Heffernan, Chada, Wilcoxson, Holohan, and Golden were struck. Among the worst hit was Corporal Ligon, who was shot in the stomach. He would die of wounds the following day. During the height of the battle, few of the casualties could be evacuated, and even many of the wounded fought.

The furious attack lasted for thirty to forty-five minutes before the Chinese were beaten off. Over a hundred enemy dead lay to the front of the Ranger positions. The 2nd platoon had been slowly driven from position. As they began to withdraw, Lieutenant Waterbury, the platoon leader, was concussed by a grenade explosion and in a state of shock. The bulk of the platoon then destroyed its 57mm recoilless rifle, took its machine guns and weapons, and withdrew to the beach. At Anderson's position there was one-half box of machine-gun ammunition remaining, and an average of sixteen rounds per M-1 rifle and thirty rounds per carbine—no grenades remained. He attempted to cover the 2nd platoon position with the 3rd squad of the 3rd platoon, but the enemy had the location under enfilade fire. The continuing rain and fog prevented air support.

When Anderson's position was no longer supportable, he radioed Regiment for permission to withdraw, and 7th Cavalry replied that Company I was landing on the beach and would join him on position, bringing ammunition. Anderson was then to take his combined force and attack Objective 80. The 7th Cavalry Regiment was prepared to ferry additional forces over the reservoir to build up the attack force. At about 1630, as Anderson was preparing to carry out his instructions, he received orders to cancel the attack and return to the landing site. Company I would cover the withdrawal.

General Hoge had wanted a quick, surgical operation, but this was now turning into a situation that could require the commitment of large numbers of troops. "Bring them back," he ordered.

There was anger on the hill—the Rangers had beaten off the Chinese, Company I was ashore, and other units were in position to cross—but Captain Anderson could only shrug his shoulders in resignation; the orders were clear. Covered by Company I, which fought off another Chinese attack, the Rangers disembarked, followed by Company I. At 0126 hours on April 12 the last American reached the point from where the operation had begun. Material to support the attack was now arriving in quantity.

The Hwachon dam loomed large. Like the gates of Rome were to Hannibal, to the 4th Rangers the dam would always be "so close and yet so far."

Chapter 13

For the Devils of the 8th Airborne Rangers, all the days of April blended into one.[1] They received missions, were briefed, test-fired weapons, and spent the nights patrolling in front of their lines. Conversation centered on clean socks, a package from home, and the hope for a hot meal. It was difficult to tell what the Army was doing. Now and then someone would ask, "Are we advancing or retreating?" A soldier could fight for a week, back and forth, and find himself in the spot he started from.

We ate C rations or "Charlie Rats," as they were often called. The olive-drab cans contained approximately eleven ounces of solid food such as frankfurters and beans, ham and lima beans, spaghetti and meat balls, sausage patties, and corned-beef hash. A smaller can would contain crackers and cocoa. There was jam and a can of fruit. Accessories included matches, toilet paper, instant coffee, a cream substitute, sugar, and salt. The cans were opened with an ingenious device called a P-38, a small can opener about the length of the first joint of the thumb. Folded flat, it was worn around the neck on the identification dog-tag chain. Like the two identification disks, it was taped to prevent noise.

Few men gained weight eating C rations. Eaten cold, as they often had to be, the best that could be said was they kept one going. There was a monotony to them. Still, with the lid laid back as a handle, a can of lighted Sterno underneath, and the juices bubbling around the sausage patties, a man could feel comfortable.

Each man had his preference and the trading was constant.

"Anyone have franks and beans?"

"I'll swap a ham and lima beans for spaghetti."

Those with corned-beef hash cursed their fate and waited for a better day. Hash lovers were rare, and even a Chinese prisoner rejected it.

Though the C rations contained a plastic spoon, it was too delicate an instrument and prone to melting. Many Rangers carried a large mess-kit spoon stuck down inside the top of a boot. If a can of peaches came into one's life, he wiped the dust off the spoon with his thumb, opened the can with his P-38, and dug in.

At 0700 hours on 15 April 1951 the three platoons of the 8th Ranger Company waited in concealed positions along the main line of resistance of the 24th Division's sector. Each platoon would operate independently on this mission.

Constant patrol activity had provided the 24th Infantry Division with valuable information regarding the location of enemy strong points. On April 10 the 19th Regiment had relieved the 5th Regiment on the west sector of the division front. On the morning of April 11 the 19th and 21st regiments had begun an attack named Operation DAUNTLESS. Despite initial heavy resistance, the attack moved forward. By April 14 it appeared the enemy was withdrawing to more favorable positions while screening his movements with reconnaissance forces. Such a battalion from the XX Corps, 3rd Chinese Field Army, was reported operating in the area.

Alerted for action at 0400, the 8th Rangers ate a quick C-ration breakfast, checked equipment, were briefed, then moved into platoon assembly areas behind the 1st Battalion, 19th Infantry. It was a fair day. Sunrise had come at 0558 hours, and the temperature, which had been in the high thirties overnight, would climb to 67 degrees during the afternoon. The wind was calm, with visibility one mile in the smoke and haze.

Platoon sergeants Moore of the 1st platoon, Ellis of the 2nd, and Lieutenant Strong, leader of the 3rd platoon, checked their watches and signaled their men forward. At 0800 hours the Rangers crossed the line of departure. The 1st platoon passed through Company C, 1st Battalion, 19th Infantry, the 2nd through Company B, and the 3rd through Company A.

The 1st and 2nd platoons scoured their areas of operation, but the enemy was elsewhere. After checking for mines on trails that would be used in the next attack, the patrols returned to friendly lines, the 1st platoon arriving at 1230 hours, the 2nd at 1245 hours.

The 3rd platoon was in high spirits. Despite the early hour, their war dance had been performed and a rough harmony achieved by singing "That Old Black Magic." Prior to moving out, there was time to brew a cup of C-ration coffee and to sharpen teeth on an iron-hard cracker.

Weapons were checked, including personal sidearms such as Browning, Parabellum, and Beretta pistols. Most popular was "The Old Equalizer," the Colt .45 which had proved reliable since 1911. Ammunition was difficult to obtain for the foreign makes but readily available for the .45-caliber automatic.

As Lieutenant Strong and Platoon Sergeant Cox held last minute discussions with the squad leaders, the men began to "saddle up." E. C. Rivera donned his harness and SCR 300 radio, though the addition of a brightly colored aircraft recognition panel seemed like double jeopardy.

Rifleman Jimmie White was depressed. He had been detached from his squad to carry machine-gun ammunition. Though still with his platoon, being removed from his inner circle of friends was disturbing. Friendship was the rock to which men in battle clung.

A man gave a thumbs-up signal to automatic rifleman Antonio Velo, of Oxnard, California. At Colorado Springs Tony had avoided the night spots because he had a girl back home.

Lieutenant Strong gave the signal. The 3rd moved out with "Silent" Pete Torres, lead scout, on point. The men of the 19th Infantry looked up from their foxholes as the Rangers passed. The only sounds were the scuffing of boots against the earth, or the soft slap of sling against rifle. The trail led downward to the valley floor, then through intermittent low ridges and hills leading toward distant high ground.

Using cover and concealment to its best advantage, the platoon passed without making contact through what had been presumed to be enemy strong points. Standard procedure was to use a different route to return to friendly lines. As the 3rd platoon turned to make its return home, a smattering of fire from the left front sharpened their senses and brought their weapons off safe.

Elements of the 19th Infantry, Intelligence and Reconnaissance (I&R) Platoon, were conducting a reconnaissance patrol near Hill 299. As the Rangers watched from concealment on a flanking ridge, the men of the I&R Platoon broke contact with a Chinese force and passed from a woodline going left to right across an open stretch to the front of the Rangers, then disappeared into the woods beyond. To their rear came a large force of Chinese moving in quick but silent pursuit. The men of the 19th gave no indication they were aware of this force. Waiting until the Chinese were midway across the open space, Lieutenant Strong gave the signal. The Rangers opened fire with devastating effect. The Chinese behind the lead element returned this fire. At this point the action was pure infantry, automatic rifles and machine guns setting the pace. The din of battle was deafening. The I&R Platoon reported "heavy" firing. Men on the main line of resistance recalled the constant crackle and roar of weapons.

Pete Torres was hit, shot in the right side of the face about two inches below the eye. The bullet passes through his mouth and neck to lodge in his shoulder. Previous to this engagement, the 8th's casualties had occurred at night. Covered by darkness, it was difficult for another soldier to gauge the impact of the wound. The sight of Peter Torres's torn and bloody face burned itself in the memory of his friends.

Radioman E. C. Rivera, who was near Lieutenant Strong, held out the handset.

"Sir, Battalion wants to talk to you."

"You talk to them," replied Strong. "I'm busy."

Strong, whose youthful face seemed at odds with the Combat Infantry Badge he wore from World War II, was constantly on the move, exhorting his men.

"When I throw the grenade," he yelled, "everybody goes." And that is how it went.

In a series of charges, constantly firing, the Rangers drove the Chinese force rearward. From the recollections of the hectic battle, vignettes remain:

Antonio Velo and E. C. Rivera killing a Chinese soldier in

the act of reloading a drum in an "American" Thompson sub-machine gun.

Nick Tisak was changing magazines in his Browning Automatic Rifle when his assistant Leroy "Willie" Williamson yelled in warning. "There's a Chink!"

"Well, kill him!" replied Tisak.[2]

Williamson fired one round, a snap shot from his M-1 rifle, killing the Chinese soldier in the act of throwing a grenade. As the Communist fell back with arms extended, his lifeless fingers released a grenade that soared upward to explode above the Chinese position.

As the platoon continued forward, medic Gill Gregory came to the aid of the wounded Torres. Blinded by blood and holding his rifle with bayonet affixed, Torres waited. At the sound of approaching footsteps, he struggled to defend himself. Gregory's reassuring voice put him at ease. Setting to work, "Doc" Gregory used a bayonet and fingernail clippers to remove the bullet, rigged bandages for the wounds, then, as the platoon had gone on, began to guide Torres back to friendly lines.

The 3rd platoon continued its attack, driving the enemy before them. As the action progressed into the area of the main enemy line, the Chinese began to gain an appreciation of the size of the force they opposed. Enemy fire from prepared positions increased, and Rangers Waldecker and Washburn were hit. Chinese mortar rounds began to fall like rain.

A Chinese counterattack pushed in from the right flank. Automatic rifleman Antonio Velo met this threat head on with magazine after magazine of withering fire. Fighting a covering action for his comrades, Velo was severely wounded in the upper thigh. A tourniquet was rigged, and Leonard Wiggins, Tom Uldall, Rudy Belluomini, and Norman Erb took turns carrying Velo.

Reversing their direction, the Rangers began to withdraw to their own lines. The Chinese fire continued as enemy elements tried to encircle the Rangers.

On the valley floor the heat seemed oppressive. Exhaustion was total, and even the sight of bullets striking near one's feet was insufficient to inspire faster movement. There was only heat, thirst, and the dusty path stained with the blood of our wounded.

A Chinese machine gun covered an open space of rice paddy that had to be crossed. Squad leader Dan Rivera recalls that as a wounded man crossed, the machine gunner would hold his fire. For the unwounded, crossing the paddy was a run through a gauntlet of death. Jimmie White, the "Little Tiger," died there, his life ended by a Chinese mortar. Tony Velo died of shock and loss of blood.

The 1st Battalion 19th dispatched troops forward to assist, but they had not cleared the forward slope by the time the Rangers closed on friendly positions at 1309.

The 24th Infantry Division Command report for April 1951, summed up the action as follows:

> The 8th Ranger Company conducted three platoon-sized patrols in the 19th Infantry area, with two making no contact and the third engaging an estimated two enemy companies. All patrols returned to friendly lines prior to darkness. The 3rd platoon killed an estimated seventy enemy, fifty of which were counted dead. Patrol losses were two killed and three wounded, all of whom were brought back with the patrol.

The morning report closed with the words, "Weather fair, morale high." The action known as "the 299 Turkey Shoot" was history.

Chapter 14

On 21 April 1951 United Nations positions were anchored in the west at Munsan, below the 38th parallel. Proceeding east, they followed the course of the Imjin River, then traced northeast to Yonchon and continued east above Hwachon to Taep'ori.

The goal of the Eighth Army was to seize the "Iron Triangle," an area formed with Chorwon and Kumhwa at its base and Pyongyang at the apex. The Iron Triangle contained key road junctions that made it important to both sides. While the Eighth Army advance drove forward, there was caution; prisoners and increased activity behind the line gave the indication that the enemy was preparing his long expected Fifth Phase Offensive.

In I Corps the 24th Infantry Division had continued in the attack, with armored patrols from the 6th Medium Tank Battalion striking northward toward Kumwha while the 19th and 21st regiments secured objectives along line "Utah."[1] On April 20 the 5th Regimental Combat Team relieved the 21st Regiment on line, and the 21st Regiment then moved to reserve positions along line "Kansas," an Eighth Army designation for a stretch of defensive terrain above the 38th parallel.

On April 21 the 5th and 19th regiments advanced one to two thousand meters. Up to two thousand meters in front of them, the 8th Rangers were operating and finding good hunting. Two enemy patrols were ambushed and twelve enemy were killed without a Ranger loss.

The Rangers often worked by the eight-million candlepower beams of American carbon-arc searchlights. Mounted on two 1/2-ton trucks, these powerful lights would send out their beams from positions deep behind friendly lines. Their great light would be reflected from low hanging clouds or high hills. The light was helpful to the line infantry in illuminating the ground to their front, but to the Rangers the light could present a danger. On some patrols, Rangers moving under cover of darkness were suddenly exposed to Chinese view when the searchlights came on.

On April 22 a prisoner revealed the Chinese would attack at dark. In late afternoon Chinese artillery and mortars began pre-paratory fire whose heavy volume was itself indicative of something big brewing. With the coming of night, tension increased along the line. Men gripped their rifles and peered anxiously north. A radiant moon crept stealthily higher, providing excellent visibility for the approximately 350,000 North Korean and Chinese troops that awaited the order to attack.

Not everyone was coming south. Two platoon-size combat patrols were scheduled for the 8th Rangers. One patrol was to pass through 19th Infantry lines in the east, while the other would cross through the 5th Infantry on the west, along the right flank of the 25th Division.

Lt. Berk Strong's 3rd platoon made last minute checks, then began to file northward, passing through the forward line of foxholes. The movement was interrupted by the sound of a vehicle horn and flashing lights as a jeep swept into the forward positions.

"Get back in here," screamed a 24th Division staff officer. "They're coming in waves on the right flank; they'll hit us soon."

The words of that brave officer were soon fulfilled. As the Ranger platoons quickly dug in with the forward rifle compa-nies, the Chinese struck the 24th Division. The attack came at a center ridge occupied by the 2nd battalions of the 5th and 19th infantry regiments, then flowed like water along the 24th Divi-sion line. The whole front was a roaring crescendo of fire.

Throughout the long night, the attacks continued, positions lost, regained, and lost again. A battalion commander who had been with the 24th Division since it landed in Korea said he had seen more Chinese in this attack than he had seen since his arrival.

At 0250 hours on April 23 came a chilling piece of information: the 6th ROK Division, located on the right flank of the 24th Division, had broken. The Chinese were exploiting a situation that could shatter the Eighth Army.

The 5th and 19th regiments began pulling back, under a curtain of American artillery fire. On that day the division artillery would fire 15,712 rounds. The Chinese dead piled up, but live Chinese kept coming.

The 21st Infantry moved into blocking positions along line Kansas. At 0855 hours the 24th Division was also ordered to withdraw to line Kansas and defend. The division established its line with the 19th Infantry on the left, the 21st Infantry on the right, and the 5th Infantry in reserve.

At 1000 hours on April 23, the 8th Rangers were ordered to withdraw. A new mission was in the offing. I Corps had informed 24th Division that the nearest friendly troops on the division's right were approximately 13,000 meters to the division's rear. The fog of war had settled on the right flank of the 24th Division. Something was developing out there, and the Rangers would be sent to find out what it was.

Throughout April 23, the Rangers were constantly on the move. At about 1600 hours they arrived in an assembly area near Munnumi-ni where trucks waited to carry them to the jump-off point. Supply Sgt. Joe Hosch issued ammunition. Weapons and equipment were checked. Boxes of hand grenades were nearby, and the men began to hang them on pack harnesses or stuff them into field-jacket pockets.

Only one thing remained before the company moved to action: the mess truck was standing nearby, loaded with various supplies (including sacks of flower), and the company mess section had prepared the first hot meal the men had seen in days. It was a simple meal—meat, potatoes, and gravy, with a slab of cherry pie on top and a canteen cup full of steaming-hot G.I. coffee—but it would be difficult to remember a meal that looked so good. Ravenous men hurriedly extended their mess kits for the food. The first men through the line found a box or a rise of ground to sit on, or ate using truck beds or fenders as tables.

Ranger Bill Wehland was a big man both in stature and heart. Mild mannered and gregarious, he was a good friend, except when it was his turn to sleep in the foxhole. Then his propensity to snore with the decibel power of an air-raid siren made even his closest friends angry. Chinese from the 38th parallel to the Yalu River knew where the sleeping Bill Wehland's position was and therefore—to the consternation of his friends—the position of those who shared the hole with him.

Wehland was always on the lookout for more food, and asked the mess team for a loaf of bread he could carry with him on the mission. Told he could get a loaf from the mess truck, Wehland, carrying weapon, ammunition, grenades, and filled mess kit, climbed over the flour sacks and secured the bread. Coming off the truck, he jumped rearward—and then screamed.

Some men say the handle on a grenade at his belt caught in a flour sack and snapped; most believe the circular pull ring caught on an obstruction and was pulled free.

Encumbered by his equipment and the items in his hands, Wehland tried desperately to get the live grenade from his belt. Recognizing he would be unable to save himself, he shouted, "Get back!" and turned his body away from his friends.

The grenade exploded, the force lifting and hurling Wehland backward. Men were splattered with blood, and three were slightly wounded. Wheland shouted, "Oh, Christ!" and died.

A numbing chill swept over the company. Almost as one, hardened men threw away their food, filed mechanically past the immersion heaters to wash their mess kits, then loaded onto the trucks. There was little conversation. Death in battle was acceptable, but this waste of a good man's life in a tragic accident left a feeling of utter desolation.

This was the low point in the existence of the 8th Airborne Ranger Company.

As the Rangers moved to the 24th Division right flank, the extent of the disaster of the 6th ROK was not known. It would be three days before Gen. Chang Do Young would write in a letter of apology to South Korean President Rhee, "It is a great regret to me that we have lost about twenty-one miles." The general did not mention the eighteen howitzers; over 3,300 rifles, carbines, and submachine guns; eighty-four machine guns; eighty-six trucks; and enormous quantities of other equipment captured by the Chinese in this disgraceful rout.

At 2000 hours 23 April 1951 eighty-seven enlisted men and three officers of the 8th Rangers passed through 2nd Battalion,

21st Infantry, lines and began the long, difficult climb to the high ground on the right flank of the 24th Infantry Division. The planned route of march included Hill 628, Hill 1010, and Hill 1168.

The men carried heavy burdens for such a climb. Combat packs included two days' rations and mountain sleeping bags. Each rifleman had four bandoliers of ammunition with forty-eight rounds per bandolier. Each Browning Automatic rifleman carried his twenty-pound weapon and twelve magazines with twenty rounds per magazine. Each of the three machine guns had four boxes of ammunition with 250 rounds per box. There were two sixty mm mortars at 45.2 pounds apiece. Fifty-six rounds of high-explosive mortar ammunition were distributed among the men. Most of the Rangers carried four to six fragmentation grenades, though some men had as many as twelve. A shortage of radios hampered communications. Two SCR 300 radios had been borrowed from the 2nd Battalion, 21st Infantry Regiment.

At 0230 hours on April 24, the Rangers made contact. Locating a Chinese patrol, they called in artillery fire on the enemy without revealing their position, then continued to climb. After several hours of hard climbing, the Rangers neared the top of Hill 628 and waited on the narrow trail while scouts checked out the summit. Several ROK soldiers, left behind by their fleeing comrades, were located. By 0600 the company had the 2nd and 3rd platoons occupying the crest of the hill with the 1st platoon on a ridge that led west.

The men rested and ate. At about 0730 hours activity was seen on Hill 830. SFC James McNeely, squad leader of the 2nd squad, 1st platoon, led a reconnaissance patrol and made contact with a patrol from L Company, 21st Infantry Regiment, on Hill 830. The 21st had no knowledge of 6th ROK Division units but had seen the enemy to the east of Hill 628.

At about 1000 hours on the April 24 the Rangers began the ascent to Hill 1010. It was an arduous four-hour climb. The narrow ridge swept ever higher, affording excellent observation. It was obvious the enemy had made a major penetration. American air strikes were being put in to the front and rear of the Rangers. Some of those visible were an estimated five miles to the rear of the Ranger location.

Reaching the top of Hill 1010, the men found previous occupants had dug positions, many of which were still usable. A perimeter was established with the 3rd platoon facing north toward Hill 1168. The 1st platoon was oriented to the west, and 2nd platoon to the east. The 1st and 2nd platoons also covered the approach from Hill 628. White phosphorous grenades were used to burn off high grass areas on the ridge to Hill 1168.

Hill 1010 was a critical terrain feature, with ridgelines that offered natural avenues of approach southeast into the 6th ROK Division area and southwest into the right flank of terrain occupied by the 21st Infantry Regiment.

Several hours after reaching Hill 1010, MSgt. Phillip Moore led a patrol toward Hill 1168. The mission objective was to make contact with the enemy. A squad of Chinese was observed, and the patrol opened fire, hoping to get the Chinese to reveal the extent of their number and their position, but the Chinese did not take the bait. The patrol returned to Hill 1010, from which large numbers of Chinese could be seen passing to the east.

The U-shaped gap between the U.S. 24th Infantry Division and the 1st Marine Division now threatened the entire Eighth Army front. The 7th ROK regiment had attempted to form a line some eight thousand meters south (rear) of Hill 1010, but this plan went awry as the 7th joined the 2nd and 19th ROK regiments in pell-mell retreat.

While the 8th Rangers monitored enemy movement into this gap, Eighth Army moved to withdraw the front. While the 24th and 1st Marine divisions began to re-fuse their flanks, the 27th British Brigade from IX Corps reserve and the 5th Cavalry Regiment were committed to seal off the base of the penetration.

Elements of the 40th, 20th, 27th, and 26th Chinese Field Armies were, in that order, pouring through the hole in the line between the 24th and 1st Marine divisions. Like water, the Chinese attack flowed along the route of least resistance, exploiting the disintegration of the 6th ROK Division.

When the 35th ROK Regiment was dispersed by Chinese forces, the 2nd Ranger Company moved in and held the position while the regiment reorganized.

Enemy attacks were continuing in the 19th Infantry sector. At 0807 hours on April 24, the 19th Infantry reported their position untenable. A battalion of the 5th Regiment was sent to assist. To protect the increasingly exposed right, the 21st Infantry Regiment had re-fused its flank. Now, the 24th Infantry

Division moved the 3rd Battalion, 5th Regiment, to the right rear (south) of the 21st Regiment. This position was approximately four thousand meters to the rear (south) and two thousand to the right (west) of the Ranger position on Hill 1010.

Facing due east, the 3rd Battalion of the 5th Infantry blocked to prevent the flow of the Chinese attack from breaking into the division rear. The frontage was too large to prevent infiltration.

On Hill 1010 the Rangers observed large formations of Chinese passing south through the valley. Enemy patrols began to probe the Ranger position at dusk, hitting several locations. Movement was particularly heavy in front of Sgt. Keith Smith's 3rd squad, 2nd platoon. Artillery flares were requested but not forthcoming, but some fragmentation grenades brought a cessation to the Chinese movement. A Ranger outpost killed two Chinese soldiers and withdrew to the perimeter.

Around midnight Ranger reconnaissance patrols were dispatched. Commanders on both sides were seeking the relative strengths on the opposing hills. In the darkness Ranger and Chinese patrols passed each other, each pursuing its own mission.

A patrol led by Cpl. Mike Rosen went back down the slopes to Hill 628 and found it occupied by enemy infiltrators. Though blocked by the Rangers from coming by way of Hills 1168 and 1010, the Chinese had used the thousands of meters of open expanse to the east to move into position.

With the wide gaps between units under heavy attack, and with the division right flank open, the situation was ideal for infiltration by Chinese units. The rear positions of the 24th Division soon came under attack. At 0245 on April 25 the division switchboard came under fire, as did the division airfield ten minutes later. At 0330 hours the 5th Infantry rear command post was hit, and at approximately the same time, artillery units in the 25th Division sector reported they were under attack from the rear.

At about 0230 hours the first of several small carrying parties arrived on Hill 1010. One came in under the guidance of Cpl. Tom Uldall of the 3rd platoon, who had been enjoying the pleasures of an I Corps rest hotel in Seoul when the battle began. Uldall promptly headed north, thumbing rides and seeking information on the location of the 8th Rangers. He arrived at the 2nd Battalion, 21st Infantry, just as a party of Korean Bearers under the control of a corporal of the 21st Infantry were being formed to carry food, ammunition, and water to the Rangers. Uldall accompanied this group. When the soldier from the 21st Infantry was killed, Uldall continued on and brought the much needed supplies through to the company.

From atop Hill 1010 interlocking tracer fire could be seen coming from battles along the 24th Division front to the west. But to the north, east, and south, and in the 6th ROK Division sector, the night was ominously dark and still.

Just prior to dawn, a group of twelve to fifteen men approached the Rangers' perimeter. Unresponsive to challenge, they were taken under fire. The Rangers were well aware of the North Korean and Chinese tactic of posing as ROK soldiers. These men, however, were South Korean soldiers who had been bypassed by the enemy. As they were taken into the perimeter, several of them said repeatedly in stumbling English, "Many, many Chinese!"

The Chinese had good reason to be jubilant in the early hours of April 25. Their attack had fallen heavily upon the positions of the 1st ROK Division and the U.S. 3rd, 24th, and 25th divisions. It was the collapse of the 6th ROK Division that was their greatest success, however, leaving, in the words of an Eighth Army report, "the naked right flank" in I Corps and forcing Eighth Army to order its forces to withdraw to line "Delta."

Delta, as amended, allowed for the ground lost and generally followed a trace below the 38th parallel from a point on the Han River near Karyon-ni in the west, on to Chunchon in the center, then east to Chumunjin on the Sea of Japan.

At 0500 on April 25 forward elements of the 24th Division began receiving orders for the daylight withdrawal. The pressure of the enemy attack and fluidity of the situation are reflected in the following series of instructions sent by the 24th Division G-3 to the 21st Infantry Regiment:

0421: Pull back Ranger company from Hill 1010 to Hill 628 and join 5th Inf. Upon contact with 5th, Rangers become attached to 5th.

0502: Take Ranger company out with 21st Inf.

0650: Ranger company is detached from 21st Inf. and is attached to 3rd 5th Inf.

At approximately 0700 hours the Rangers were ordered down from Hill 1010. At this point the 21st Infantry with Company C, 6th Medium Tank Battalion attached, was beginning to withdraw its 1st and 3rd battalions through the 2nd Battalion.

Despite attempts by both the Rangers and the 5th RCT, there was no radio contact between them. Messages were relayed through the 2nd Battalion, 21st Infantry. Communications with the 5th was critical, as they were firing on the Ranger route of withdrawal. Sunrise on April 25 came at 0541 hours. The night, which had seen a low of 35 degrees, now gave way before a sunny day in which temperatures would move into the high sixties. Visibility was excellent: three to five miles, despite haze and smoke.

The Ranger descent began with Master Sergeant Moore's 1st platoon leading the way down the southeastern ridge. Rangers Baldridge and Barley were to the front on point. The 3rd platoon was in the center, with the 2nd platoon as rear guard. One radio was with Captain Herbert behind the 1st platoon, the second with the executive officer, Lieutenant Giacherine, toward the rear of the column. Halfway between Hill 1010 and Hill 628 a message was received from the 2nd Battalion, 21st Infantry, to avoid Hill 628. A friendly patrol had met heavy resistance in that area.

Shortly thereafter, a message from Division G-3, relayed by 21st Regiment S-3, instructed Captain Herbert to continue south along the ridge across Hill 628 to prevent the 3rd Battalion, 5th RCT, from being cut off by the enemy. As the company approached Hill 628, approximately fifteen enemy were observed digging in on lower ground. Captain Herbert ordered these be taken under fire. Machine-gunner Anthony Fiore opened the battle.

At the rear of the column 1st Lt. Alfred "Jack" Giacherine had taken a moment to admire the calm and deceptively peaceful aspect of the valley to the right of the ridge. Giacherine was an experienced soldier and a veteran of World War II. While enjoying the freshness of the morning, he studied the terrain. One of his considerations was the best route off the ridge. Some distance to the front he saw a stream bed that offered cover. "That," he decided just before the firing started, "is how I will go out, following the stream bed and nearby trail to the main road."

Ranger fire struck among the enemy and was immediately and fiercely returned, initially from the front, then the right front and left flank. It was immediately obvious that a large enemy force was on Hill 628 and the adjoining ridgelines.

The narrowness of the ridge and its steep sides prevented the establishment of the traditional base of fire and maneuver elements. A misstep, and a man would tumble from the ridge. In several locations the trail was so narrow it was necessary to move single file.

Close to Hill 628 the 1st squad, 1st platoon, found space to move into a skirmish line and advance by marching fire. As the 1st squad took casualties, the 2nd squad found space to join them on line. The 3rd platoon ran down the ridgeline to assist. Where possible, the men fired from the higher elevation in support of the 1st platoon attack. Enemy machine-gun fire from the left flank raked the 3rd platoon. Lieutenant Strong and Master Sergeant Cox deployed their men to return this fire. The ridge was littered with large outcroppings of stone, and interlocking streams of Chinese tracers ricocheted off the faces of the outcroppings.

The rangers were still wearing their packs, most with rolled sleeping bags attached. As one man raced down a ridgeline, a bullet cut the tie cords. The sleeping bag trailed out, leaving him feeling very conspicious, like a bride at some macabre wedding.

The din was deafening, a constant crackling roar like a raging forest fire. Soon this was punctuated by the crash of high explosive as Chinese mortars came into play.

At 0750 hours the 2nd Battalion, 21st Infantry, reported to regiment, "Ranger company fighting way off Hill 1010, have contacted 3rd Battalion, 5th Infantry." The 3rd and 1st battalions of the 21st were withdrawing through the 2nd Battalion, the former under fire from the front and left flank.

On the ridgeline from Hill 1010 to Hill 628, the duels between Browning and Degtyarva weaponry continued. Ranger Dan Rivera saw a Chinese machine-gun emplacement where gunner after gunner was killed. Another Chinese soldier always came forward to take the fallen man's place. Rivera's squad was pinned down by a Chinese machine gun. Cpl. Rudy Belluomini's Browning Automatic Rifle was malfunctioning, so he took an M-1 rifle from one of the wounded, a grenade launcher, and rifle grenades and crawled to a higher elevation. From there he fired with deadly accuracy, knocking out the machine gun and killing its crew.

Rangers Manuel Diaz and Jesse Cisneros were working as a team. Diaz had loaded an M-1 rifle clip with tracer ammunition. Diaz would spot an enemy automatic weapons position with the tracers, then Cisneros would take the enemy under fire with a Browning Automatic Rifle. Both noted that dead Chinese gunners were quickly replaced.

The 3rd platoon, then the 2nd, fought their way down the ridge. Park Hodak and George Wheeler brought up the rear of the Ranger column, exchanging shots with an enemy force coming down from Hill 1168 to attack the Rangers from the rear. Toward the front, sergeants Moore and Chagnon had just killed some Chinese and were running forward to rejoin the 1st platoon when Moore was shot in the thigh. The force of the impact knocked Moore from the ridgeline, sending him rolling down the slope. Moore resumed firing, while the medic Potter bandaged his wound. In this exchange Moore's map case was shot away.

Ranger Paul Snavely was shot through the head. Snavely, who had often joked on return from patrols that he had "saved Uncle Sam the cost of his life insurance," died quickly. Moments later a cursing and snarling Mike Rosen, furious at his friend's death, took the enemy position under fire.

Fighting from behind bolders and from folds in the earth, the Rangers kept up a heavy fire. Men fought standing, sitting, or kneeling, as the ground permitted. Leonard Wiggins saw a Ranger on the open hillside whose Browning Automatic Rifle had fouled. Under fire, the man removed his fatigue jacket, spread it out, disassembled the weapon and cleaned it, then put it back together, put his jacket on, and resumed firing.

Man after man was hit. Emanual Rish, Harold Hooks, and Marco Sparko were wounded. Bill Tiemeyer and another Ranger were hit simultaneously and tumbled down the side of the ridge together. Ron Smith's hair was parted by a bullet. Many Rangers shucked their packs, keeping only ammunition. Some of the Korean bearers dragged the packs into a deep gully and began to rifle them, oblivious to the battle that raged above.

Richard Strand was hit, as were Donald Weyant and John Finke. Lieutenant Strong led a charge that included Ismael Ve-

lasco, Victor Jorgenson, Dan Rivera, and others. Jorgenson was
wounded. George Hall attacked the crew of a Chinese machine
gun and killed them with a grenade, Sergeant McNeely and
another Ranger crawled forward and eliminated another. Rudy
Belluomini continued his accurate fire and killed the crew of yet
another machine gun, his second of the day.

The 1st platoon employed rifle grenades on the more distant
positions to clear a path. One Ranger dropped into a depression
and was firing his Browning Automatic Rifle when he felt a tug
at his sleeve. One of the Korean soldiers who had entered Ranger
lines was pointing, talking excitedly. The Ranger looked in the
direction he was pointing and saw a squad of Chinese advancing
up a gully, presenting a lineal target. The Ranger emptied a
twenty-round magazine from front to rear of the Chinese and
turned to the Korean with an exultant shout. The ROK soldier
lay sprawled at the back of the depression, a neat blue hole
centered in his forehead.

There were approximately seventeen ROK soldiers on the
ridgeline. They fought well, and several were killed defending
their homeland.

The limitations of terrain and enemy fire coming from many
locations hindered organized maneuvers. All over the ridgeline
Rangers fought as individuals and groups—attacking here, defending there, engaging at two hundred yards in one place and
firing point-blank at another. Casualties mounted. Thomas In-
gram, Paul Chagnon, and John Allen were hit. Harry Trout, a
former medic, had braved a hail of fire several times to help
wounded men. He was killed by Chinese machine-gun fire, his
jacket burning from the tracer bullets that pierced his body.

The 1st platoon came under fire from a bunker on the opposite side of a ravine. Under covering fire from Jim Barley, Rangers Simpson and Davis went down the ravine and began to scale
the other side. The enemy dropped grenades, but the grenades
fell past the Rangers and exploded harmlessly below. Barley
could hear his friends cursing because the face of the cliff was
too steep to allow them to let go and throw their own grenades.
The Rangers continued climbing, and the enemy fled.

Slowly but steadily the Rangers fought their way down the
ridgeline and onto Hill 628. At 0821 hours, 25 April 1951, the
2nd Battalion, 21st Infantry, reported to Regiment, ''Ranger
Co. completely surrounded, still in radio contact with them.''

With the 1st and 3rd battalions of the 21st Infantry withdrawing through the 2nd Battalion, the right flank of the 24th Division formed an inverted ninety-degree angle. The 2nd Battalion, 21st Infantry, held the horizontal (east–west) leg, the 3rd Battalion, 5th Infantry, the vertical (north–south). The 8th Rangers were located at the right corner and at a greater range, engaging forces that threatened the north flank of the 3rd Battalion, 5th Infantry, and the east flank of the withdrawing 21st.

Throughout the morning acting communications chief E. C. Rivera used the Ranger call sign of "Old Rose," trying repeatedly to establish direct communication with the 5th Infantry. At 0728 the 3rd Battalion, 5th Infantry, journal shows a message received from a station identifying itself as "Old Rose." The 3rd of the 5th was suspicious and asked questions: "Who is Betty Grable's husband?" Rivera was under heavy fire, but responded "Harry James." Not satisfied, the 3rd of the 5th asked, "What does Sammy Sneed do?" Rivera was a superb soldier and knew popular music, but he was not a golfer and failed the question. The 3rd of the 5th closed the transmission and made no checks of the Signal Operating Instructions to determine that "Old Rose" was the 8th Ranger call sign.

The 3rd Battalion, 5th Infantry, journal records the following message at 0830 hours: "Company L to move N on ridge to contact Rangers believed to be in trouble by Division. Two Plats to go."

The Journal shows that at 0935 hours the two platoons crossed the line of departure approximately 2,500 meters south of the Ranger position. At 0945 hours they were under heavy small-arms fire. At 1008 hours they withdrew.

On the ridgeline from Hill 1010 the Rangers were using their heavy firepower to grind their way forward, but at a price of continued casualties. The forward observer from the 52nd Field Artillery was hit, as was his sergeant. Ranger Joe Chaney was struck, then Lieutenant Strong. Captain Herbert, who had constantly put himself at risk to direct the battle, went down, hit hard in the neck and shoulder.

Medics Gregory, Hardground, Johnson, and Potter continually exposed themselves to fire to assist wounded men. Corporal Hardground sheltered the wounded under an overhanging ledge. On occasion the medics found it necessary to take up weapons and fight for their lives and the lives of their patients.

The antenna on the radio that accompanied Lieutenant Giacherine had been broken on brush. Issuing instructions for the 2nd platoon to keep moving forward, Giacherine passed through the 3rd platoon to the 1st platoon. As he was moving forward he slipped and fell down a steep slope. A bullet tore his fatigue jacket but passed through without hitting him. Seeing that the company was drawing fire from the right, Giacherine decided to take the 2nd and 3rd platoons off the ridge, where they were exposed to accurate, enemy machine-gun fire. Several Rangers remained on the ridge to cover the move.

Giacherine then saw E. C. Rivera with the SCR radio, the last workable communications link with friendly units. With Rivera, Master Sergeants Ellis of the 2nd platoon and Cox of the 3rd, Giacherine established a command post from which he placed men on the ridge and formed a perimeter. He established radio contact with the 2nd Battalion, 21st Infantry, and called for artillery fire on the enemy position to the right.

With E. C. Rivera on the radio, Sgt. Keith Smith began to direct the fire of the 52nd Field Artillery. As Smith walked the artillery in close to the Ranger position, the American howitzers pounded the Chinese with devastating effect.

Giacherine sent Cox over to the knoll to pinpoint enemy positions and Ellis to a vantage point from which fire could be adjusted. Giacherine then moved forward again and found that Captain Herbert had been seriously wounded. With Cox, Ellis, and Rivera, Giacherine now directed artillery fire on Chinese positions to the southeast of Hill 628.

Chinese mortars peppered the Ranger positions, and the sheer energy of high explosive was so powerful that it felt like the fillings in teeth were rattling. Scattered firefights raged all around the ridgeline and the slopes of Hill 628. Rangers gained the crest and repelled several banzai charges by small groups of Chinese. The terrain and varying actions had an impact on the ability of both sides to consolidate. At times Ranger platoons were forced to fight separate actions, and one small group would split off from the main force.

Though the fire from the high ground to the southeast had been silenced, it continued unabated from other locations. Rangers Ralph Simon, Edward Otts, and Delbert Slaughter were added to the list of wounded.

At 0910 hours the 2nd Battalion, 21st Infantry, received the following message from the 5th Infantry S-3: "Send message to Ranger Company. Get out best way possible."

At 0921 hours the 2nd Battalion, 21st Infantry, recorded that five wounded Rangers had arrived—this was the small group that was separated from the main body. At 1005, with the rest of the 21st clear, the 2nd Battalion of the 21st Infantry was in the process of withdrawing. Two platoons of Company C, 6th Medium Tank Battalion, were in the valley, forward of the 21st's position, covering the move by fire. At 1026 hours the 2nd Battalion reported all their troops were on the road.

The fight was still in progress on and around Hill 628, and the Chinese units poised on the division flank pressed their attack. Someone called out that tanks were in the valley floor. Not knowing the tank unit's call sign, but knowing they must be monitoring the 21st Infantry frequency, E. C. Rivera kept calling on the radio. "Tankers, this is Old Rose, tankers, this is Old Rose, do you read me?"

Lieutenant Giacherine said, "Tell them if they don't stop for us, Old Rose will be No Rose."

Unable to make contact, Rivera climbed to the top of Hill 628, and immediately came under direct small-arms fire. Nick Tisak accompanied Rivera to provide covering fire with his BAR, and while Rivera tried to establish contact with the tanks, Tisak sat on the open hillside exchanging fire with some Chinese.

"I got one in the leg," Tisak said.

"How do you know you got him in the leg?" queried Rivera.

"Not him," replied Tisak. *"Me!"*

Rivera informed Giacherine that communication with the tanks was established. Satisfied that the enemy position to the right (northeast) was silenced, Giacherine decided that, even though it meant going deeper into territory now occupied by the enemy, the route he had selected earlier was the best way off the ridge. He requested a linkup with the tanks in one hour at a point some three thousand meters northeast of the Ranger position. The message was acknowledged. At 1105 hours the tank liaison officer with the 21st Infantry reported, "3rd platoon of Company C, 6th Tanks, remaining at CT 558055 to assist Ranger elements that will be down in about one hour."

Giacherine now began to execute a fighting withdrawal. A six-man force under Master Sergeant Ellis was dispatched to serve as point; the wounded went next. Few men could be spared to assist evacuating the wounded, and men walked off the hill holding their entrails to prevent their spilling out of gaping stomach wounds. Captain Herbert's neck wounds were in such a location that bandaging was difficult. Herbert jammed his fingers into the bullet holes to stanch the bleeding and came down off the ridge.

For a number of men covering the withdrawal, movement in any direction required running a gauntlet of enemy positions. For some it was a race down the slopes, firing into enemy foxholes on each side.

Under fire, Joe Slavinski drove off a ridgeline and slid on his stomach to the bottom. The slide was comparatively easy, and when he stood up he saw why: he had been sliding on his grenades. Linking up with the wounded Joe Chaney and John Finke, Slavinski continued downward. He came upon a trail at the same moment as an enemy soldier a short distance away. The man was looking in the opposite direction, and Slavinski shot him. The man seemed to disappear behind a boulder, so Slavinski lobbed a grenade over the top, then checked the results. The enemy was dead. Slavinski signaled his small party forward.

Lieutenant Giacherine kept tight control on the main body. Four or five automatic riflemen were with him as security. A similar-size group of automatic riflemen moved a short distance to the right and took up firing positions. Men seemed to gravitate toward Giacherine. Later they would recall, "He knew what he was doing." One combat veteran of World War II said, "If it hadn't been for Lieutenant Giacherine, we'd probably still be laying up there on that hill."

The anticipated enemy attack came quickly. The enemy boiled over the ridge to be met by the impromptu reverse-slope defense of the Ranger rear guard.

Ranger Oral Lee Baldridge remembers seeing white uniforms while others saw dark garb, but whatever uniform they wore, the Chinese seemed to boil over the surface of the hill. The automatic riflemen fired as one, sweeping the crest. The Chinese fell back, and the rear guard began to withdraw.

A Ranger looked back toward the crest of the hill. Seemingly suspended in the sky was a black Navy F4U Corsair. The aircraft swept from right to left across the Ranger's vision and released a cylinder. Moments later the flames of napalm appeared above the crest. An artillery observation aircraft appeared overhead, and soon after, the enemy came under accurate and deadly fire. The rear guard broke contact and moved to catch up with the main body of Rangers.

The route to the rendezvous with the tanks passed Hill 341. Giacherine noticed enemy on the hill, but they did not interfere with the Rangers' passage. When they reached the road, however, the tanks were not yet in sight. Giacherine deployed a perimeter around the wounded, and one man recalls hearing him say, "If we can't get help, we'll fight it out here."

About fifteen minutes later the tank platoon arrived. They had been delayed when they had taken fire from the high ground to the northeast of the road. Some men of the 1st and 3rd platoons had moved ahead and were riding beside the turrets.

The courage of the men of the 3rd platoon of Company C, 6th Medium Tank Battalion, deserves recognition. Unescorted by infantry, the crews of four tanks remained some 3,500 meters in advance of friendly forces to aid the Rangers. They did this with the knowledge that friendly forces had withdrawn and enemy troops were occupying the vacated positions.

The wounded were placed on the tanks, then the other Rangers and ROK soldiers climbed on board. The grilles over the tank engines were so hot, they burned the soles of the Rangers' feet through their boots. As the tanks raced south, Ranger weapons faced outward and the tanks' 90mm guns swung about menacingly. The Chinese made no move to interfere.

The 5th Infantry Regiment had the mission of covering the division's withdrawal. Their S-3 journal reported the 2nd Battalion, 21st Infantry, passed through 5th Infantry lines at 1130 hours. At 1150 hours, the journal records, the Rangers came through the valley with tanks.

The S-3 journal of the 6th Medium Tank Battalion shows the following message from C Company at 1200 hours: "3d Plat on his way back, 107 men with him, 25 WIA."

The disintegration of the 6th ROK Division had created a massive gap in the U.N. line and a desperate situation for the 24th Infantry Division. Ordered to "move to contact," ninety men of the 8th Ranger Infantry Company (Airborne) went into the teeth of the enemy attack. For thirty-six hours they reported enemy locations and blocked a key avenue of approach into the division right. The Rangers then attacked the enemy, drawing off forces that were in position to strike both the 21st Infantry and the 3rd Battalion, 5th Infantry, in the flank. Enemy casualties were estimated at two hundred.

Maj. Gen. Blackshear Bryan, commanding general of the 24th Infantry Division, congratulated the 8th Rangers, telling Giacherine that the Rangers had revealed to him that the entire division right flank had been exposed and the Ranger action had prevented the 21st Infantry Regiment, if not the entire division, from being cut off.

Chapter 15

May 1 found the first thrust of the Communist offensive stalled to the north of Seoul as U.N. troops were deployed along "No Name Line." These positions began north of Seoul, went northeast to Sabangu in the center, then continued at a sharp angle northeast to Taep'o-Ri.

While "No Name Line" was being heavily fortified, U.N. forces began a limited attack to regain lost territory and resecure the advantageous terrain of line "Kansas," near the 38th parallel. The attack progressed well, but stiffening Chinese resistance was a harbinger of another enemy offensive, one that would be known to the U.S. 2nd Division as the "May Massacre."

On May 1, the 1st Ranger Company returned to the battle area. At 1130 hours the company had been detached from control of the 38th Infantry Regiment and attached to Task Force Zebra. This force changed composition frequently: on April 30 it had been reformed to include B Company, 9th Infantry; F Company, 38th Infantry; and the 72nd Tank Battalion.

The Ranger Company moved into defensive positions along ridgelines north of Chuchon-ni. Contact was made with the French Battalion, which occupied the left, and with Republic of Korea Forces, which were on the right. Company strength was now 107.

While in these positions, the company conducted aggressive patrols and captured a POW. On May 5 the company was alerted to join the Task Force Zebra Reserve. Relieved by K Company,

9th Infantry, the Rangers moved into a reserve perimeter with B Company, 72nd Tank Battalion.

On May 7 Lieutenant Herman, who had been on temporary duty with Japanese Logistical Command for twenty-one days, returned to the unit. More replacements and men returning from the hospital also joined the unit.

On May 9 the company remained at Saemal in Task Force Zebra Reserve. The 1st platoon patrolled to Sachi-ri to contact the 7th Republic of Korea Division. The 2nd platoon provided security for a forward displacement of the 37th Field Artillery, while the 3rd platoon kept watch over a platoon of the 2nd Engineers who were engaged in road construction. These security missions continued for several days, affording a break in the patrolling routine. Other men were being sent in groups of four on temporary duty to Japan for rest and relaxation.

On May 14, the company was further attached by Task Force Zebra to the 2nd Battalion, 23rd Infantry Regiment. The company departed Saemal at 0930 hours and established a defensive line in the vicinity of Antiwi-Gol. Elements of the 23rd Infantry were on the left, elements of the 5th ROK Division on the right. The 1st Rangers closed into position by 1030 hours. At 2330 hours an enemy patrol was taken under fire and dispersed.

Chinese attacks were increasing on the ROK divisions to the right of the U.S. 2nd Division. Beginning early on May 16th, the Chinese attacks would collapse the ROK front and expose the east flank of the 2nd Division.

The Rangers remained in their positions until May 17. Chinese patrols again attempted to penetrate the perimeter at 0430 hours on May 15 but were driven off by automatic-weapons and mortar fire. One Ranger was lightly wounded but remained on line. At 0130 hours on May 17 retreating forces of the 35th ROK Division blundered into defensive mine fields and booby traps, and several were killed. Those Korean soldiers that could be stopped were put into the position. During patrol actions Ranger Louis Oluich was killed.

The 2nd U.S. Infantry Division was deployed along "No Name Line," with the 9th Infantry Regiment occupying the left sector of the division front, the 38th Infantry the center, and Task Force Zebra the right.

A major enemy attack was developing—the second thrust of the Chinese Fifth Phase Offensive, which was designed to drive the U.N. forces into the sea. The 3rd Chinese Army Group, consisting of twelve divisions (approximately 120,000 men), would lead the attack, while elements of the 12th and 27th armies would be used to break through the 5th and 7th ROK divisions. These forces would then turn west, striking the 2nd U.S. Infantry Division from the east (right) flank in a deep penetration designed to destroy the 2nd Division's communications and cut off its forward forces.

Simultaneously the 15th and 60th Chinese armies would attack the center of the 2nd Division at positions held by the U.S. 38th Infantry Regiment and attached Netherlands Battalion. The two Chinese armies would attack in column. The 15th in the lead would strike, break the crust of the defense, then sidestep to the right and left and execute a double envelopment. The double envelopment was a favorite tactic of the Chinese and a maneuver as old and ubiquitous as warfare itself (it had been used by Hannibal and the Zulu). As the 15th sidestepped, the 60th would punch forward into the broken crust of the defense.

Eight Chinese divisions waited in reserve to follow up the attack. Though the Chinese plan would fall far short of its ultimate objectives, for those American units at the point of impact, it succeeded all too well.

At 1630 hours on May 17, the 1st Ranger Company was released from attachment to Task Force Zebra and attached to the 38th Infantry Regiment. By 2145 hours the Rangers were at the 38th Infantry Regiment command post, which was coming under increasingly heavy attack.

As the Chinese moved forward at night, their path was frequently marked by stones daubed with luminous paint which had been placed along the trails by reconnaissance units.

The 38th Infantry was under heavy attack throughout the night of May 16, the main blow falling on the 2nd Battalion and A Company, which was located on the strategically critical Hill 1051. By the early morning hours of May 17, the 2nd Battalion of the 38th had been withdrawn after E Company had been decimated. By dawn on the seventeenth the situation of the 38th Regiment was critical. Completely surrounded, A Company was overrun as the Chinese stormed the crest of Hill 1051. American artillery was employed to maximum advantage on these long columns of Chinese. The result could only be described as a slaughter, yet the attack continued.

Called from division reserve, the French Battalion fought superbly. The Dutch Battalion was assigned to plug the hole at Hill 1051, as the Chinese were pouring into that gap. This counterattack, made late and from the wrong line of departure, was unsuccessful, and the Dutch began to pull back.

While the 23rd Infantry Regiment fought to hold the division right flank, the 38th scrambled to stem the tide coming through the gap left by the bulk of its forward units and the withdrawal of the Dutch. By 2230 hours on May 17, the 1st Battalion, 38th Infantry command post was under attack and out of communications with Regiment. The 1st Battalion was fragmented: thirty men from Company A and fifteen from Company C held Hill 957 while L and K companies of the 38th were under attack, with K Company reporting that the Chinese were walking right through the mine fields and over the barbwire. It was in this chaotic situation that the 1st Ranger Company was ordered to move forward to regain positions originally occupied by 1st Battalion, 38th Infantry, and vacated by the withdrawing Dutch Battalion.

It was past midnight when the Rangers moved forward into the gap, and as they climbed the dark slopes, they met Dutch soldiers pulling back. The Dutch told the Rangers not to go forward, that there were many enemy soldiers, but the Rangers continued on their mission. On the trail up to the vacated positions, the Rangers came under heavy fire. SFC Herbert E. "E.V." Robertson was killed, dying in the arms of his friend Anthony "Luke" Lukasik. Dropping their packs and moving steadily upward, the Rangers attacked and accomplished their mission of securing Hill 710. Throughout the remaining hours of darkness, a steady series of Chinese counterattacks was beaten off. Clinging to their positions, the Rangers provided time for the 2nd Division to adjust its forces in the face of the continued onslaught.

The Chinese were paying a horrendous price for their successes. In their attacks across the U.S. 2nd Division front, soldiers of the 44th and 45th Chinese divisions were cut down by the thousands. The 181st CCF Division made a successful penetration between hills 1051 and 914, but the cost was so great that the division was unable to continue to function as a unit. To the rear of the 181st was the 179th CCF Division, a unit

decimated by American artillery before it even reached the
battle line.

In the first twenty-four hours of the Chinese attack, 2nd Division artillery fired 30,149 rounds of ammunition, causing an
estimated five thousand enemy casualties. The Chinese dead lay
in windrows. Daylight brought a cessation in Chinese assaults
on the Ranger position. Sprawled across the hill and on a forward knoll, the Rangers occupied bunkers and emplacements
built by former occupants. Other hills dominated their positions—hills occupied by the Chinese.

Throughout the daylight hours of May 18, the Rangers clung
to the hill. Though under heavy sniper fire, they were not attacked. Long columns of Chinese forces were executing a double envelopment of the remnants of the 1st Battalion (38th
Infantry) and the 1st Ranger Company.

The Rangers were engaged not only by the enemy, but also
by two U.S. Marine Corsairs that swooped down to mistakenly
strafe the Ranger position. On the knoll, Ranger Robert Morgan
clung to earth as the guns of the fighters blew his bunker apart.
Dashing from his position, Morgan seized an aircraft recognition panel and vainly tried to attract the fighters' attention. The
Chinese were quick to spot his action and opened fire on him.
Diving to escape the heavy barrage, Morgan rolled over and
over down the hillside, ending up in a pile of Chinese dead. He
remained there until firing quieted, then returned to his position.

Gordon Voss had been hit in the hand and head by shrapnel.
Taken to a bunker on the rear side of the hill, he found Wayne
Sharp asleep in a pool of his own blood. Voss woke Sharp, and
the two stopped the bleeding. Sergeant Girolimo, who had been
shot in the hip, was also brought to the position. The company
was running short of ammunition, so the wounded crawled about
taking water and ammunition from the dead to redistribute to
the living.

At 1830 hours the 1st Ranger Company was designated as
rear guard for the withdrawal of the 1st Battalion, 38th Infantry.
By this time the Chinese envelopment had succeeded. Individually and in small groups the Rangers and men of the 1st of the
38th began to attempt to infiltrate back to friendly lines.

For each man, the ensuing hours became a private hell. Many
would die. The withdrawal required running a gauntlet of fire.
For most Rangers, this began with small groups racing down

the hill together. Waiting till it became the turn of his group to exfiltrate, Ranger Lew Villa was ordered to return to the top of the hill and destroy the company's SCR 300 radio. Villa returned to the command bunker only to find it occupied by Chinese, who surrounded and captured him.

Ranger Morgan made it to the base of the hill but found himself alone; the only Rangers he saw were dead. In front of Morgan groups of 2nd Division soldiers were trying to cross an open space under heavy fire from Chinese machine guns. Some of the Indianhead Division soldiers had panicked and were being cut down by the Chinese. Morgan waited, studying the pattern of fire, then raced across the open space toward friendly lines during a lull between bursts from the machine guns.

At the point of impact, the enemy's numerical superiority was so great that the air seemed solid with bullets. Man after man was killed. Alfred Herman, who had led the company successfully until the arrival of Captain Carrier, was shot through the head and died on the hill, as did Rangers James Clopton, Roy Evans, Harrison Fraser, John Girolimo, and Robert Kettlewell.

Other men were beginning a different ordeal. Ranger Earl Baker found a way through the curtain of fire and began the trek south. Wounded at Chipyong-ni, Baker was struck again, this time as burning American ammunition trucks exploded. Despite his wound, Baker continued south and made his way safely into the reforming American lines.

The redoubtable Glen Hall, winner of the Distinguished Service Cross at Chipyong-ni, was wounded. Rangers Laydon, Bach, and Bagnell were killed, and John Pointeck, the gunslinger, shot it out in his last gunfight.

Men of the 2nd Division were scattered about the hills in groups that would flow together then break apart under fire. As the surviving Americans tried to reach friendly positions, the Chinese killed or captured large numbers.

Ranger Bob Morgan had made a new friend, a 2nd Division soldier with plenty of fight left in him. As Morgan and this soldier rounded a bend in a trail, they came upon a column of American prisoners guarded by three Chinese. One enemy soldier, his arms loaded down with captured American weapons, yelled and signaled with his head that the two Americans should join the group of prisoners. Morgan and the other American responded with a burst of fire that killed all three Chinese.

Howard Thompson was killed, as were SFC Gordon Lewis and MSgt. Paul Lotti. Captain Carrier was captured, and Lieutenant Vismore killed. PFC Robert Mastin constantly risked his life to help others. Mastin, a rifleman who had been assigned to the company as a replacement only a few weeks before, had once been a medical corpsman. He was repeatedly struck by enemy fire as he continued to bring wounded men under shelter and tend their injuries, and at length his severe wounds stilled his courageous heart. Mastin, who was posthumously recommended for the Medal of Honor, would be awarded the Distinguished Service Cross.

The Chinese attack that had fallen so heavily on the 1st Ranger Company would break like a wave against the rocks of American positions farther south, but the Communists enjoyed the brief taste of victory while they could.

For Bob Morgan, the direct route south seemed suicidal. He watched while a number of Americans died trying, then moved east. Morgan was alone again, his new friend from the 2nd Division having been killed. A group of several hundred Americans were in a valley, milling around as leaders attempted to restore order to attempt a breakout. Morgan's automatic rifle had jammed, but he continued east alone, hearing Chinese on the ridgelines taunting the Americans to "come on up." With some semblance of organization achieved, the Americans attacked.

Trusting his own ability and training, Morgan disregarded the attack and continued east. By a seeming miracle he came upon his best friend, Ranger Joseph "Lefty" LaFontaine, who was also making his way independently to American lines. Teaming up, the two friends observed the routes taken by other groups, determining which were successful and which were not. Then the two Rangers followed the successful routes back to the American lines.

For squad leader Anthony "Luke" Lukasik, events took a different turn. Running down a trail from the hill, Lukasik met Ranger Alexander Ramatowski. They were near the point where the Rangers had first dismounted from trucks to move into position. Light was fading, but the two Rangers could see men standing at the dismount point. The Rangers yelled to the men below them, who promptly yelled back in Chinese and opened fire. Fire also came from the bush around the two Rangers as they attempted to run back up the hill. Ramatowski was wounded and captured. Lukasik ran to the left into brush and concealed himself.

When daylight came, Lukasik could see Chinese walking around shooting fallen Americans. Lukasik then slowly crawled to the top of a hill and peered over. Some distance below he could see American tents with vehicles parked around them. He began to cautiously move in that direction, but his movements had been observed by the enemy. Chinese soldiers soon arose from the brush about him and took him prisoner. The tent area, which had been the command post of the 1st Battalion, 38th Infantry, now was held by the Chinese. Taken there by his captors, Lukasik observed the Chinese loading boxes of material and records into the captured trucks. The bodies of a number of American officers and enlisted men of the battalion headquarters lay about. They had been stripped of sidearms; many Chinese now wore .45-caliber automatics.

Lukasik was taken to a small village and placed with a group of approximately a hundred American prisoners, including Ranger Villa. About dusk the men were moved along a trail littered with American dead. An ordeal of twenty-eight months' captivity was about to begin. Several days later they would see Captain Carrier, the company commander. Beaten, tortured, and confined in a wood cage, Carrier did not recognize his men. The other prisoners later learned he was taken to an infamous North Korean interrogation center known as "Puks Palace," from where it was said few returned alive. Two Americans who endured captivity with Captain Carrier for eleven months described him as "a great man—a wonderful officer." They told of how the Communist's kept the captain tied up in a hole, questioning him at night and harassing him all day, trying to break him down. Each day at dawn he was forced to climb mountains with a bag of rice on his back; at night, when not being questioned, he would be bound hand and foot and thrown into a pit. When the rains came, he would be left lying in deep mud. They would tie him by the arms and pass a line around his throat then over a beam. The slightest movement would choke him.

Still the Ranger captain would not break. He told the Communists over and over again, "You've got my name, rank, and serial number—that's all you'll get."

When dragged out of the mud pit to resume his torture, he would hold his head high and proudly tell the other prisoners not to give in.

After eleven months of this torture failed to break his spirit, the Communists killed him.

Throughout May 19, men of the 1st Ranger Company who had evaded captivity infiltrated through enemy lines and began to assemble with the 38th Infantry Regiment at Yasidae-re. Tragically, Glen Hall, who had safely evaded the enemy, was killed by friendly forces as he and a friend attempted to enter American lines.

At 1300 the remaining members of the 1st Rangers were moved by motor convoy to Hoengsong. The Rangers began to reequip and prepare to receive replacements. Sixty-two men were present for duty.

The 1st Ranger Company and the 1st Battalion, 38th Infantry, had taken the brunt of this Chinese offensive. Though badly mauled, they succeeded in buying time for United Nations forces to adjust and strike back.

The Chinese offensive was smashed. The Communists suffered a defeat so bloody that the name "May Massacre" is indeed an apt description. A U.S. 2nd Infantry Division report estimated 2nd Division casualties at 900, with the Chinese losing 35,000 men.

Besides those Rangers killed or wounded, eight (including Captain Carrier) were captured in this battle and endured the hell of the Communist prison camps. These men were Rangers Lukasik, Villa, Ramatowski, Rhatigan, Rollins, Lutz, and Dansberry.

The 1st Ranger Company would receive its second Distinguished Unit Citation for this action.

Less than a week after its ordeal in the May Massacre, the 1st Rangers were back in action. On May 24 a four-man Ranger patrol captured two POWs near Kunmul-Gol and turned them over to the POW camp.

On May 30, after reequipping and training, the 1st Rangers departed Hoengsong, traveling twenty-five miles by motor convoy to Sinae. The mission was to clear and hold the area until arrival of the 2nd Infantry Division headquarters.

Chapter 16

While the 1st Ranger Company was undergoing its ordeal, the other Ranger companies had also been heavily engaged. The 2nd Rangers spent the early days of May in defense of the high ground near Chinon-ni. On May 8 the attachments were released to the 17th, 31st, and 32nd regiments. The needs of war were breaking down the color barriers.

With 123 men present for duty, the 2nd Rangers occupied an outpost position on Hill 258, south of the Hongchon Gang River. Daily, platoon-size patrols crossed the river to protect the right flank of the 31st Regimental Combat Team and to make contact with the 5th Marine Regiment.

On May 17 the 2nd Rangers began a long foot march leading to an attack. The front was in flux as the Chinese hammered at each soft spot in the line. Masters at reconnaissance, the Communists were frequently able to learn the locations of positions by drawing fire and identifying the flanks of platoons, companies, and higher organizations. Favorite points of attack were the ''seams'' where units tied their flanks together. Seams between American and South Korean units were particularly vulnerable to this tactic.

The Chinese had seized a critical terrain feature named Hill 581. The 2nd Rangers, eager for a fight after their stint in training newcomers, swarmed up the hill killing fifty Chinese and wounding ninety. The attack began at 1500 hours on May 20. Two hours later Hill 581 was in Ranger hands. Ranger Ralph

Sutton was killed in the attack. Herman Jackson was seriously wounded, and six others received light wounds.

As night follows day, so counterattack would inevitably follow the attack. The Rangers dug in, prepared interlocking fires, established artillery concentrations and barrages, tested communications, and performed the multitude of tasks trained infantrymen do before rest. An hour before midnight the Chinese counterattack struck.

The Chinese, sparing no manpower, threw an estimated regiment into the attack against the 2nd Rangers. The fighting was furious, with the Rangers and Chinese fighting hand to hand. First Lt. "Big Jim" Queen called for artillery support and walked the fire in until the last rounds were falling on the Ranger positions. The battle raged until 0645 hours, when the Chinese withdrew. Sixty of their dead littered the hillside, but they were unable to penetrate the 2nd Ranger position. Ten Rangers were wounded.

Ranger Bill Weathersbee and some of his friends were cleaning their weapons when a rifle company from the 7th Infantry Division came through their positions to continue after the Chinese. The rifle-company commander was astounded at the level of carnage he found. He halted his company and asked the Rangers questions about the action. The company commander then faced his unit and said in a loud voice, "I want all of you to look around. This is what happens to the enemy when soldiers don't panic." The company commander then faced the Rangers and said, "Gentlemen, I salute you." With a snappy salute, he moved his men on.

From Hill 581 the 2nd Rangers moved to relieve elements of the 7th Marines. On May 24 they were back on the attack, seizing Hill 545 from the Chinese and killing fifteen in the process. Two Rangers were seriously wounded.

The 4th Ranger Company had the onerous duty of keeping watch on IX Corps headquarters. The duty was boring, but the Rangers had liberated the horses of a Chinese cavalry unit and found some unattached boats, so patrols took on a new flair. First Sgt. James Way confided in his diary that the unit should properly be known as the 4th Ranger Infantry, Mounted, Naval Company (Airborne).

On May 11 the 3rd and 5th Rangers moved to Kimpo Airfield, where they participated in parachute training jumps. The need to keep Ranger companies current in Airborne training was a sore spot with the infantry divisions to which they were attached. The division staff had a tendency to look upon these exercises as distractions from the real business of the war.

At 1200 hours on May 13 the 5th Ranger Company became part of Task Force Hamilton. Named after Major W. T. Hamilton of the 89th Tank Battalion, the task force was comprised of:

Company A, 89th Tank Battalion
5th Ranger Infantry Company (Airborne)
Artillery Forward Observer Team
Reconnaissance Platoon, 89th Tank Battalion
Assault Gun Platoon, 89th Tank Battalion
Engineer Detachment, 65th Engineer Battalion
Tactical Air Control Party
Medical Detachment

The mission, commencing with daylight on May 14, was to conduct a reconnaissance in force along the axis Uijongbu–Songu-ri, to locate the enemy's main line of resistance, capture prisoners, and inflict maximum destruction on the enemy. The task force was instructed to return not later then one hour prior to darkness.

Moving through the 1st Cavalry Division's sector, Task Force Hamilton slashed northeast. Tank guns scoured the valley floor, and 25th Division artillery provided close support.

Some five thousand meters northeast of Uijongbu, the fighting became fierce. The valley narrowed, allowing a concentration of enemy fire from well-prepared fortifications. Tanks were being lost to well-concealed mines. With forward movement virtually at a standstill, the Rangers dismounted to sweep the high ground on each side of the road.

Lt. Joe Ulatoski led his 3rd platoon in a hill sweep and found resistance growing increasingly heavy as they neared the crest. Task Force Hamilton could not be raised on the radio, so artillery and air support were not available. Even had communications been established, close air support would have been hampered by the limited visibility of the overcast day.

The large numbers of Chinese were spoiling for a fight. As the Rangers reached the crest, Chinese mortars showered the hill, taking advantage of the protection of the fortified Chinese positions and the exposed position of the attacking Rangers. On the reverse slope an estimated company-size force was preparing to counterattack.

Lieutenant Ulatoski saw four Chinese setting up a machine gun to his front. Pulling the pin from a fragmentation grenade, Ulatoski was preparing to throw when a Chinese mortar round exploded behind him. Seriously wounded and partially unconscious, Ulatoski fell to earth, the armed grenade still in his hand.

Seeing his platoon leader's plight and quickly recognizing the danger, Ranger John Hammond shouted, "The grenade, lieutenant, the grenade!" Hammond threw himself on the wounded officer, locking Ulatoski's hand around the grenade with his body and hands. As Ulatoski regained full consciousness, Hammond pried the grenade from his fingers and used it to destroy the enemy machine-gun crew.

Hammond then dragged Ulatoski to safety, administered first aid, then returned to the action, where he was himself wounded.[1]

The Rangers' attack was a day-long slugfest, with casualties heavy on both sides. Master sergeants Owen, Claycomb, and Donald White were killed in action, as was Sgt. Nicholas Gallo. Lieutenant Ulatoski and Rangers McGlins, Hardway, Kelleher, Teel, Arena, Casey, and Hammond were seriously wounded. Those with lesser wounds were Rangers Derham, Romagnoli, Bundy, Worden, Midkiff, Gagnon, and Sharp.

Though the cost was heavy, the Rangers accomplished the mission. The area in which the battle took place was determined to be the Chinese main line of resistance, the prisoners 25th Infantry Division headquarters wanted were captured, and Task Force Hamilton returned on schedule, the Rangers herding their prisoners before them.

On May 23, with seventy-eight men present for duty, the 5th Rangers took up blocking positions near Sanung-ni. There they would remain until the 25th Division decided to launch Operation DETONATE.

The mission of Operation DETONATE was to launch a major raid behind enemy positions, accomplish major destruction to the enemy rear, and establish a base of operations until U.N. forces could link up with the raiding party. Selected to lead the raid was the famed Col. Welborn G. Dolvin of Columbus, Georgia, commanding officer of the 89th Tank Battalion and the same officer who led the task force in November 1950 when the Eighth Army Ranger Company made its gallant fight. The new Task Force Dolvin was comprised of four teams:

1. 25th Division Reconnaissance Company (-)
2. Company D, 89th Tank Battalion, plus one platoon of the 5th Ranger Company
3. Company A, 79th Tank Battalion, plus two platoons of the 5th Ranger Company
4. A reconnaissance platoon and an assault-gun platoon

The task force attacked at 0625 hours on May 29. Throughout the day the attack went forward with light enemy resistance. This success resulted in additional forces being attached to TF Dolvin, including an infantry battalion and tank and engineer companies.

The morning of May 25 brought heavy fighting, as an aroused enemy tried to prevent the task force from moving forward. At a deep stream and later at a narrow defile, the Chinese tried to ambush the column. These efforts were defeated in fighting that was often hand to hand.

The force of the American attack punched a hole in the Chinese line, enabling the 25th Division to press the attack with the 24th and 35th infantry regiments, the Turkish forces, and the 25th Canadian Brigade. The division advance carried some forty miles and crossed the 38th parallel toward the critical area of Kumwha.

The 5th Rangers distinguished themselves during the operation, killing many Chinese and taking twenty-six prisoners. As so often happened when the regiments the Rangers were attached to went into reserve, there was no rest for the weary Rangers. Instead, the Rangers were attached to another unit on line. On May 28 the 5th Rangers were patrolling to the front of the 35th Infantry, and on May 29, to the front of the 24th Infantry. There were sharp, nasty little firefights which were unremarkable save for those good men who bled.

Rangers Schultz and Hayden were seriously wounded near Nagksa-Dong, with lesser wounds being suffered by Rangers Benson, Conklin, Craig, Edwards, Goldbaum, Hale, Schultz,

The Battle Honors Flag of the Association of the Ranger Infantry Companies (Airborne) of the Korean War.

A Ranger squad with equipment.

A Ranger platoon with equipment.

A Ranger company with equipment.

Members of the 9th Ranger Company take judo training at Fort Benning, Georgia—1951.

Members of the 1st Ranger Company in training at Fort Benning—
1950.

Rangers training with pack mules in Colorado—1951.

Rangers in mountain training in the Colorado Rockies—1951.

Members of the 8th Ranger Company readying for a mission in Korea—April, 1951.

Lt. Berk Strong, platoon leader of the 3rd platoon, 8th Ranger Company, sounds the hunting horn as the company prepares to move out on a combat mission—April, 1951.

The 3rd Ranger Company (attached to the 3rd Infantry Division) attacking a communist position—1951.

Rangers of the 2nd Ranger Company in action with a light machine gun—1951.

Rangers Henry (L) and Cisnieros (R) of the 8th Ranger Company providing close support with a 60mm mortar—May, 1951.

A dead Chinese soldier who was killed when he tried to sneak through the 2nd Ranger Company's position near Bonji-ri—May 21, 1951.

Rangers and tank units were used to make deep, slashing attacks behind Chinese lines during the summer of 1951.

Capt. (later Brigadier General) James Herbert (L), commander of the 8th Ranger Company, confers with his executive officer, Lt. Alfred Giacherine (R) and an unidentified officer—April, 1951.

The author in Korea, 1951.

The author today, at the Airborne Walk Monument at Fort Benning, Georgia. (*photo credit: Joe Holloway*)

Memorial to the 146 Rangers who gave their lives during the Korean War. The monument is located at Fort Benning, and was made possible through funds raised by Ranger Glenn Dahl under the leadership of Ranger Emmett Fike.

and Gustafson. On May 30 Sgt. Charles D. Barcak was killed
and Sergeant Kavin wounded.

For the 8th Ranger Company and the 24th Division, the month
began with a devastating salute. Division artillery marked the
Communist May Day celebrations on May 1 with a massive,
time-on-target salvo that poured shrapnel on the Chinese parade. Beginning on May 2 the 8th Rangers operated with Task
Force Plumley, named after the captain commanding Company
D of the 6th Medium Tank Battalion. The task force included
the 8th Rangers, the 24th Division Reconnaissance Company,
and a platoon of the 52nd Anti-Aircraft Artillery. From May 2
through 17, this force conducted aggressive patrols and maintained contact with the 25th Infantry Division.

On May 9, eleven enlisted men arrived from the United States
and were assigned to the 8th Rangers. The men were promptly
introduced to their platoons. Ranger Charles E. Ouimette, (pro-
nounced we-met) reported to the platoon sergeant of the 3rd
platoon, William "Wild Bill" Cox.

"What's your name, soldier?" Cox asked.

"Ouimette, Sergeant," the new arrival answered.

"I don't give a damn if we met or not!" growled the redoubtable Cox. "I asked you what your name was."

On May 18 Task Force Byorum (named for the commanding
officer of the 6th Medium Tank Battalion) was formed. The task
force consisted of two tank companies, the 8th Airborne Rangers, and a company of the King's Shropshire Light Infantry. The
task force formed in an assembly area at 0600 hours and moved
to cross the line of departure for a deep probe of enemy positions. The order of march (with vehicles spaced at fifty yards)
shown below is representative of Task Force Byorum's several
operations.

1st platoon of Company C, 6th Medium Tank Battalion
    (MTB)
Forward observer tank
Six M39 personnel carriers with Rangers and Combat Engi-
    neers and two quad-.50 machine-gun half-tracks
Commanding officer's tank
One platoon of Company C, 6th MTB

Eleven M39 personnel carriers with King's Shropshire Light
  Infantry and four quad-.50 machine-gun half-tracks
S-3 tank
Three M39 personnel carriers with twenty Rangers and two
  quad-.50 machine-gun half-tracks
One tank-dozer
¾-ton ambulance
1 Jeep for C.O. and S-3 officer

Task Force Byorum moved through the lines into enemy territory and patrolled west and north. Mine fields were encountered, and there was sporadic fighting with withdrawing Chinese
forces. Frequently the tank commanders would open their
hatches and discuss the route of attack and suspected enemy
locations with the Rangers. These conferences would often receive fire from Chinese automatic weapons and machine guns.
As the bullets ricocheted off the tank hull, the tank commander
would drop his hatch, disappearing behind his steel shield. The
Rangers had long since learned that with only a fatigue jacket
as armor, an infantryman must be constantly aware of places he
could leap for that would provide some protection from enemy
fire and an opportunity to shoot back. When the enemy positions
were located, they would promptly be taken under fire. On one
such occasion several Chinese were flushed from their positions
and one ran up a hillside, making for a small cave. As the man
disappeared into the small opening, the tanker fired his 90mm
main gun, using high-explosive ammunition. The round passed
cleanly through the cave entrance and exploded with devastating
effect. There was much speculation on the precise point of
impact on the Chinese soldier.

On May 19 the task force encountered an estimated battalion-
plus of Chinese. Approximately one hundred of the enemy attempted to destroy the tanks in a defile, dropping from trees and
crawling along gullies to get close enough to plant charges on
the tiger-faced tanks. The fighting was close, with the Rangers
and British fighting to protect the tanks and the tankers engaging
with main and coaxial guns. The tankers kept their hatches
closed and hosed down other tanks with machine-gun fire.
Ranger Norman Erb killed a Chinese soldier just as the man was
placing a Bangelore torpedo under a tank tread.

A Chinese soldier leaped upon the sloping front of an American tank, seized the the coaxial machine gun in both hands with the muzzle toward his stomach, and attempted to pull the weapon from the tank. Peering through his periscope, the tanker caressed the trigger of his machine gun and ended the ambitious Chinaman's life.

Some 150 of the enemy were killed and over two hundred wounded. A prisoner revealed the Chinese were from the 180th Division. American losses were minimal, though three tanks were disabled. The Rangers enjoyed working with the King's Shropshire Light Infantry. On one occasion, when the British were on a hill to the right flank, several tanks mistakenly took them under fire. The British withdrew to the rear of the hill but were unable to make radio contact, so the heavy fire continued on their hill. When it became apparent the shooting would not stop, a British officer sauntered around the side of the hill carrying a recognition panel under his arm. Though he seemed to be walking on tracers, he continued his slow, deliberate pace. At the center of the hill he unfolded the panel, spread it on the hillside, bowed from the waist, and strolled back to his position.

From May 20 to 24 the 8th Airborne Rangers were once again part of Task Force Plumley. At 0330 hours on May 22 the task force set out to seize the town of Chonggang-ni and nearby Hill 112. Moving through hills and swales, the task force encountered early contact with retreating Chinese forces who covered their withdrawal with strong rear-guard actions.

At each strong point the hills would be worked over by tank and machine-gun fire, then the Rangers would move in and root the enemy from his position. The Chinese replied with automatic-weapons fire and 120mm mortars. Snipers were a constant harassment.

Despite their large numbers, it was unusual to see the enemy. Fire would be received, the flat, cracking sound of bullets whiplashing overhead or kicking up plumes of dust. Someone would yell, "They're on that hill," or "It's coming from that treeline," and the men would unload with all the firepower they could bring to bear. It was said some line units had men who would not fire, but that was not the case with the Rangers. In dust or rain or fog or snow, there was always the yammering of weapons, men yelling directions, running, falling, calling for the medic, shooting, and cursing and snarling over jammed weapons. The crash of Chinese mortars contributed the incredible violence of high explosive to the scene, violence that could shake a man to the marrow of his bones. The Chinese were damn good mortarmen. Sometimes, lying in a foxhole on the end of some razorback ridge, it seemed that the mortar rounds came like rain. Many men believed that a 60mm or 82mm mortar round could not be heard coming in, but there was no question about the 120mm mortar—it always announced its approach, though with scant warning. Many men, crouched in their holes in the earth while the high explosive searched for them, found refuge from fear in religion. There were many promises made to God and as many or more requests. Men argued their case for survival before the Lord, and fervor often displaced logic. *"Please don't kill me God, I've never had an American girl!"*

Soldiers, even those with long experience in battle, are subject to group hysteria—to panic. One night when the 8th Rangers held a hill forward on the line, a rifle company from a superb American regiment was scheduled to take over their positions. As the company came up the road under cover of darkness, a Chinese sniper fired three rounds in their direction. The entire company panicked and fled to the rear. They were soon back, their officers and noncommissioned officers filling the air with curses.

After battle, the Rangers could relax, usually with a cigarette, which were often carried in a spare first-aid pouch on a cartridge belt. This was a generation unaware of the hazards of smoking, and even if this were not so, to men at war, future danger was not an issue. We inhaled deeply on our Camels and Lucky Strikes. At night the cigarette would be lit under a poncho, keeping one eye closed to retain night vision. Then, back on watch, the cigarette would be held close, cupped in the hand to prevent its glow from disclosing one's position.

In the stress of combat, it was a frequent occurrence for men to mistakenly fire on friendly forces. Distance, poor visibility, inexperience, and lack of fire discipline are among the many factors that contribute to this phenomena. For the 3rd squad, 3rd platoon of the 8th Ranger Company, a dreadful experience was about to begin.

The squad was on the extreme right of the company, attacking a wooded hill. Trees and a fold in the ground separated and obscured the squad from the remainder of the 3rd platoon. Pete

Torres, who had been shot in the face on April 15, had gone
AWOL from the hospital to rejoin his friends. His homecoming
party was memorable. Suddenly the air seemed filled with a
howl that tore at a man's soul, a sound like a thousand freight
trains rushing by. Trees on the crest above the men began to
disintegrate as the swath of fire marched down the slope toward
the squad. The half-track-mounted quad-.50 machine guns in
the low ground below had opened a concentrated fire on the
hill.

A slight depression, a wrinkle in the earth, held the only
chance for survival, and as one, the Rangers leaped for the depression. There was barely time for them to press their bodies
to earth before the ground began to convulse. All about them
trees were chopped to pieces, showering the men with splinters
and branches.

Ranger Ronald Henry crept forward inch by inch until, some
distance away, he was able to clear the line of fire and proceed
to a point where he could warn and call off the "friendly" fire.
To be caught under enemy fire is unpleasant; to be subjected to
concentrated American firepower is an experience one never
forgets.

Later there would be speculation as to whether the eight quad-
.50s had been firing two .50-caliber machine guns at a time for
a total of sixteen, or all four guns for a total of thirty-two. The
argument dissolved under the press of business. Either sixteen
or thirty-two—like Mercutio's hurt—" 'twas enough, 'twould
suffice."

After the friendly fire was properly redirected, the Rangers
swept up and over the hill. The surviving Chinese fled, covered
by snipers and stay-behinds in spider holes. Jackie Baker saw
the muzzle blast as a round spanged off a tank only inches from
his head. The Chinese soldier disappeared, but Baker called the
nearest tank to his assistance. The tank halted over the position
and spun its tread, grinding its fifty tons down into the Chinese
soldier's hiding place.

Hill after hill was taken, and as the attack continued, Chinese
120mm mortar fire rained down on the task force. Crossing a
wide expanse of open paddy, the enemy shells bursting about
them, the Rangers walked in the tank treads to avoid mines.

At a stream with an expanse of sandy beach, several Rangers
threw themselves facedown in the water to drink. Spurts of water

around them made them aware they were under fire. The only cover was a nearby quad-.50 half-track. The track's gunner was confused as to the enemy location and kept spinning his gun console in a circle. The driver panicked and gunned his engine, pulling away from the Rangers. A Ranger thrust his M-1 rifle through the side port and held the muzzle to the driver's head while he uttered a terse "slow down." The Rangers stayed on the protected side of the half-track while they made their way off the beach.

The Chinese resistance was stubborn. Squad leader George Hall of Pittsburgh was killed while checking the positions of his men. A deeply religious man, Hall had time to say his prayers before he expired. Robert Shinavier was seriously wounded and would lose a leg; others were wounded in lesser degrees. A number of Chinese prisoners were taken, of which Ranger Bill Varnell had a particularly large group.

The final attack of the town of Chonggang-ni had all the aspects of a firepower demonstration at Fort Benning: artillery, tanks, quad-.50s, and the many infantry weapons of the Rangers poured out a relentless stream of destruction. Those enemy that survived, fled. The task force reported the enemy force at a battalion-plus, with the enemy taking four hundred casualties.

The 8th Rangers closed the month of May with a bang as a platoon of Rangers and a platoon from division reconnaissance discovered and blew up a large enemy ammunition dump containing a considerable store of mortar ammunition.

As the war progressed and the front surged back and forth, it became increasingly dangerous to walk about. The land was filled with booby traps and mine fields emplaced by people (usually Americans) who, when withdrawing, would leave these lethal remainders lying in wait. The problem was that records were not properly kept or exchanged, and when another American unit attacked to regain the terrain, they faced the same uncharted mine fields and booby traps.

At the Ranger Training Command, May opened with jeeps being turned in, to be replaced by sedans. The Army was finding it difficult to meet the needs of its combat units.

On May 6 a composite Ranger company formed an honor guard for Secretary of the Army Frank Pace. The guard uniform included the "newly adopted" black scarves and white boot laces.

On May 9 nine men were returned to their parent organizations for ineptitude or unacceptable traits of character.

Two days later Dutch and Saudi Arabian officers visited the command, to be followed by members of the women's advisory council.

On May 11 and 12, the 6th Rangers moved from Harvey Barracks at Kitzingen en route to Grafenwohr for spring field training. The 6th Rangers had developed a superb training program which included testing the security of American military forces. In one such raid, the 1st squad, 2nd platoon—led by SFC Jack DaSilva and consisting of corporals Philip Lovoie, Raymond Malone, Louis Cotter, and Jay Simmerman; PFC Joseph Lawrence, squad scout; PFCs Alfred Kelly and Marcantonio Lacatena; and privates John Glenn and David Hux—penetrated the security of an Army airfield and made off with key documents from the base headquarters. The documents included a roster of base personnel, number and type of aircraft and armament, and a map of the facility. The men of the 6th also infiltrated into 1st Division artillery positions while on maneuvers and stuffed the muzzles of the artillery pieces with mud and notes that read, "Kilroy was here. So were the Rangers." Thereafter, base security in Europe saw much improvement.

Colonel Van Houten was deeply concerned. The employment of Rangers as companies under division control was a method of organization he opposed. Now a new option was being discussed, one Van Houten felt equally faulty. On May 16 he wrote a personal letter to Maj. Gen. Maxwell D. Taylor, Office of the Assistant Chief of Staff G-3, Department of the Army. Van Houten told Taylor that he had in Korea a competent staff officer, Lt. Col. James Y. Adams, acting as an observer of Ranger activities. Adams had reported that Eighth Army had under study a plan to form the six Ranger companies in Korea into a provisional battalion under Eighth Army control and attach this battalion to the 187th Airborne Regimental Combat Team for operations, training, and logistic support.

Van Houten noted that this plan was predicated in part on reports received from division commanders: the 2nd Division wanted to keep their Ranger company; the 7th Division wanted the size of its Ranger company increased to a battalion. Van Houten tiptoed around the treatment of the 4th Ranger Company by the 1st Cavalry Division. The other Ranger companies had arrived too recently for an adequate judgment. Van Houten pointed out that the Ranger Training Center/Command had felt from the beginning that after adequate testing, company-size units with divisions would possibly not be the final solution, and that perhaps battalion-size units under a headquarters higher than division would produce better results.

The colonel added that if a provisional Ranger battalion was placed under the 187th for operational control, it would become just another Airborne infantry battalion. In fact, since the 187th was in need of replacements, it was likely the Rangers would be drawn off for that purpose.

Van Houten expounded his views as follows:

> I am convinced that Rangers, as they have been selected and trained, can accomplish the missions visualized by General Collins, provided they are utilized as intended. Since the interest of divisions is largely confined to a relatively shallow depth behind the front lines into enemy territory, it may well be that a battalion-type organization, capable of considerable self-support and operating under the control of Theater Army of Corps, can be more profitable than company units with divisions. Further, I think that the Airborne capability of Rangers may well have been given too much emphasis in the thinking on Korea. Our emphasis in their training has been to develop individuals and units capable of rapid, accurate, and stealthy cross-country movement at night to attack, destroy, and harass, to gain information and return to friendly lines. Ranger training and capabilities differ from normal Airborne units in these respects, and these are the assets I fear will become lost if Rangers are merged too closely with other Airborne units. I see no real objection to attachment of Ranger units to Airborne units for logistical support and for such Airborne training as may be necessary to retain their Airborne capability and pay. Although the parachute drop has not been employed in Korea as yet solely as a means of Ranger entry into enemy rear areas to accomplish a typical Ranger mission, I am convinced it can be so employed whenever the need arises and conditions warrant. Two Ranger companies

were attached to the 187th for the Munsan drop, and gave a fine account of themselves on a typically Airborne mission.

In summation, I believe that the organization of a provisional Ranger battalion under Eighth Army control may be a sound idea. I do not believe that such a battalion should be placed under the operational control of an Airborne unit, unless needed to perform Ranger-type missions for a specific operation. I do not feel that Ranger units in Korea, with few exceptions, notably in the 2nd Division, have been utilized as they were intended sufficiently to constitute a conclusive test as to their value.

I recommend that immediate steps be taken either to ensure the utilization of a Ranger battalion under Army control be tested or that Ranger companies with divisions be further tested with emphasis on their employment on Ranger-type missions for which they were designed and trained.

In hope of achieving his goal, Van Houten submitted a draft Table of Organization and Equipment for the Ranger battalion he proposed.

On May 17 plans for two model training companies were started by Ranger Training Command. One would be an officers' company, the other to be comprised of noncommissioned officers, each of approximately 150 men.

On May 18 the command was visited by several general officers, including Major General Kendall, Inspector of Infantry, who inspected A Company in ranks. The 14th Rangers demonstrated combat formations, and the 13th Rangers demonstrated techniques of fire. The same day, the 7th Ranger Company arrived back at Fort Benning after completing mountain training in Colorado. To round out a busy twenty-four hours, a "washout" committee disqualified another twenty-one trainees from continuing training.

On May 23 the Department of the Army lowered the aptitude area II score to eighty for Ranger volunteers. Unofficial information on this was published in the *Army Times*. More pleasing to those Rangers-in-training was nationwide publication of photographs by the famous photographer Hy Peskin. The shots showed Rangers in a stream-crossing while TNT charges exploded all around them.

On May 24, the ''washout'' board dismissed another twenty-eight trainees.

On May 27, thirty-eight potential Ranger volunteers were received from the U.S.-based armies. These were the first of a desired twenty-six officers and 303 enlisted men expected to make up the fifth Ranger training cycle.

On May 29 the 15th Ranger Infantry Company (Airborne) was designated for the 47th Infantry Division, and the 9th Ranger Infantry Company (Airborne) for the 31st Infantry Division. Both companies were activated on this date and began Airborne training. The 9th Ranger Company (second activation) was headed by Capt. Billie Mitts and 1st Sgt. Henry Hand, a veteran paratrooper who was promptly tagged ''Top Hand.'' The men of the ''Dixie Rangers'' had started with six hundred volunteers; by the time they began Ranger training, that number had been ruthlessly honed to 165.

On May 31, three Greek officers who had served with the British Commandoes in WWII visited the training.

Chapter 17

Early June found the Communist armies on the run. American infantry sensed that victory was now at hand. The movement north was through hills littered with Chinese dead. With the enemy in flight, Van Fleet sought to bring the war to a successful conclusion, and he requested several more divisions. Operating on a peninsula against a retreating foe, and having control of the air and sea, the divisions could be landed behind the enemy. Enemy forces would be cut off as during the Inchon invasion; the Chinese would have no choice but to retreat beyond the Yalu, reuniting Korea.

General Ridgeway, however, did not agree with Van Fleet's assessment. He agreed the drive to the Yalu could be made, but thought the price in blood would be too high and the result would be a longer front for U.N. forces and shorter supply lines for the enemy, while the Chinese homeland armies would remain intact to continue the war.[1] Both Ridgeway and Van Fleet would have carried out orders to continue the attack, but the President and the Congress no longer sought victory. The American people were tired of the war and wanted out. European allies kept up steady pressure on Washington to quickly negotiate an end. Van Fleet's request was denied. Orders were received that would limit the advance without prior approval of the U.S. Joint Chiefs of Staff.

Thus victory became an orphan, shunned by those United Nations whose joining together had made it obtainable.

* * *

By June 12 U.N. forces controlled Chorwon and Kumhwa, the bottom cities of the Iron Triangle. On June 20 the U.N. line was north of the 38th parallel by approximately twenty miles. On June 24 the Russian delegate to the U.N. announced that a cease fire was possible; China said the U.N. forces were beaten and agreed that a cease fire was now acceptable.

With direction from Washington, General Ridgeway broadcast a 30 June 1951 message to the enemy stating a desire to talk of a cease-fire.

On June 3 the 8th Rangers made a practice jump at Yoju airstrip. On June 5 they relieved the 4th Rangers as the security force for the IX Corps Forward (Tactical) Command Post.

The beginning of June found the 1st Ranger Company clearing and holding the area of Sinae, awaiting the arrival of the 2nd Infantry Division headquarters. Lightly wounded men were returning from the hospital. On June 6 assigned strength was 107 men with ninety-two present for duty. Second Lt. Robert Bodroghy from the 9th Ranger Company arrived on June 7. On the eighth, Capt. Charles Ross, who had previously commanded the Eighth Army Ranger Company, arrived and took command of the 1st Rangers.

The 3rd Rangers spent the early days of June in reserve or support missions, while replacements were received and wounded men returned to the company. The Rangers were frequently moving, as the 3rd Division assigned a variety of missions. Early in the month the company was eating breakfast prior to moving out on a mission when it was shelled by Chinese 120mm mortars. Corporal Tracy was sitting on a duffel bag when a piece of shrapnel hit his wrist, almost severing the hand.

Sometime later a patrol from the 3rd Rangers was clearing a small village of civilians who were in the line of fire. Some of the Koreans were deathly ill, and the Rangers saw children vomiting tapeworms more than a foot long. One Ranger went for an ambulance, and men began assisting those who most needed help. Two civilians were seen remaining in the village. Ranger Dave Rauls returned by himself to help them, but when he arrived at the village, they had disappeared. As Rauls searched among the houses, two Chinese soldiers stepped from hiding and leveled their weapons at him. A third Chinese appeared, probably an officer.

The Chinese immediately began to march Rauls to the southwest, following footpaths along the Hantan River until they came to a ford and crossed over. The leader spoke English and briefly attempted to interrogate Rauls, but Rauls refused to answer. The Chinese leader said that perhaps Rauls "would tell them more later," and moved his group on. They were joined by another Chinese, then traveled several kilometers until they reached a small scout vehicle that contained a Chinese driver guarding an American prisoner. The two Americans were placed on the vehicle and forbidden to talk to each other.

The Chinese moved with caution and with frequent stops to check out their surroundings. Shortly after turning onto a larger road, they joined two more vehicles carrying Chinese guards and American prisoners. There were now some twenty Chinese and fifteen prisoners, the latter with their hands tied behind their backs.

The three vehicles moved off, trying to hug the high slopes beside the road to avoid detection by aircraft. Soon it was necessary to enter a small valley. Ahead was a cut that offered protection.

Just before the vehicles reached the cut, two American fighter aircraft streaked downward, strafing them. Chinese and Americans alike jumped from the trucks, which immediately exploded and burned, and both Chinese and Americans were struck by the fire. The aircraft soon left in search of another target.

Now the surviving Chinese began to vent their rage on the prisoners, shooting them, clubbing them with rifle butts, and bayoneting them. Rauls remembers the barrel of a Chinese burp gun coming toward his head. His next memory is of awakening in an American hospital ward. Left for dead, he was found, fortunately, by a friendly unit.

During June, the 2nd Rangers were frequently on the move. On June 1 they were released from attachment to the 1st Battalion, 32nd Regimental Combat Team, and attached to the 2nd Battalion, but within three days they were reattached to the 1st Battalion. Some men looked upon this wandering about the battlefront as an educational experience; after all, it was observed, travel broadens the mind.

June 8 found the 2nd Rangers back in action with a mission

to assault and secure Hill 772. By early evening the hill was in Ranger hands, with eight enemy killed and thirty wounded. Seven Rangers were lightly wounded in the action.

The 2nd Rangers continued the attack on June 11, seizing a critical piece of high ground near Sanying-ni and killing five enemy while wounding several dozen more. Eight Rangers were lightly wounded and Corporal James Petteress, Jr. was killed.

The 5th Ranger Company received fifteen replacements on June 1; 103 men were now assigned with eighty-four present for duty. The 5th had been attached to the 89th Tank Battalion, but on June 2 was attached to the 27th Infantry Regiment in preparation for an attack.

The objective for the 5th Rangers was a Communist strongpoint on Hill 722. In the operations order it was called "Objective Sugar."

June 4 was overcast and the steep slopes of the objective were wet and slippery from previous rains. The men gathered in the assembly area, waiting to cross the line of departure with the private thoughts that all men who await the coming of battle know. Some men are anxious for conversation, others seek quiet—all check and recheck the equipment on which their lives depend.

Ranger Pat Brady cleaned and recleaned his M-1 rifle; the once-trusted weapon was beginning to show a tendency to misfire. All the men sensed that this would be a tough fight. Equipment was snugged down, bayonets fixed, then came the signal to move out. The war was losing its mobility; enemy positions were increasingly well fortified, and men began to recall the stories told by fathers who had fought in the trenches of World War I.

Avoiding the frontal attack, the 5th Rangers struck from the flank, but the enemy had prepared a masterful defense: Communist soldiers were concealed in "spider" holes, covered positions from which they would remain concealed until the Americans drew close or passed, at which point the Chinese would rise and shoot.

Pat Brady saw the ground in front of him seemingly explode as a Chinese soldier armed with an automatic weapon threw off his concealment and prepared to engage. Brady and the Chinese soldier swung their weapons toward each other. Brady squeezed the trigger, only to hear the sickening sound of the bolt slamming forward into a misfire.

The Communist soldier was beginning the trigger squeeze that would end Brady's life, when suddenly a nearby Ranger with an automatic rifle turned and fired, shattering the enemy soldier's skull. The Rangers were now among the Chinese positions, locked in close combat. Fred Hoy bayoneted a Chinese soldier then fired to ensure the kill and assist in freeing the bayonet.[2] Other Rangers were employing the same tactic. American casualties mounted swiftly. Lieutenant McAbee was wounded; Rangers Conklin, Ted Edwards, Eckhardt, Drinkwater, Farcier, Hayden, Zambos, Rodriguez, May, and Hardway were hit.

Chinese mortars came into deadly play. The incessant rattle of small-arms fire and the bone-jarring shock of high explosives filled the air. Cpl. Timothy Ontayabbi was killed. Ranger Fred Hoy was caught in the open and looking for cover. Running hard, he dove into a hole occupied by Rangers Edward Keeler and John Wray.

Wray yelled, "Find your own damn hole. This one is only big enough for us two!"

Hoy jumped from the foxhole and began running across the fire-swept slope. Suddenly he was slammed to earth by the force of an explosion. A Chinese mortar round had landed in the hole he had just vacated, killing Keeler and Wray.

The skillfully prepared Chinese defense began to prevail. Dragging their wounded, the Rangers withdrew to the base of the hill, reorganized, and attacked again. The Chinese brought up additional reinforcements and increased their mortar fire. Still the Rangers fought their way up the crest.

Near the top of the slope the battle was fought among huge boulders. Furious grenade fights erupted; flights of Chinese stick grenades filled the air, coming on the Rangers as many as twenty at a time. The Rangers carried grenade pouches or grenades affixed to pack straps and cartridge belts; most Rangers carried as many as six grenades apiece. The Rangers replied to the Chinese barrage in kind, heaving flights of the heavy, corrugated cast-iron fragmentation grenades up and over the crest.

Cpl. Edward Durney was killed; wounded were Rangers Goldbaum, Evens, Wofford, Kandziore, Gross, McDonald, Jones, Wilson, Butler, McGlothin, Laird, Jubeck, Brady, and

Derham. Lieutenant Sansalone was down with a serious wound to the chest.

Decimated, the 5th Ranger Company tried once again to reform to continue the attack, and requested reinforcements. Instead the company was ordered to withdraw. Reinforcements were not available.

On June 11 the 1st Rangers began security patrols for the 2nd Division. Lt. William Cole led a team consisting of Sergeant 1st Class Olsen, sergeants Dahl, Simpson, Morgan, and Corporal Meyer, on a mission to train Korean Rangers until July 7.

The 5th Rangers spent June 10 through 14 screening and maintaining flank contact for the 15th and 27th infantry regiments, running contact patrols, and locating suitable fording sites on the Namdae-chon River. Operating with tanks, the company continued its screening missions until the night of June 20 when it conducted a raid on the town of Tipo-Dong then reverted to a reserve role for the remainder of the month.

In the course of their many operations, the Rangers were frequently called upon to use their own resources to cross rivers, many of which possessed treacherous currents. On the night of June 14 a reconnaissance patrol from the 4th Ranger Company set forth on a mission to cross the Imjin River, lay up for a day behind enemy lines observing enemy activity, then return. The route was difficult, involving three water crossings, only two of which were fordable. The five Rangers and a Korean interpreter who made up the patrol had an inflatable rubber boat to make the final crossing.

Near the riverbank the Rangers worked quickly and silently to inflate their craft. The night was dark, devoid of stars to aid navigation. The wet and slippery grass made movement difficult. Stepping off into the river, the men could immediately feel the powerful surge of the water. The equipment and weapons were placed on the raft, but there was insufficient room for all of the patrol. SFC Lester V. McPherson and Sgt. Thomas A. Ward would remain in the water to help guide the craft across the river.

With the others on board, McPherson and Ward pushed off from shore. They immediately encountered a stiff current and soon lost the river bottom from beneath their feet. In a matter of moments the boat was wrenched from their hands and swirled away downstream with its occupants, weapons, and equipment. McPherson and Ward had to swim for their lives.

In the cold dawn the two Rangers located each other on the enemy shore. There was no sign of the remainder of the patrol, which had safely returned to friendly lines. Laying low, McPherson and Ward took stock of their situation. Their only weapon was a trench knife, but they had a map and knew the mission. Even if heavily armed, they could not outshoot the Chinese Army. The mission required stealth, and two could do that as well as six. They decided to continue the mission. The distant sound of armor only added an additional element of suspense. Moving under cover, the two Rangers found a dirt road occupied by men of the 8th Cavalry Regiment, who had crossed the river on a tank probe. There were anxious moments until identification was made. The officer-in-charge offered to take the two Rangers back, but they were determined to complete the mission and settled for some food and water.

The tank-probe route went part of the way to the Ranger objective, so McPherson and Ward rode with the cavalrymen, then, at a concealed point, dropped off to make their own way. By the next morning they had reached the predesignated point of observation, and per their orders, spent the day observing Chinese emplacements and activity and marking it on the map. They knew the information they had was valuable, and they were impatient to get it back to friendly lines.

They began their return shortly before dark, but the hills seemed alive with Chinese. They passed through position after position, but always there was another. Finally a Chinese outpost saw them and opened fire.

Then began a race for life. The two Rangers ran hard through the night with a Chinese force in hot pursuit and Chinese soldiers to their front and flanks alerted. The chase lasted until first light. Ward and McPherson found themselves in a hollow of ground much like a small amphitheater. There were Chinese troops on the ridges, but the two men hoped they had not been seen. The ground was barren save for a small clump of bushes. With full light coming, the two Rangers crawled into the bushes and concealed themselves as best they could.

Soon they heard the sound of the Chinese who had been pursuing them. Chinese on the ridge began to yell to those entering the hollow, and suddenly the bushes were shredded by automatic-weapons fire. Miraculously, Ward and McPherson were unhurt, but the hunt was over. With hands raised, they stood up.

A Chinese soldier pressed a pistol against Ward's head and hissed one word in English, *"Agent."* Another Chinese prepared to strike Ward's head with a stick grenade. McPherson was getting the same treatment. At that moment a Chinese soldier yelled a single word and the enemy scattered. Ward later learned the word translated as, *"Airplane."*

There was no escape for the Rangers, but as everyone flattened themselves to earth, Ward and McPherson had the presence of mind to bury the map marked with Chinese positions. The action probably saved their lives. When the aircraft was gone, the Chinese searched them, found nothing suspicious, and started them under guard for the prison camps.

On June 17 the 1st Cavalry Division reported Ward and McPherson captured. They would survive several years of captivity.

Though it did not come on a routine basis for Ranger companies, mail call was a welcome relief from the routine. News from home sometimes sounded foreign, as though written from another planet: "The church had a picnic, Uncle Bill lost his job, your cousin Bobby has joined the Marines and is now in Korea, be sure and look him up." You could feel the love and caring behind the simple phrases. Those who were lucky enough to have wives and girlfriends sought privacy for their reading. It was observed that the company cooks received stacks of mail that were in feminine hand and perfumed. Their secret was not revealed for a long time. The women in the United States who packed the eggs that were being sent to Korea often wrote their names and addresses on the eggs, along with messages encouraging correspondence. The cooks got first crack at the eggs and the women.

On June 17 the 3rd Division formed Task Force Ferret, consisting of the 3rd Ranger Company, the 3rd Reconnaissance Company, a company of infantry, a battery of artillery, an anti-aircraft platoon, and a tactical air control party. This force established a patrol base about six miles forward of the line and conducted sweeping patrols to clear the area of enemy.

On June 23 the 2nd Rangers were perched on a high-ground observation post when they saw in the distance a platoon of enemy soldiers unaware that they were being observed. Without disclosing their position, the Rangers called artillery fire on the Chinese, causing numerous casualties.

The constant probes that were designed to keep the enemy "off balance" took a terrible toll of American youth. Gone were the days of maneuver. The Chinese excelled at field fortifications; to survive under American air and artillery power they had learned to burrow deep.

On June 24 Task Force Croft—tank-infantry elements of the 1st Cavalry and the 4th Rangers—began a probe some twenty miles into Chinese territory in the Iron Triangle area. The Rangers were riding the lead tanks. Engineers used mine detectors to clear the road, but these would only detect metal. As the force approached a village with high ground to its rear and flank, the lead tank had its tread blown off by a wooden box mine. The Rangers dismounted as the column came under fire and took cover in a roadside ditch. They quickly learned the ditch was occupied by small anti-personnel bombs—which, fortunately, the Chinese had disarmed—previously dropped by the U.S. Air Force.

Lieutenant Johnson and Sergeant Johnson of the 1st platoon moved toward the village when suddenly both men were hit by automatic weapon fire. Sgt. George Vidrine went to their assistance and carried both men to safety. A tank retriever attempting to extract the stricken tank hit another box mine and was itself knocked out.

The Chinese were directing accurate mortar and artillery fire from the hills. A Ranger pinpointed the location of the Chinese forward observer, and a tank blasted the position with one round of 90mm high explosive. Parts of clothing and bodies were hurled aloft in a cloud of dust. The Chinese fire slackened.

When Chinese positions were located, the task force had no intention of lingering in the area. Yet the Rangers were ordered to attack through the town and seize the heavily fortified hill beyond. Captain Anderson protested the needlessness of seizing the terrain when it would be immediately given up, but was told, "You have your orders!"

Anderson planned to use one platoon for a base of fire and

attack with two, but the men were angered by the senselessness of the mission. Platoon Sgt. Gregory Matteo walked openly down the road, disregarding enemy fire. With the tanks supporting by fire from the road, the 4th Ranger Company moved as one. Crossing a narrow stream and then moving through the village and a rice paddy on the other side, all three platoons went on-line. Shouting, "Let's go, Buffalo!" they assaulted the hill. Many men were hit, but they kept charging until they were on the Chinese. Unable to use his jammed weapon, Sgt. Frederick Fuhst drew his entrenching tool and hacked a Chinese soldier to death. Those Chinese that did not run were killed. As the Rangers seized the Chinese positions, they saw the tanks begin to leave. Their rising anger abated when they learned that half of the tanks were pulling back a few miles for refueling. As they had foreseen, the Rangers were now ordered down from the hill, which the Chinese reoccupied.

As the Rangers rejoined the tanks, the Chinese struck the column hard with accurate mortar and artillery fire. Many more men were hit.

On Task Force Croft the 4th Rangers lost Sgt. Paul J. Gotney, and fifty-seven Rangers were wounded to take an objective and then pull away. In his diary 1st Sgt. James Way asked the question: "Worth it?"

To be an attached unit in the U.S. Army is to experience the lot of the orphan or the poor relation. On several occasions Ranger units went without rations as they were transferred from one regiment to another. The Rangers had five truckloads of equipment to move and one truck to move it with. When requests through official channels were filed or refused, it became a matter of self-preservation. The 1st Ranger Company had men get in the drivers' line as vehicles were being offloaded at the Pusan docks. Bluffing their credentials, the Rangers drove off with the quantity of jeeps they needed.

Each Ranger unit had its own technique to secure transport. The 8th Rangers, for example, found the rear area made the best hunting preserve. Security was at a lower level, men were less inclined to shoot on sight, and rear-echelon units had many vehicles. The rear area also had outdoor theaters, consisting simply of a slope with sandbag seats and a plywood screen located at the lower elevation. At dusk, men from surrounding units would drive in, park their vehicles at the top, then move down the slope and take a sandbag seat to watch the film.

Military vehicles are not equipped with a key lock. A careful driver chained his steering wheel or removed the distributor cap, but many drivers were not careful. One night as the film was in progress, shadowy figures came down from the hills, and one by one, vehicle engines came to life. At the "Devil" camp, men waited with cans of olive-drab and white paint, stencils, and brushes. In a matter of minutes each vehicle would be repainted and stenciled with parachute wings, 8th Ranger, and 24th Division markings.

Soon the area surrounding the Ranger camp began to resemble a motor pool. Each draw and depression was used as a source of concealment, but greed resulted in too many vehicles to hide.

Throughout the corps area vehicle security rapidly improved. Men charged with responsibility began to carefully lock and maintain surveillance on their equipment.

Airborne Ranger convoys began to appear on the roads making frequent trips to shower points and ration dumps. Motorized patrols were established. Fred Willis and Jim Kennedy took a trip to 1st Ranger country; 2nd, 4th, and 5th companies were visited by other men of the 8th Rangers.

The 2nd Rangers generously provided Combat Infantry Badges to the 8th Rangers that had long since been earned but were not forthcoming through the units to which the 8th company was attached.

After several weeks the vehicle caper came to an end— probably as the result of a hot pursuit by MPs that led too close to home, though some believe it was because a leading Korean police official's vehicle had been lifted.

Officers from a variety of units began to arrive and scan the motor park. Captain Eikenberry was a genial host; on one occasion he dumbfounded an irate Air Force Officer with the bland remark "Thank you for the loan."

At 0530 hours on June 26, the Devils were back in action. Friendly elements were stalled at a roadblock. The Rangers moved forward, cleared the block, then moved on and seized two objectives. Before the day was complete, the 8th Rangers joined the 24th Reconnaissance Company and elements of both the 6th Tank Battalion and the 5th RCT tank Company for a

patrol. A quantity of enemy material was destroyed and prisoners were taken.

Things were not going well for the Chinese. Strewn across
the slopes of the Korean hills were the dead bodies of their young
men. The corpses did not resemble forms that had once held
life; they were foul-smelling offal, lumps of filth that stunk of
the putrid, rotten corruption of death.

The forms lay in a variety of poses, some showing their last
desperate flight for life. Bodies sat upright in foxholes or were
buried with only a rotting leg or arm showing. Often the corpse
was burned black by the horrible fire of napalm.

Death was so commonplace, the sight and smell of rotting
corpses so frequent, that the living looked upon them not as
dead men but as battlefield trash. One Ranger decided that the
leg of a dead Chinese, protruding from the earth some distance
from his foxhole, made an excellent target for pistol practice.
Another Ranger found it necessary to clear the body of a na-
palmed Chinese soldier from a position he was to occupy; as he
inserted a shovel under the lower extremities, a putrefied leg
broke off. His friends laughed, and one of them took a photo-
graph of the Ranger holding the rotting leg on a shovel and
grinning.

Occasionally men sat on a fresh corpse to keep off the wet
ground, but generally the more recent dead were checked, then
ignored. The North Koreans on occasion mutilated Ranger (and
other) dead. The Rangers did not reply in kind. It was enough
to kill them.

The four horsemen of the apocalypse rode the unhappy hills
of Korea, and death was not confined to soldiers. During a reconnaissance patrol, the 3rd squad of the 3rd platoon, 8th Rangers, entered a small valley. In the midst of war it seemed a place
untouched by destruction, a place of peace, so quiet that there
was an unreal quality to the air. At the base of the valley was a
small village of approximately fifteen houses. The Rangers moved
cautiously and uneasily. Near one of the houses the patrol saw
an old man and a teenage girl. They were slumped forward, the
hand of death having closed quickly on them. Silently, the patrol
moved through the village, checking the interiors of the houses.
It was a village of the dead; some plague had swept over them,
sparing neither young nor old. Entire families lay in rows within
the houses, as though they had gone peacefully to sleep. Here

and there were the single bodies of those who had died at the daily chores of life. Men hardened to the many faces of death wiped tears from their eyes and hastened from the valley.

On June 27 the Devils continued in the attack with elements of the 19th Infantry. The Rangers went forward at 0600 hours, riding tanks from the 5th Regimental Combat Team. At 0800 hours they split into a three-platoon force to accomplish varying missions. One platoon seized objective "Victor" after a stiff fight. Another platoon assisted B Company, 19th Infantry, on its objective, while the final platoon blocked.

By afternoon the company had reunited and seized hills named objectives "George" and "Able." As darkness fell, the Rangers dug into positions that were several thousand meters in front of the main line of resistance. The Rangers occupied central screening positions while B Company, 19th Infantry, was on the left, and the 5th RCT Tank Company covered low ground approaches to the right. Other companies of the 19th Regiment operated behind this screen, destroying enemy fortifications and supply dumps and locating weapons caches.

At 0745 hours on June 29 the Devils moved from their positions to secure high ground along the route of the 19th Regiment's withdrawal. The Ranger mission was to fight a delaying action back to the main line of resistance. The mission was successfully accomplished.

The attack netted one enemy howitzer, thirty-three mortars, 135 rifles and submachine guns, and a large quantity of ammunition.

The 6th Rangers spent six weeks at Grafenwhohr, firing weapons and conducting squad and platoon exercises. On return to Kitzingen, they staged a river crossing. Armed Forces Radio was present. The announcer commented on "how quietly they enter the water." Just then a man got caught by the current and there was a cry of *"Help!"* followed by, *"Throw him a line."* The announcer quickly left. Despite this minor aberration, the 6th was setting an example of training, bearing, and discipline, which resulted in the phrase "Sharp as a Ranger" being used in American units in Europe.

Captain Cain was justifiably proud of the accomplishments of his men and inclined to enumerate them over drinks at the officers club. To prove to the doubters the incredible physical conditioning of his men, Cain led the 6th Ranger Company on a speed march covering forty miles in eight hours.[3] The march was made with full combat pack, bedroll, and individual weapons. In addition, all crew-served weapons of the company were carried for the first fifteen miles.

June 4 began the sixth week of training for the fourth cycle. Hand and rifle grenades, platoon night attacks and defenses, aerial resupply, and submachine gun mechanical training were featured. *Popular Mechanics* magazine sent a writer to do an article on training.

At 0400 hours on June 5 a fire swept through building number 4469, which served as 12th Ranger Company's orderly and supply room. No one was hurt, but the building was destroyed. Damage was estimated at $35,000.

Additional volunteers, numbering 161, were received from the regular Army. The seventh week of training for the fourth cycle was highlighted by day parachute jumps, village fighting in Dixie Village, foreign and silent weapons, and squad and platoon tactics.

From June 12 to 15 Colonel Van Houten attended conferences at Army Field Forces at Fort Monroe, Virginia, and Washington D.C.

The RTC newsletter *The Ranger* published a letter from Captain Carrier written just prior to the May Massacre.[4] Carrier wrote of the importance of night fire-control and the use of tracer ammunition for the base of fire during night fire and movement. He reported that the 1st Rangers were practicing the use of assault boats, and it was his intention to have each Ranger know how to drive a tank and fire its weapons.

Statistics for the fourth cycle showed the average age to be 22.2 years. The average 13th Company Ranger was 23.8 years old; 12th Company was the youngest, with an average age of 21.

The eighth and final week of the fourth training cycle commenced on June 18. All units began five days of parachute jumps and intensive field training.

On June 20 the men of the 10th and 11th Ranger companies sailed from Seattle, Washington, aboard the *General Simon B. Buckner*. They would arrive in Yokohama on July 1 to join the 40th and 45th divisions and continue training.

On June 23 the 9th and 15th Ranger companies completed Airborne training and received their silver wings.

On June 26 the men of training companies A and B, the 12th, 13th, and 14th Ranger companies, celebrated; graduation day had come, and now and for ever more they would be *Rangers*. Some 550 Rangers in khaki uniform with black scarves and white boot laces paraded on French Field.

One whose spirit was present at that review was Ranger Robert Luttrell of the 14th Rangers. On his seventh jump Luttrell fell eighty feet after a brush with another trooper and suffered serious injuries, including a broken back. The doctors predicted he would not walk again. Though he could not be at graduation, Ranger Luttrell did learn to walk again and promptly volunteered for Korea. He would lose a leg to a land mine, but not his Ranger pride.

The 12th, 13th, and 14th Ranger companies departed Fort Benning for three weeks of mountain training at Camp Carson, Colorado, on Thursday, June 28.

Payday brought a new innovation in the 14th Ranger pay line. Ranger Joe Holloway had jumped with Lt. John Carney and his 2nd platoon, 14th Rangers. Holloway was experienced with the radio directional finder and was designated to guide the platoon from the drop zone. Holloway blamed mechanical malfunction after the platoon traveled in precisely the wrong direction. On payday Lieutenant Carney was the pay officer. Everyone else marched face-forward to his pay, but Lieutenant Carney required Ranger Holloway to back up to the table.[5]

Chapter 18

As July began, the Chinese and North Korean armies were in desperate straits. The April and May attacks had cost them over 160,000 casualties. Their total casualties for the first year of the war were estimated at 1.25 million men. For the U.N. fighting men, the sweet smell of victory was in the air.

On July 1 the Communists agreed to Ridgeway's request for a meeting. They desired the talks to be held at Kaesong, an area within Communist lines. Washington hastily agreed to this site on July 2. Thus the Chinese were able to foster the impression that they were the victors forcing the defeated allies to come to them to sue for peace.

The propaganda war now began—a war fought not only over people and territory, but over the positioning of tables, chairs, and miniature flags. It was a war at which the Chinese were clearly superior.

Behind a screen of propaganda the Chinese skillfully played on the American and European people's desire for a quick solution. Through agreeing to truce talks, they were able to bring the U.N. forces to a halt. Given the respite they had been denied under Van Fleet's attacks, the Communists now began to funnel more men and material to the front. The war now changed from one of maneuver to a static front.

It was World War I, Oriental style. The Chinese were master diggers, and soon the Korean hills were mazes of bunkers, obstacles, and fortifications. The Russians provided them with large quantities of artillery, which the Chinese had previously lacked.

Ground that could have been taken without resistance in May and June became killing zones where the youth of America bled and died for the conquest of mere yards.

To the individual soldier, July 1951 was a bewildering period. Ordered to halt while the enemy fled, men watched the Communist foe gain the breathing space to regroup and fortify. Hills that could have been taken without cost soon bristled with barriers and gun emplacements. As the talks dragged on, attacks were ordered to seize heavily defended terrain features. After costly success, the wounded and dead were brought down and the newly won positions often ordered evacuated without enemy pressure.

As the dead Americans were carried down from the muddy mountains and razorback ridges, they were taken on stretchers, their bodies covered by ponchos. But the poncho was never long enough, and the boots always were exposed—the scuffed, scratched, muddy, heel-worn infantry boots that once carried a vibrant young man, an American youth with a family, hope, and aspirations.

War is always a waste and a tragedy, but it has proven better to win the wars we are called upon to fight than to ask men to "die for a tie," or to have them put their lives at risk without the backing of the nation that sends them to war. Debate should precede war or follow it, but while a war is in progress, those who fight it are entitled to the attention and support of their homeland.

The Rangers cursed the enemy—called him "chink," "gook," "slant," or "geek"—but respected his fighting ability and courage. Rangers did not see that kind of respect coming from Washington.

On July 10 Department of the Army Message 95587 directed the inactivation of the Ranger companies in Korea. The message was promptly passed by Eighth Army to I Corps, IX Corps, and X Corps, then on to the divisions. The message stated that the Rangers would be transferred to the 187th Airborne Regimental Combat Team.[1] It stated the Rangers had been chosen because of their record as volunteers for service who emphasized high qualities of mental alertness and physical stamina. This would ensure that the 187th would have a full compliment of highly qualified personnel.

The startling reason for inactivation the Army recommended to be given the press was:

> The fact that deep patrol missions by small units, for which the Rangers are intended, are made most difficult in the Far East Command by reason of the racial differences between the Oriental and the Caucasian.

The face of the enemy had not changed, yet it took the Department of the Army more than a year to publicly come to the conclusion that the enemy we were fighting in Korea was racially different than the American soldier. The message went on to say that the new utilization of the Rangers in the Far East was not expected to effect the training program at the Ranger Training Command at Fort Benning. The Rangers knew there was no truth in this statement either.

The *Army Times* of July 14 carried an article in which Gen. Mark Clark, chief of the Army field forces, predicted that the Army's present program of Ranger training would be expanded "when some of the present physical limitations are relieved."

Columnist Peter Edson questioned if the move was being done because the Marines were jealous of the Army Rangers and saw the Ranger program as an attempt to incorporate the Marines into the Army.

It was not the Marines that were the foe of the Rangers but, rather, the old guard of the Army. This was personified in remarks by Maj. Gen. Reuben E. Jenkins, Assistant Chief of Staff G-3, Department of the Army. General Jenkins was opposed to the formation of what he termed "prima donna" type units. He stated that the formation of such units lowered the standard of regular infantry units by draining them of their best soldiers. He was opposed to extra pay for Ranger-trained personnel. From Europe and the Far East, the old guard rallied to the cry that they would "prefer to have the high-class personnel normally assigned to the Rangers distributed equally among their combat units in the positions of leadership that they would ordinarily occupy."

The recommendations of the three division commanders who employed their Rangers and wanted them retained were glossed over, as were many recommendations to form battalion-size units. The companies were to be inactivated.

The opposition to Ranger and other "special" type units did not begin (or end) in the Korean War. Since the 1700s such units have been viewed by American traditionalist officers as a drain on the regular establishment. Roger's Rangers was a temporary unit, as was Darby's. Through the centuries, the existence of the Rangers and other special forces has been threatened more by the generals of the American army than by the generals of the enemy.

Between July 10 and 20 the 3rd Division withdrew its forces from several key hills in the triangle area. Hills 682 and 717 were left vacant except for a platoon of the 3rd Rangers. The mission of the Rangers was to create the impression that a large force remained on the hills. During daylight the Rangers observed locations suitable for night-ambush patrols, then set their traps under cover of darkness. On July 25 a morning patrol engaged a Communist force, killed five and captured twenty grenades. One Ranger was wounded.

Other men of the 3rd Rangers were engaged in passing on their expertise. Instructors for the 3rd Rangers trained three companies of the 90th ROK Division in Ranger tactics. The 3rd Division reported the training very successful and the ROK units much improved.

Additional men had joined the 1st Ranger Company, and the unit was spoiling for a fight. Time and time again the company petitioned division for missions, but the front had changed to fixed-position warfare. One last chance occurred. On the night of July 17–18 two all-volunteer platoons, each consisting of two officers and forty men, patrolled to the front of the 23rd and 38th infantry regiments. It was the last hurrah of the 1st Ranger Infantry Company (Airborne).

The 5th Ranger Company spent the first half of the month in I Corps reserve with the 25th Infantry Division at Kumo-ri. From July 17 to 25 the 5th Rangers were in defensive positions along the Imjin River, and on July 26 and 27 the company did combat patrolling across the Imjin. Enemy were sighted, but not at rifle range. Artillery was used to satisfying effect. On July 29 the company moved to 25th Infantry Division replacement company. Inactivation was completed on 1 August 1951.

During the month of July the mission of the 24th Division and the attached 8th Ranger Company was preparation and active defense of line "Wyoming," to the northwest of Hwachon. Patrol activity was heavy, with a battalion-size patrol base established forward of the line.

On July 2, the 8th Rangers conducted combat patrols forward of the 21st Regiment sector, then established ambush positions on the night of the second. July 3 found the Devils ordered to join the 2nd Battalion, 21st Infantry, for a combined attack on Hill 851.

The Devils, now at a strength of 108, led the attack, with the battalion following approximately thirty minutes later. The attack was made through dense fog and heavy rain. The route of approach was over heavily vegetated razorback ridges with chimney rock and sixty to seventy degree slopes that were slick with mud and difficult to traverse.

The Rangers scouted the approaches and led the battalion to an assembly area near Hill 1118. As the 2nd Battalion, 21st Infantry, moved into positions for the assault, the 8th Rangers blocked enemy routes from Hill 1118 and held open the route of supply.

The attack by the 2nd Battalion was successful. The enemy counterattacked with a battalion-size force but was beaten off with the aid of artillery.

The enemy effort that began at 0526 hours on July 6 was defeated by 0545 hours. During their counterattack the Chinese had used white phosphorous, and a number of the American soldiers were badly burned. There was a numb hatred at the futility of our effort when orders were received to withdraw from the hill.

An infantryman faces many adversaries in war besides the enemy. Weather and terrain are often the most difficult of foes. In Korea monsoon rains and high mountains made movement a torturous task.

From the viewpoint of the individual Ranger, his role seemed to be that of a beast of burden. Men looked in vain for the brawny mules of Camp Carson; all ammunition and supplies had to be transported on human shoulders. Mortars and automatic weapons devoured ammunition, and many trips were required to carry heavy loads up the steep and slippery slopes. Some men wrote on their fatigue caps: "You call, we haul, that's all."

Bleeding piles and dysentery were commonplace, abetted by the torrential rains that left even the soul clammy. Men would claw their way up the muddy trails, soaked to the skin and shivering, clutching at branches for support. Frequent stops were required, but there was no solid waste to pass, only blood.

Faint with exhaustion, one Ranger visited the 21st Infantry aid station for examination. "Ah, yes," the doctor said. "What we have here is an acute case of bleeding piles. If you ever get off the line, we can fix you up."

On July 11 the 8th Rangers passed through 21st Regiment lines. Their first assignment was to secure a blocking position that would facilitate the 21st Regiment's attack. The Devils accomplished their mission by 1345 hours, then continued forward to seize Hill 1118. Scaling steep slopes, they gained the summit without being detected. The surprised enemy fled from the hill. At 1120 hours the objective was secured.

During the night the Rangers occupied blocking positions southwest of Hill 851. Shortly after midnight an attack from enemy forces on 851 was beaten off. At 0305 the Rangers directed artillery fire on Hill 851. While the 21st Infantry continued in their attacks on Hill 851 with the 8th Rangers blocking, artillery and mortars were employed by both sides and sniper fire was heavy. The Rangers were firing 60mm mortar shells off of rifle grenade launchers, and also manhandled .50-caliber machine guns to the crest of their positions on Hill 1118 and used them effectively as sniper weapons on Chinese messengers who thought they were out of rifle range.

At 0044 hours on July 14 a heavy mortar barrage fell on the 3rd platoon, 8th Rangers. One round landed close to Captain Eikenberry's position.

Concerned for his commander's safety, a Ranger crept close and called out, "Captain, are you okay?"

The only response from the unflappable Eikenberry was a sonorous snore.

At 0514 hours the enemy made an attempt to penetrate the Ranger's position. The 24th Division records note, "The Rangers had a small firefight with good results."

During the night of July 14–15 the Chinese used three-man teams to pinpoint Ranger positions. Their efforts were unsuccessful, and when they attempted an attack, it was quickly beaten off.

The 24th Division G-3 sent orders to the 21st Infantry to begin withdrawing to the main line of resistance. At 0600 hours on July 15 the 1st and 3rd battalions began their withdrawal. The 8th Rangers screened the movement, fought a successful delaying action, and covered the withdrawal. At 1500 hours the company arrived back at base camp. Ranger casualties were light, though close calls had been frequent. Jesse Cisneros carried two bullet holes in his soft cap. The Chinese were not as fortunate, suffering over eighty casualties.

On July 16 the 8th Rangers were preparing for another mission when Captain Eikenberry was summoned to a conference at G-3. When he returned at 1000 hours it was with the sad news that the Rangers were being inactivated.

During the first week of July, fifth-training-cycle companies underwent administrative processing. The word ''Airborne'' was added to the title of the Ranger Training Command.

Col. John G. Van Houten gave his welcoming address to Rangers of the fifth cycle on Friday, July 6. He spoke of Ranger history and the Ranger mission. Van Houten no doubt suspected the end was near for his command, but he probably did not know that this would be the final training cycle.

On July 9 the first week of the fifth training cycle began, consisting of 9th, 15th, and A companies, with 7th as the demonstration company. Training featured individual tactical training, the M-1 rifle, mechanical training, and demolitions.

Engineer units of Fort Benning were building bridges for practice, and they had a difficult time completing the work. The Rangers had plastic explosive left over from demolition classes and were constantly searching for something new to practice on. The bridges became favorite targets. Ranger Ed Therens was supply sergeant of the 7th Rangers. Unlike most supply sergeants, Therens never had a shortage. With his supply clerk, Ranger Corbin, he prowled bivouac areas as soon as units pulled out. The material left behind made excellent trading items for whatever the 7th Rangers needed.

On July 12 Colonel Van Houten was informed that he had been nominated for promotion to brigadier general.

The second week of training was highlighted by day and night patrolling, communications, and night parachute jumps. In the third week, the Browning Automatic Rifle, mechanical training and firing, night vision, battlefield illumination, and platoon tactics were stressed. On July 24 thirty-six trainees were dropped from training and returned to former units.

On July 30 Colonel Van Houten was promoted to brigadier general. The fourth week of training for the fifth cycle stressed squad exercises, rubber boat crossings, and specialist training. Meanwhile, far across the Pacific Ocean, the 10th Ranger Company made history with the first Ranger parachute jump in Japan. The 10th had also created a minor international incident when they took a large carved wooden bear from in front of the city hall of Sapporo, Japan, and placed it in front of their company commander's tent.

Chapter 19

The opening of August 1951 saw the dissolution of the Ranger companies in Korea. By tradition, philosophy, and training, Rangers are designed to fight for victory. A man experiences too much in the process of becoming a Ranger to accept half measures or limited effort. In a war the United States and its allies decided not to win, there was no place for the spirit of the American Ranger.

Under the provisions of Eighth United States Army, Korea, General Order number 584, dated 25 July 1951, the 1st, 2nd, 3rd, 4th, 5th, and 8th Ranger companies were to be inactivated by the commanding generals of the various divisions to which they were attached. The inactivation would occur on 1 August 1951. Personnel rated and designated as parachutists were to be reassigned to the 187th Airborne Regimental Combat Team.

On August 3 a train carrying the 3rd and 4th Ranger companies left Inchon. At Yongdungpo it picked up the 5th and 8th Ranger companies, and that evening the train reached Pusan, where trucks took the men to the replacement company where 1st and 2nd Ranger companies were waiting. This was the first time that the Airborne Ranger companies who fought in Korea had ever been assembled. The men set about making the most of it.

Many men were frustrated and angry. All of them had volunteered for something special, had proved themselves on the field of battle, and were immensely proud of the effort they had put forth. But what the Chinese and North Koreans could not do, the Department of the Army was bringing to pass. The city of Pusan caught the brunt of the anger. Fences surrounding the

Rangers' compound were demolished and the party began. As night fell, the sky glowed red and there were sirens and shots, shouts and screams. The military police were distraught.

The next morning there was a formation. The companies were formed in a large square, and a lieutenant colonel with a Japanese Logistical Command patch on his shoulder began to harangue them with choice statements, referring to them as animals and wild men utterly lacking in discipline.

"Officers and gentlemen fighting with their fists!" shrilled the shocked staff officer. He was referring to an altercation between two Ranger captains. Captain Eikenberry had been one of the offenders. "I'd like to get *you* alone," Eikenberry snarled under his breath to the officer. The sun was hot, many men had hangovers, and many had decided to leave the Army at the earliest opportunity. The men in the ranks began to growl, and the formation was quickly dismissed.

The Rangers were taken out of Pusan in long open-bed trucks called cattle cars. The Rangers mooed as each truck pulled away. The men, standing packed like cattle, saluted the camp commander with the cry of, "Forty-eight, forty-nine, fifty—*some shit!*" and a sharp jab of the index finger.

All the sweat and effort and sacrifice; the close friendships formed under adversity; the love and pride of being a Ranger, of being part of the best that America had to offer, was being taken from the men. They were now officially known as *replacements.*[1]

Ranger companies continued to exist in Japan, Germany, and the United States, but information about the breakup was having its effect. Men felt betrayed. The 12th and 13th Rangers returned to their parent divisions—the 12th joining the 28th Division at Camp Atterbury, Indiana, and the 13th rejoining the 43rd Division at Camp Pickett, Virginia. The commanding general of the 43rd Division had promised the men of the 13th Rangers that they would receive home leave before the beginning of a maneuver named "Exercise Southern Pines." The general did not keep his word. A Ranger officer posted a sign-out sheet in the company area that was headed: ALL MEN GOING AWOL SIGN OUT HERE. Approximately seventy Rangers signed the absent-without-leave sheet and left for home. All the men returned in time for the exercise and willingly faced the commanding general's wrath through reduction in rank.

The two-star plate of the major general commanding the 43rd

Division disappeared from his automobile. Friends of the Rangers in other units made certain there were no replacement stars locally available. The plate remains a trophy of the 13th Ranger Company.

In Japan, the 11th Ranger Company jumped from C119 aircraft over Matsushima Air Base with the 40th Division. Showing their versatility, the 11th Rangers were also involved in amphibious training aboard the USS *Menard*. The Rangers saw Japanese beaches the hard way from August 13 to 20.

In Germany, on August 4, officers of the 1st Infantry Division claimed they had made aviation history when ten men of the 6th Rangers participated in a mass free-fall parachute jump from 1,900 feet altitude. The event was the climax to the Organization Day ceremonies for the 1st Infantry Division. Lt. Cecil Kidd led a stick composed of Cpl. Donald Traynor, Pvt. Williard V. Moore, Cpl. Walter E. Kimmel, and PFC Alfred F. Kelley. First Sgt. Joe Dye led the stick consisting of PFC Lawrence R. Brown, Cpl. Jesse E. McDonald, PFC Virgil R. Hill, and SFC Howard Griggs.

At Fort Benning the month opened with training featuring squad night-attacks and defense, platoon exercises, and stream crossing. At a retreat parade on August 7, Brigadier General Van Houten made his farewell remarks. Col. Wilbur Wilson assumed command of the Ranger Training Command (Airborne).

Twenty-four men were dropped from training and returned to their former units. Training in the last week of the fifth training cycle began on August 27 and consisted of three forty-hour tactical problems.

The Department of the Army recognized that there was a need for Ranger-trained individuals in divisional combat units. Therefore, the restructuring of the Ranger program would continue Ranger training, yet satisfy those who wanted Ranger units disbanded. The Ranger Training Command would be inactivated and reconstituted as the Ranger Department of the Infantry School. The Ranger Department would be responsible for continued study and training in Ranger doctrine, tactics, technique, and organization. Ranger courses would be established for infantry officers and NCOs assigned to infantry units.

On August 30 Col. Henry C. Learned, Jr. of the infantry

school staff was appointed president of a board to increase the efficiency of small-infantry-unit leaders and further the development of Ranger doctrine. Lieutenant Colonel Copley and Major Bond of the Ranger Training Command were appointed to the board.

Chapter 20

On 1 September 1951 the fifth and final Ranger training cycle ended. On September 4 the Rangers of B Company were transferred to A and 7th companies. Seventeen men were returned to their former units for failure to meet the standards of the Rangers. On September 8, at a ceremony on French Field, Lt. Ralph Puckett, Jr. received the Distinguished Service Cross and Lt. Robert Sanders the Silver Star. The Ranger companies at the command continued training while awaiting disposition instructions from Department of the Army. The companies served as honor guard for dignitaries visiting Fort Benning and turned in property.

September 10 was a day of celebration for the 6th Rangers. Captain "Sugar" Cain was promoted to major. In exercise after exercise the 6th Rangers had proven themselves a potent force, raising havoc in the rear areas. Their success at infiltration was only thwarted on one occasion, when they encountered guard dogs.

In Japan, by orders dated September 13, the 11th Ranger Company was directed to inactivate. The 10th Rangers received the same instruction.

On September 29 a Department of the Army message was received directing the inactivation of:

6th Ranger Infantry Company (Abn) in European Command
7th, 9th, and 15th Ranger Infantry companies (Abn) Fort Benning, Georgia

12th Ranger Infantry Company (Abn), Camp Atterbury, Indiana

13th Ranger Infantry Company (Abn), Camp Pickett, Virginia

14th Ranger Infantry Company (Abn), Camp Carson, Colorado

The final words of the diary of the Ranger Training Command read:

Ranger training will be continued as an adjunct of the Infantry School, Fort Benning, Georgia, under a Ranger Department, where selected individuals will receive a course of instruction in Ranger tactics and will return to their parent organization to serve as Ranger Instructors therein.

All things have their end. One by one the Ranger companies furled their guidons and departed from the rolls of the Army. Like the Rangers that proceeded them in history, they had accomplished much in the brief, bloody period allocated to them.

Chapter 21

Long after the Rangers had been disbanded, one small group remained in Korea. They were the Rangers who were prisoners of war.

The Department of the Army, in a message published 17 July 1984 for National POW/MIA Recognition Day, gave the following statistics:

In World War II, the United States had 130,201 of its service personnel captured or interned. Of that number, 14,072 died while prisoners. In Vietnam, 836 were captured or interned and 101 died while being held prisoner. During the Korean War, 7,140 men were captured or interned and 2,701 died while in Communist hands. The percentages show the ferocity with which Communists treated prisoners in Korea. Close to three of every seven Americans taken prisoner died in the camps.

Anthony "Luke" Lukasik and Lew Villa had been wounded at Chipyong-ni and had scarcely returned to the company at the time of the "May Massacre." William Rhatigan had recently come from the United States. Captured separately on 19 May 1951, the men would share the ordeal of twenty-eight months of captivity.

Villa was captured after trying to help wounded escape. Lukasik had reached the headquarters of the 1st Battalion, 38th Infantry, only to find it was in the hands of the Chinese. Lukasik and others were made to lay facedown in a ditch while the Chinese fired burp guns over their heads. He remembers thinking, "What a hell of a way to die." But someone yelled in Chinese and the firing stopped. An officer speaking fluent English told the men to get up, and said, "Welcome American soldiers, you have been liberated."

Villa was wearing a soft cap with parachute wings. He saw an officer going through the prisoners, carrying a book; from the rear Villa could see the book was *Identification of American Insignia*. He quickly removed his wings, scuffed a hole with his boot, and buried them.

The small group Lukasik was with was taken to a hillside where there were seventy-five to a hundred American prisoners, including officers, noncommissioned officers, and enlisted men. Many were wounded, and American dead lay sprawled about. Near Lukasik was a dead American. Shot through the face, he lay on his back, eyes open and staring at the sky. He had been stripped of his equipment. The Americans were confused and frightened, and men kept asking, "How could our intelligence have been so bad? How could so many Chinks be in front of our lines without our knowing about them?"

Soon Chinese guards began to herd the prisoners along the trail, forcing them to carry captured American weapons. One American was barefoot, his feet torn and bloody from walking on rocks. He kept walking, crying from his pain. As the prisoners crossed a small bridge, a Chinese column was coming from the opposite direction, and they used their rifle butts on the prisoners as they went past.

The men were astounded at the number of Chinese they saw. They could hear heavy firing behind them but had no way of knowing the Chinese attack was failing, though they knew the Chinese were paying a high price. Lew Villa remembers continuous columns of Chinese bearers bringing their wounded to the rear on bicycle litters.

After two or three days of forced march, the prisoner column, which by this time numbered 150 or more, was halted in front of a mine shaft, which the men were told to enter. The captives had to drop down through a hole in the earth to a platform, then down again to a lower level. Lukasik was near the front of the column, but on a hunch, stalled his entering the shaft, to remain closer to the entrance. Men were packed into the confined space.

The worst place was at the back of the tunnel; there the space narrowed and men were pressed together four abreast.

Men at the back of the mine soon began to suffocate. There was panic and calls to the Chinese that there was not sufficient air to breathe. An American officer tried to get the men to put their faces close to the ground and conserve air. Another officer crawled to the entrance to ask the Chinese to remove the men from the mine. He was beaten with rifle butts.

Some twelve to fourteen hours later the survivors were permitted to leave the mine shaft. Their lungs sucked in the fresh air, but they were quickly moving north again.

About ten P.M. a Chinese officer called out Lukasik and two others, and soon these three prisoners, escorted by the officer and three guards, were marched back toward the front. This gave the Americans hope that they would be released. The group passed large columns of Chinese troops, mule trains, and 2½-ton trucks pulling 105mm howitzers, all heading south. The American air force was dropping flares, trying to locate the enemy, but the bombs that followed fell wide of the trail.

Lukasik and his companions were taken to a cave that served as a Chinese command post. They could hear heavy fighting to the south. Exhausted, the Americans fell asleep. When they awoke, they were given a bowl of rice, their first food in over three days. The Chinese then force-marched them north again. Large numbers of Chinese were now heading north. Planes of the U.S. Air Force passed overhead again, but the column seemed to remain unnoticed.

Lukasik had learned a few Chinese phrases, so when the column halted in the darkness, he asked a soldier for a cigarette, and the Chinese handed one over. Lukasik then asked for a match. The Chinese lit the match and found himself looking into the face of an American. He began screaming with rage and had his burp gun up and ready to shoot when the guards stopped him. Thwarted, he vented his anger by dashing the cigarette from Lukasik's mouth and crushing it to the ground.

During the day the Chinese went to ground to escape the pummeling of American fighter-bombers. They were adept at concealment, hiding under trees and in caves. Their mules rested with their packs concealed nearby.

As night fell the forced march began again. Faint with thirst, Lukasik drank up several handfuls of water from a rice paddy, and within a few hours he was seized with cramps and dysentery. He soon stunk so badly from involuntary discharge that Chinese guards avoided him. Desperate, Lukasik ate ashes from the Chinese fires in the hope of stopping his sickness. Several days later a Chinese doctor gave him some pills that eased the dysentery.

The march continued and the men were now well inside North Korea. Their food consisted mainly of millet and sorghum, though Lukasik remembers some rice and, on one occasion, small pieces of meat the Chinese identified as dog.

One night Lukasik and three other prisoners and a Chinese guard were sent to pick up rice from a distribution point. En route they encountered a North Korean soldier. The Korean had his bayonet fixed and intended to kill the prisoners, but the Chinese soldier butt-stroked the Korean and knocked him down. The Chinese then shoved the muzzle of his weapon into the Korean's face and cooled his ardor.

There were other prisoners nearby, men with 2nd Division patches, but the two groups were not allowed to communicate, and 2nd Division men were not seen again. Russian soldiers manned rear-area anti-aircraft artillery positions; the Chinese called them "White Chinese," and Lukasik talked with one who could speak Polish.

Fourth Rangers Ward and McPherson had, by virtue of burying the map, probably saved their lives, but the Chinese suspected they were something more than strayed foot soldiers. The two men were taken to a Chinese headquarters and put in separate huts for interrogation.

An officer with a book of American insignia came by and began pointing at American unit patches. The men knew they could safely divulge assignment to the 1st Cavalry Division but must not admit to being paratroopers or Rangers. Chinese soldiers tied their ankles together then tied their hands behind their backs. A long rope was tied from their wrists and tossed up and over a beam. The Chinese officer approached Ward and asked, "What is your unit?"

Ward responded with his name, rank, and serial number, then added, "Anything else you want you will have to get on your own." Almost immediately the Chinese interrogators pulled on the rope, hauling Ward aloft by his hands tied behind his back. The pain was excruciating. A Chinese soldier jumped on Ward's back, almost tearing his arms from their sockets, while another began to use a club on the front of his body. After hanging in agony for some time, Ward was lowered to earth and again showed the insignia. He nodded toward the 1st Cavalry Division. The interrogation was over.

Ward and McPherson were then taken from their separate huts. Their hands were wired together and they were connected by a short rope, with a lead rope around each of their necks. Relays of Chinese guards began to run the men through the night. It was a grueling run. The Chinese guards enjoyed changing off, but the Americans were forced to continue northward through the night. In the morning they were stopped at a temporary Chinese camp where they endured a week of interrogation. Though McPherson was a master sergeant, he had come on patrol wearing a jacket without stripes. The Chinese believed he was an officer and kept him in a hole with a badly injured American Air Force pilot who had been shot down. Ward had torn off his stripes, but the outline still showed on his fatigues. He was placed in a hole with a Korean prisoner.

The interrogations continued. Thinking to embarrass the prisoners, the Chinese switched hole mates, placing Ward with the Air Force officer and McPherson with the Korean. Thus, by conversing with the officer, the two Americans were able to keep their stories similar. They were stood at attention for long periods while questioned, then moved again to another prison camp. This Ward remembers as a former Japanese camp. The land was thrice terraced, with buildings on the two higher terraces and a village on the lower level. Here Ward and McPherson met some of the 1st Rangers who shared their captivity.

The men discussed the possibility of escape. The Chinese guards walked a route that brought them face to face before they retraced their steps. When the guards were eyeball to eyeball there was a brief period when the men could go down the terrace wall. Patiently waiting for their chance, Rangers Ward, McPherson, Ramatowski of 1st Company, and three men of other units evaded the guards and escaped to open country.

Their joy at escape was short-lived. They were scarcely free when the monsoon rains began. Constant rains blotted out the sun and stars and turned every brook into a raging torrent. Land navigation was impossible. Through the endless rain they tried to work their way south. They were starving, and when they chanced upon a cornfield, they devoured everything, corn, husk, and stalk. Within half an hour they were wretchedly sick. At one point they came upon an isolated hut with only a Korean man and woman, who nervously fed them. Soaked and weary, they continued in the direction they thought was south. After several days they chanced upon what they thought was another isolated hut. Again nervous Koreans provided some food, but this time the hut was not isolated. There was a village out of sight around a hill, and while the Americans ate, the Koreans sent for the soldiers. The house was soon surrounded. At the end of their resources, the Americans were recaptured. Kept separate from the other prisoners, the men spent three weeks with their arms tied behind them at the elbows. Then they faced trial. The Chinese accused Sergeant Ward of being the escape leader and sentenced him to six months hard labor. The other men got three months each. They dug latrines, cleaned the death house, and picked vermin from the clothes of the dead.

In July 1951 the men were moved to another camp called "the pine camp," then on to a place near Pyongyang known as "the mining camp." This camp included a schoolhouse with a high wall around it. Close to four hundred men were packed inside these walls. One of them was Sgt. Norman A. Grimm, who had been captured in January. Grimm was a disease-ridden shadow of his former self. He told the newly arrived Rangers that Sgt. Reginald King had died in January. Rangers Spence, Lublinski, and Waters had been marched farther north.

The men slept on the floor without blankets. The death rate was about ten a day. The survivors would pile the dead in the hall to clear some space. Those who buried the dead were so weak they could barely scratch out a hole big enough to cover the corpse. Villa remembers that though they were young men, there was no talk of women. When men talked it was always about food.

Lukasik's legs swelled to twice their size. Some Rangers from 1st and 4th companies and some men from the 187th Airborne looked after him until the swelling went down. Several Rangers died here. In July Corporal Lutz of the 1st Rangers passed away. In August Sergeant Grimm died and was buried by his fellow Rangers. The Chinese fed the surviving prisoners some sorghum then put them to work on wood-chopping details.

Each day the prisoners were forced to listen to propaganda lectures. They were told they were stooges sent to Korea by capitalists to kill the peace-loving Chinese and Koreans. The Chinese executed an American soldier as a war criminal. Lukasik remembers the man's name as James Ellerson. Machine guns were posted at the four corners of the compound, but the camp did not have barbed wire. Only a flag and a ditch marked the outer limit, but the prisoners were too weak to escape. One Chinese officer laughed at the idea, saying, "How far do you think you would get with your blue eyes and big noses?" Other Chinese told the men, "The peace talks are in progress, any day the war will énd. You will soon go home. Why risk being killed in an escape?" The men lived ten to a hut, in space so confined that at night one could not turn over.

In the camps the heavy rains of the monsoon overflowed the latrines. The sorghum the men were fed was infested with worms. Their unwashed bodies crawled with lice, and each day began and ended with picking the lice from their rags. The camp was a breeding ground for disease, which struck with sudden swiftness. Some 180 men died before the epidemic of dysentery and fever ended.

Surrounded by death and despair, Lukasik wanted to live. He set himself a goal—he intended to make it home so that he could buy a brand new car, a fully equipped Chevrolet Bel Aire. He spent hours dreaming about every aspect of his vehicle-to-be. He was determined he would not die.

Villa and Rhatigan saw so many die that they could predict the hour of a fellow prisoner's death. All that could be done was to endure. On one occasion they saw a Chinese truck driver drive over a Chinese woman; the truck driver stopped, but only to check his load. The prisoners felt if the Chinese had so little regard for the lives of their own people, they obviously would not care about American lives.

The Chinese kept up a drumfire of propaganda about how lenient they were to prisoners of war. The prison camp was not identified so it could not be recognized from the air, and in September 1951 Air Force fighters bombed and strafed the compound. The Chinese propagandists saw this as heaven-sent ammunition for their cause. "You see," they cried. "Your own people are trying to kill you. Wall Street and the capitalists want you prisoners of war killed. They don't want you to return home where you can tell the American people about the imperialists and the atrocities committed by them.''

Soon a Chinese officer announced that due to the American air strikes, the prisoners would be moved to a safer camp. The men were told to gather up their belongings (a spoon and the rags they wore) and prepare for the move. The wounded and those too sick to move were left behind. The Chinese said these men would be moved by truck to the new camp. The Rangers and the men of the 187th Airborne assisted each other so that none of them would be left behind.

The column of scarecrows stumbled their way up the mountain trail for over an hour before the first rest was called. As the men stopped, they heard the sound of machine-gun fire coming from the camp. None of those who had been left behind rejoined their comrades.

A march north began, which Lukasik said lasted forty-six days and Villa estimated at 350 miles. Of the approximately four hundred men who began the trek, less then three hundred would see its end. The new camp was called ''Camp Number One'' and was located on the Yalu River approximately fifty miles northeast of Sinuiju, near a place the guards called Chongsong. The prisoners who were here were dressed in blue Chinese uniforms and looked healthy.

It was November. Lukasik and his companions were issued blue uniforms, given toothpaste and a bar of soap, and taken to the Yalu River. After six months in the same filthy rags, the men were granted a river bath and a change of clothes. Next came a haircut, and following that, a long harangue about how well the Chinese treated their prisoners.

Camp Number One was a permanent prisoner of war camp with about 1,500 prisoners. The hillsides surrounding the camp showed a large number of gravesites, one of which was the grave of PFC John W. Spence. Food was better at Camp Number One. The men received rice, turnips, potatoes, and one ounce of sugar a week. Some men were suffering from night blindness. They could see in the daytime but at night had complete loss of vision.

The camp had collaborators, call ''opportunists,'' who acted as spies for the Chinese and would sell out a fellow American for a cigarette. On one occasion the prisoners talked about forming an association of POWs. This information was promptly passed to the Chinese, who considered it a threat. The American soldier they accused of fostering the idea was locked in a shed, in solitary confinement with only a small hole to peer out of, for over two years.

The Chinese would talk some prisoners into writing letters or making tapes favorable to the Chinese cause. Shortly thereafter they would publish pamphlets and distribute them throughout the camp, telling all the man said. On one occasion the Chinese asked all the men to sign a paper saying the United States used germ warfare. When the prisoners refused, they were forced to stand at attention on a freezing parade field for hours. Still they refused. Finally a Chinese officer told them: "You may stand here as long as you like and freeze, or you may return to your hut. If you return to your hut, we will consider it your admission that the United States uses germ warfare." The men stood for a while then decided since they had signed nothing, there was little to be gained by freezing to death, so they returned to the huts.

One morning two prisoners began to make the sounds and motions of playing an imaginary game of Ping-Pong. Soon other prisoners gathered to watch and follow the game avidly. Chinese guards came and were obviously made uncomfortable by what they didn't see. Then the prisoners began to invent many imaginary things. There was a corral, where horses were available for riding. Many men had imaginary pets and took great care to train their dogs and cats. Finally, when the Chinese could take it no longer, they issued orders that nothing imaginary was permitted.

Each morning the prisoners would stand in formation in the snow while the Chinese propagandists lectured them. One day the prisoners seemed to function as one. Without a word they simply broke formation and returned to their huts. After that the lecture formations were discontinued. Each hut had an English-speaking Chinese monitor. There were mandatory readings of Chinese newspapers and the *Daily Worker*. When the readings were concluded, questioning began to determine if the daily lesson had been learned. Those who were recalcitrant were placed in crude wooden boxes or cages called "dog cages." These were designed so that a man could not sit or stand and was in a constant cramped position. Some men spent months in these cages.

American officers in the camp were eventually moved to another location. Lukasik and the other noncommissioned officers were moved into their huts, but about a month later all NCOs were put on trucks and moved to another camp, Camp Number Four.

There were constant lectures on the theory and practice of communism. The prisoners were required to learn and sing the Chinese national anthem. They were required to unload barges from the Yalu River and carry telephone poles. Marching to and from the details, the prisoners would sing:

> We'll take that flag down from the pole
> and shove it up Joe Stalin's hole.
> The working class can kiss our ass
> 'cause we got the foreman's job at last.
> If I die on the Russian front
> box me up with a Russian cunt.

In April 1953 the sick and wounded were removed from the camp; later the prisoners learned these men had been exchanged. A month or two afterward the Chinese commander gave a speech about the failure of American air power. He said American pilots dared not fly above the 38th parallel because the Chinese controlled the land and sky. Just then a flight of American jets flew over the camp, so low that the men could see the pilots' faces. The Chinese ran for cover while the Americans raced into the open to cheer. A pilot waggled his wings in recognition then rejoined his formation to blow to smithereens a Chinese ammunition dump and hydroelectric dam on the nearby Yalu. When the mission was completed, the American fighters returned and each did a victory roll over the camp while the prisoners cheered. The Chinese were so furious that the prisoners were denied rations for two days. The destruction of the dam meant the loss of electricity, but the prisoners did not mind.

Tom Ward of the 4th Rangers, who had learned the foundry business from his father and grandfather, alerted his fellow prisoners to look for scraps of aluminum. He created a small foundry in the camp, making knife handles, bowls, and even tobacco pipes.[1]

One day in August 1953 the prisoners were lined up in front

of movie cameras. The Chinese announcer said the war was over and the men were going home. Lukasik and his friends put their hands over their faces to spoil the pictures. After a ride on trucks, the prisoners were given some canned beef and placed forty men to a boxcar for the train ride south.

Unloaded at Kaesong, the men could see the American lines, with tanks and trucks bearing the white star. On the morning of 3 September 1953 the men were strip-searched, then loaded onto trucks and, at approximately ten A.M., were exchanged.

The Rangers of the Korean War known to have been captured, and their fates, are:

PFC John W. Spence .... Dead
Cpl. George Lublinski .... Taken by Russians
SFC Earl L. Dansberry .... Dead
Sgt. Edmund J. Dubreuil .... Returned
Sgt. Martin R. Watson .... Returned
Cpl. Eunis G. Waters .... Dead
Cpl. William H. Rhatigan .... Returned
Cpl. Alexander Ramatowski .... Returned
PFC John Lutz .... Dead
Sgt. Charles E. Rollins .... Returned
Sgt. Lewis J. Villa... Returned
Sgt. Norman A. Grim.. Dead
Sgt. Frank King, Jr. .... Dead
Sgt. Anthony J. Lukasik .... Returned
SFC Lester V. McPherson .... Returned
Capt. Charles L. Carrier .... Dead
Sgt. Thomas A. Ward.. Returned

Epilogue

The Korean War was very small to history, but very large to the men who fought it. Coming so soon after World War II, it did not arouse a patriotic fervor in the American people. Only a small percentage of families had men at the front. It was as rough and dirty a war as has ever been fought—an infantry mountain war in a merciless climate against an enemy with a reputation for brutality—but it was not a national war, not a war with popular support.

Throughout history, it has always been a small percentage of men who have stepped forward to set the example, to lead the way. At no other time in American history was the volunteer spirit better expressed than in the Rangers of the Korean War, who were volunteers for the Army, the Airborne, the Rangers, and repeatedly for combat. They were a disciplined band on duty. They worked hard and, in their brief times of relaxation, played in the same fashion. They were young men in superb physical condition, preparing for a life-and-death struggle. In the spring of their lives they gave their all.

Approximately one of every nine Rangers who served in Korea died there.

The men who fought in Korea came home to apathy and lived with it for many years. On return from war to the small town of my birth, I entered a clothing store where my family had often shopped. The clerk looked up in surprise. "Hello, Bob," he said pleasantly. "I haven't seen you around for a while. Have you been out of town?"

The returning soldier found little interest in his war experience. Ours is a Western culture. It is one thing to say you were wounded at the crossing of the Rhine, but tell a man you were shot in the guts at the battle of Sangdok-ni, and he is more likely to laugh then commiserate.

Later, returning from Vietnam, I, like others, was cursed and reviled by those who stayed behind in the States. It wasn't pleasant, but at least we had their attention. To come home and be ignored, to have people look through you, was the welcome of the Korean War veteran. There were no parades, there was no victory. The politicians claimed the nation did what it set out to do, but the men knew that if such were the case, we would have stopped at the 38th parallel on the first drive north. The line infantry knew that in the summer of 1951 the Chinese were beaten. The Yalu River as a boundary and the reunification of the Korean people was a worthy and obtainable goal. To "die for a tie" in the middle of Korea, as men did from the fall of 1951 to the summer of 1953, was not.

Thus the Korean War veteran was left with nothing to brag about and no one to listen. Years later, Rangers who fought in Korea would compare notes. The commonalities were that most men had been divorced and had bleeding piles. There was something more for the Rangers, however—a knowledge that we had chosen the high, hard path of the volunteer. We did all we could to stand for our nation, we went beyond the call of duty. That knowledge, that experience, and the remembrance of those who died, is ours. It is our keepsake, and is more precious than any parades and speeches.

As they were inactivated, the Rangers became the forgotten men of the forgotten war. They built a wide variety of careers. Fourteen became general officers, and dozens became colonels and senior noncommissioned officers. They became ministers, carpenters, business executives, and coal miners—but they always remained Rangers.

Thirty years after the war, in the autumn of their lives, the Rangers of the Korean War began to search each other out, to reestablish the bonds of their youth. Again the volunteer spirit made for success.

There is something special about the Rangers. They are uniquely American. They have always been a small band of brothers, their methods best described by the motto born in

battle in World War II, "Rangers lead the way." Through forests, plains, and mountains, from Atlantic to Pacific, in Europe
and Asia, this uniquely American brotherhood of the brave has
fulfilled that motto. It is my belief that even when the American
army goes out to the stars, the Rangers will lead the way.

Appendix A

Table of Organization and Equipment

TABLE OF ORGANIZATION
AND EQUIPMENT
No. 7–87

DEPARTMENT OF THE ARMY
WASHINGTON 25, D.C., *17 October 1950*

RANGER INFANTRY COMPANY (AIRBORNE) (TENTATIVE)

SECTION I

GENERAL

1. Mission.—To infiltrate through enemy lines and attack command posts, artillery, tank parks, and key communications centers or facilities.

2. Assignment.—Attached to Infantry Division, T/O & E 7N.

3. Capabilities.—*a.* Infiltrating through enemy lines and destroying hostile installations.

b. Repelling enemy assault by fire, close combat, or counterattack.

c. Maneuvering in all types of terrain and climatic conditions.

d. Seizing and holding terrain.

e. Conducting reconnaissance and intelligence operations by penetration of hostile combat zone.

f. Landing by parachute, glider, or assault aircraft.

g. The reduced strength column adapts this T/O & E to the lesser requirements for personnel and equipment during prolonged noncombat periods and for a limited period of combat.

h. Without augmentation column, company must be attached to another unit for administration, mess, supply, and organizational maintenance.

i. With augmentation column, company can operate separately for short periods of time.

223

T/O & E 7–87

RANGER INFANTRY COMPANY (AIRBORNE)

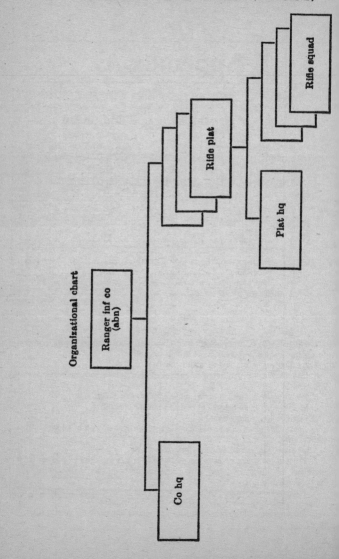

T/O & E 7–87

RANGER INFANTRY COMPANY (AIRBORNE)

Section II
ORGANIZATION

Designation: † .... Ranger Infantry Company (Airborne)

1	2	3	4	5	6	7	8	8a	9	10
Unit	Specification serial No.	Total company	Total reduced strength company	Company headquarters	3 ranger platoons (each)			Enlisted cadre	Augmentation	Remarks
					Platoon headquarters	3 ranger squads (each)	Total platoon			
Captain, company commander	31542	(1)	(1)	1						† Insert number of company.
Lieutenant, company commander				(1)						* Also as driver, truck, light. Augmentation not included in totals. Augmentation may be authorized by Department of the Army when required.
Executive	31542	4	3	(1)						
Platoon leader	31542	(3)	(3)		(1)		(1)		2	
Total commissioned		5	4	2	1		1			
First sergeant	31745	1	1	1				1		
Master sergeant	31745	(3)	(3)		(1)		(1)	3		
Platoon		10	10		1	1	3	(1)		
Sergeant, first class	31542	(1)	(1)	(*1)				(1)	2	
Communication chief	30824								(1)	
Mess steward	32745									
Squad leader	30821	(9)	(9)		(1)	(1)	(3)	(9)	2	
Supply										
Sergeant	32215	36	36		4	4	12			
Assistant squad leader	30060	(9)	(9)		(1)	(1)	(3)		(2)	
Cook, first	32745									
Leader, automatic weapon	32745	(27)	28	1	(3)	(3)	(6)		3	
Corporal	30630	37	28	1		4	12		(2)	
Clerk, company administrative	30060	(1)	(1)	(1)						
Cook, second	30057									
Medical aidman	34745	(27)	(27)	(*1)	(4)	(4)	(12)			
Rifleman		13	9				4			
Private, first class	30637	(36)	(9)	(*1)						
Medical aidman	34745									
Messenger	34746									
Rifleman	34746	(9)	(9)		(1)	(1)	(3)			
Total enlisted		100	87	4	2	10	32	14	7	
Total commissioned		5	4	2	1		1			
Aggregate		105	91	6	3	10	33	14	7	

T/O & E 7–87

RANGER INFANTRY COMPANY (AIRBORNE)

Recapitulation of SSN

((a)=company; (b)=reduced strength company)

Officer SSN	Total SSN		Grade			
			Capt		Lt	
	(a)	(b)	(a)	(b)	(a)	(b)
31542	5	4	1	1	4	3
Total	5	4	1	1	4	3

Enlisted SSN	Total SSN		Grade									
			E–7		E–6		E–5		E–4		E–3	
	(a)	(b)	(a)	(b)	(a)	(b)	(a)	(b)	(a)	(b)	(a)	(b)
30657	4	1							1	1	3	
31542	1	1			1	1						
31745	4	4	4	4								
32745	45	45			9	9	36	36				
34745	46	36							36	27	10	9
Total	100	87	4	4	10	10	36	36	37	28	13	9

Section III

EQUIPMENT

. GENERAL

1. This table is in accordance with AR 310–30, SR 310–30–1, and SR 310–30–4, and is the authority to requisition in accordance with pertinent Department of the Army directives, and for the issue of all items of equipment listed herein unless otherwise indicated.

2. For the purpose of supply planning, when there appears to be a discrepancy between the allowances shown in Section III, Equipment, total column and the "Basis of distribution and remarks" column, the amount shown in the total column will govern.

3. This unit is designated a category 1 unit (par 16, SR 310–30–4).

4. Items of clothing and equipment, components of sets and kits, spare parts, accessories, special equipment, special tools, and allowances of expendable items as contained in the following publications are authorized so far as they pertain to the allowances for the organization and individuals covered by this table:

Air Force.

USAF Supply Manual, AFM 67–1.

USAF Supply Catalogs.

Chemical Corps.

Department of the Army Supply Catalogs CML 1, 2, 3–1, 5–1, 6, 7, 8, and 9.

T/A 3–100, Allowances of Chemical Corps Expendable Supplies.

T/O & E 7-87

RANGER INFANTRY COMPANY (AIRBORNE)

Corps of Engineers.
 Department of the Army Supply Catalogs ENG 1, 3, 6, 7, 8, and 9.
 T/A 5-101, Allowances of Corps of Engineer Expendable Supplies (when published).
Army Medical Service.
 T/A 8-100, Allowances of Medical Expendable Supplies.
 Armed Services Catalog of Medical Matériel.
Ordnance Corps.
 Department of the Army Supply Catalog, Ordnance Section (see ORD 1, Introduction and Index).
 T/A 23, Targets and Target Equipment.
Quartermaster Corps.
 T/A 21, Clothing and Equipment.
 T/A 10-100, Allowances of Quartermaster Expendable Supplies.
 T/A 10-100-12, Allowances of Insect and Rodent Control Supplies.
 Department of the Army Supply Catalogs QM 1, 3-1, 3-2, 3-3, 3-4, 5, 6, 7, and 8.
 AR 30-2290, Sale of Quartermaster Property and Services.
Signal Corps.
 Department of the Army Supply Catalogs SIG 1, 3, 5, 6, 7 and 8, 7-8-10, and 10.
 T/A 11-101 (7-87), Allowances of Signal Corps Expendable Supplies for Ranger Infantry Company (Airborne) (when published).
AR 310-90, Military Publications—Distribution of Department of the Army Publications.
AR 775-10, Qualification in Arms and Ammunition Training Allowances.
 5. The abbreviations used herein are in accordance with AR 320-50, SR 320-50-1, and SR 310-30-4.
 6. Allowance breakdowns other than totals are shown as guides.
 7. Items of equipment authorized herein are the latest adopted type standard articles. Priorities of issue, issue of substitute items pending availability of later models, or in lieu thereof until exhausted, are established and authorized by current supply directives.
 8. Allowances of equipment shown in section III may be reduced by higher headquarters when the assigned mission of this organization indicates such equipment to be in excess of actual requirements.
 9. See SR 700-50-200 and SR 700-50-10 for supply responsibilities and procedures.

RANGER INFANTRY COMPANY (AIRBORNE)

Section III—Continued
EQUIPMENT—Continued

Major or key items of equipment are indicated by capital letters

1	2	3	4	5	6	7	8	9	10
Service and Item No.	Item	Total company	Total reduced strength company	Company headquarters	Platoon headquarters	3 squads (each)	Total platoon	Augmentation (not included in totals)	Basis of distribution and remarks
	CHEMICAL								
3-1	Mask, gas, M9	105	91	9	3	10	33	7	1 per indiv.
	ENGINEER								
5-1	Compass, lensatic, luminous dial, induction damped, 5 degree and 20 mil graduations, with case.	27	13	3	2	2	8		1 per off; 1st sgt; plat sgt; squad ldr and asst sqd ldrs.
5-2	Lamp, electric, portable, command post	1	1						1 per tent, CP.
5-3	Marker, luminous, radioactive, 1 inch disk	24	24			24			
5-4	Metascope, Type US/F	4	4	1	1		1		1 per 6 sniperscopes or MFCT.
5-5	Ruck, battery, charging, SS	4	4	1	1		1		
5-6	Sniperscope, M-2	4	4	1	1		1		
	MEDICAL								
8-1	Medical Kit, Individual	4	1	1	1				1 per EM (30657).
8-2	Splint set, folding splints	3	1	1					

RANGER INFANTRY COMPANY (AIRBORNE)

ORDNANCE

Line No.	Item	Allowance	Basis of issue
9-1	Bag, ammunition, M2A1	6	2 per rifle, 57-mm.
9-2	Bayonet, M1, w/scabbard, M7	27	1 per indiv armed w/rifle (SNL B-8).
9-3	Bayonet-knife, M4, with scabbard, M8A1	63	1 per indiv not armed w/rifle (SNL B-8).
9-4	Binocular, M17A1	13	1 per off; m sgt (31745); sfc (32745); sgt, asst squad ldr (32745) (SNL F-238).
9-5	CARBINE, CAL .30, M2	46	
9-6	Chain, tow, ⁵⁄₁₆" x 16 ft.	1	1 per trk, 2½-ton OS (SNL J-17).
9-7	Demolition equipment, set No. 5, individual	18	SNL R-7.
	GUN:		
9-8	MACHINE, CAL .30, BROWNING, M1919A6	3	SNL A-6.
9-9	SUBMACHINE, CAL .45, M3A1	36	SNL A-58.
9-10	Launcher, grenade, cal .30, M7A1	18	SNL B-39.
9-11	LAUNCHER, ROCKET, 3.5-IN, M20	9	SNL B-42.
9-12	MORTAR, 60-MM, M19, ON MOUNT M5, W/E&S.	9	SNL A-43.
	Mount, tripod, machine gun, cal .30:		
9-13	M2	3	1 per MG, cal .30 (SNL A-6).
9-14	M1917A1	3	1 per rifle, 57-mm (SNL A-5).
	RIFLE:		
9-15	57-MM, M18	3	SNL C-73.
9-16	AUTOMATIC, CAL .30, BROWNING, M1918A2	18	SNL A-4.
9-17	U.S., CAL .30, M1	37 (or 23)	SNL B-21.
	TRAILER:		
9-18	¼-TON, 2W, CARGO	2	SNL G-529.
9-19	1-TON, 2W, CARGO	1	SNL G-518.
	TRUCK:		
9-20	¼-TON, 4 x 4, UTILITY, M38	2	SNL G-740.
9-21	2½-TON, 6 x 6, CARGO, W/WN	1	SNL G-508.
9-22	Watch, wrist, 7 or more jewel	20 (or 23)	MBI to any of the fol when required: EM (31745, 32745, 33745, 30824) or MBI to any of the fol add when required: off WAB TOC. (SNL F-36).

T/O & E 7–87

RANGER INFANTRY COMPANY (AIRBORNE)

Service and Item No.	Item	Total company	Total reduced strength company	Company headquarters	Platoon headquarters	3 squads (each)	Total platoon	Augmentation (not included in totals)	Basis of distribution and remarks
	QUARTERMASTER								
10–1	Attachment, packboard, plywood, cargo	36	36			4	12		2 per packboard.
10–2	Axe, handled, chopping, single bit, standard grade, weight 4-lb	3	1	3					1 per trk.
10–3	Bag, canvas, water, sterilizing, porous, complete with suspension ropes and cover	1	1	1					1 per 100 indiv or MFCT.
10–4	Carrying, ammunition	54	54	1		6	18		
10–5	Bucket, general purpose, metal, galvanized, heavy weight, without lip, 14-qt. cap.	1	1	1					1 per SMG; launcher, grenade.
10–6	Burner, oil, stove, tent, M–1941	1	1	1					1 per stove, tent, M1941 WAB ZI army comd or TOC.
	Can:								
	Corrugated, nesting, galvanized with cover:								
10–7	10-gal							1	
10–8	16-gal							1	
10–9	24-gal							5	
10–10	32-gal							1	1 per set of range, fld, M1937; heater, immersion type.
10–11	Water, 5-gal	21	11	21				1	1 per 5 indiv or MFCT.
10–12	Carrier, wire cutter, M–1938	9	9	9				1	1 per cutter, wire, M1938.
10–13	Case, canvas, dispatch	1	1	1					
10–14	Chair, folding	1	1	1					
10–15	Clock, alarm	1	1	1				2	
10–16	Container, food, insulated, M–1944	3	2	3				1	
10–17	Cutter, wire, M–1938	9	9	9					

RANGER INFANTRY COMPANY (AIRBORNE)

No.	Article						Basis of distribution and remarks
10-18	Desk, field: (Empty) fiber, company	1	1	1		1	
10-19	M-1945						
10-20	Drum, inflammable liquid, gasoline, steel, with carrying handle, cap 5-gal.	4 or 5	2 or 3	4 or 5		1 (or 1)	1 per trk, ¼-ton; set of range, fld, M1937; 2 per trk, 2¼-ton. — or — 1 add per burner, oil, stove, tent, M1041, when burner is auth.
10-21	Flag, guidon, bunting	1	1	1		1	
10-22	Fly, tent, wall, large, complete (with pins and poles)	6	3	6		1	1 per set of range, fld, M1937.
10-23	Goggles, M-1944	6	3	6			
10-24	Heater, immersion type, for can corrugated	2	1	2		4	2 per trk.
10-25	Kit, barber, with case	2	1	2			
10-26	Lantern, gasoline, leaded fuel	18	18	18			4 per set of range, fld, M1937. WAB ZI army comd or TOC.
10-27	Mask, face, launcher, rocket	19	19	19	2	6	2 per launcher, rocket.
10-28	Mattock, pick, with handle, weight 5-lb.	19	18	19			
10-29	Outfit, cooking, 1 burner	36	36	36	2	6	1 per trk, 2¼-ton.
10-30	Packboard, aluminum	1	1	1	2	6	2 per squad.
10-31	Pad, shoulder	1	1	1	4	12	2 per packboard.
10-32	Paulin, canvas, large	1	1	1			
10-33	Range, field, M-1937, 3-unit	1	1	1		1	1 per trk,
10-34	Safe, field, combination-lock	1	1	1			
10-35	Screen, latrine, complete (with-pins-and-poles)	1	1	1			
10-36	Shovel, general purpose, D-handled, strap back, round point, No. 2.	3	1	3			
10-37	Stove, tent, M-1941	1	1	1		1	1 per tent, CP WAB ZI army comd or TOC.
10-38	Strap, quick release, packboard	54	54	54		3	3 per packboard.
10-39	Table, camp, folding	1	1	1			
10-40	Tent, command post, M-1945, complete (with pins and poles).	1	1	1			
10-41	Tube, flexible nozzle	3	2	3		1	1 per trk; set of range, fld, M1937.
10-42	Typewriter, portable, with carrying case.	2	2	2		1	
10-43	Whistle, thunderer	1	1	1		1	1 per 1st sgt; mess steward.

RANGER INFANTRY COMPANY (AIRBORNE)

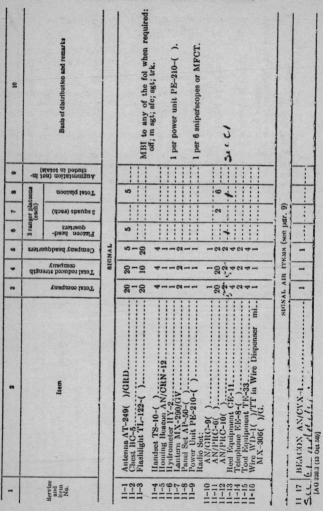

1 — Service and item No.	2 — Item	3 — Total company	4 — Total reduced strength company	5 — Company headquarters	6 — Platoon head-quarters	7 — 3 squads (each)	8 — Total platoon	9 — Augmentation (not included in totals)	10 — Basis of distribution and remarks
	SIGNAL								
11–1	Antenna AT-249( )/GRD	20	20	5	5		5		MBI to any of the fol when required: off; m sgt; sfc; sgt; trk.
11–2	Chest BC-5-( )	1	1	1					
11–3	Flashlight TL-122-( )	20	10	20					
11–4	Handset TS-10-( )	4	4	4					
11–5	Homing Beacon AN/CRN-12	1	1	1					
11–6	Hydrometer HY-2	1	1	1					
11–7	Lantern MX-290/GV	2	2	2	1	2			
11–8	Panel Set AP-50-( )	1	1	1					
11–9	Power Unit PE-210-( )	1	1	1					1 per power unit PE-210-( ).
	Radio Set:								1 per 6 sniperscopes or MFCT.
11–10	AN/GRC-9( )	1	1	1					
11–11	AN/PRC-6( )	20	20	2	2		6		
11–12	AN/PRC-10( )	4		2	4	1			
11–13	Reel Equipment CE-11	4		4					
11–14	Telephone EE-8-( )	2		2	2		4		
11–15	Tool Equipment TE-33	4		4					
11–16	Wire WD-1( )/TT in Wire Dispenser mi MX-306( )/G.	1		1					

	SIGNAL AIR ITEMS (see par. 9)								
11–17	BEACON AN/CVN-1	1	1	1					

T/O & E 7-
*C 2

RANGER INFANTRY COMPANY (AIRBORNE)
(TENTATIVE)

CHANGES ⎫   DEPARTMENT OF THE ARMY
No. 2 ⎭   WASHINGTON 25, D. C., *8 February 1951*

T/O & E 7–87, 17 October 1950, is changed as follows:

To determine authorizations for equipment, Section II, Organization, of these changes, and Section III, Equipment, of the table, correspond as follows:

    Column 7, section II of these changes, corresponds with column 3, section III of the table.

    Column 8, section II of these changes, corresponds with column 4, section III of the table.

    Paragraph numbers in column 1, section II of these changes, correspond with numbered columns in section III of the table.

[AG 320.3 (8 Feb 51)]

    BY ORDER OF THE SECRETARY OF THE ARMY:

OFFICIAL: J. LAWTON COLLINS
    EDWARD F. WITSELL   *Chief of Staff, United States Army*
    Major General, USA
    The Adjutant General

DISTRIBUTION:
    As requested on DA AGO Form 12.

---

*These changes supersede section II, T/O & E 7–87, 17 October 1950.

T/O&E 7-87

SECTION II - ORGANIZATION

DESIGNATION: ...... RANGER INFANTRY COMPANY (AIRBORNE)

INDEX / PARA LINE	DESIGNATION	MOS CODE	FULL STRENGTH	REDUCED STRENGTH	GEN	COL	LT COL	MAJ	CAPT	LT	WO	E-7 MSGT	E-6 SFC	E-5 SGT	E-4 CPL	E-3 PFC	E-2 PVT	ENLISTED CADRE	AGG
	SRC 07 087-0 00-		1															4	
05	**COMPANY HEADQUARTERS**																		
01	COMPANY COMMANDER O1N	31542	1	1					1										1
02	EXECUTIVE COMMANDER O1N	31542	1	1						1									1
03	FIRST SERGEANT E	31745	1	1								1							1
04	COMM CHIEF E	31542	1	1															
05	COMPANY AIDMAN E	32645	1																
06	MESSENGER E	34745	1													1			
			6	4														3	
06	**3 PLATOON HEADQUARTERS**																		
01	PLATOON LEADER O1N	31542	3	3						1									
02	PLATOON SERGEANT E	31745	3	3								3		3				3	
03	COMPANY AIDMAN E	33666	3																3
			9	6															
07	**9 RANGER SQUADS**																		
01	SQUAD LEADER E	31745	9	9									9					9	6
02	ASST SQUAD LEADER E	31745	9	9										27					9
03	LT WEAPONS LEADER E	31745	27	27											36	9		6	
04	LT WPNS INFMAN E	34745	45	36								4		41	36	10		9	
	TOTALS		105	91						4	1							14	40
	SRC 07 087-0 02-		1																
09	**AUGMENTATION**																		
01	MESS STEWARD																		
02	SUPPLY SERGEANT E	31816	1									1							
03	COOK E	31810	1									1			2				
04	COOPERS MGT CLERK E	33620	1																
05	SECOND COOK E	33R60	7																

T/O&E 7-87

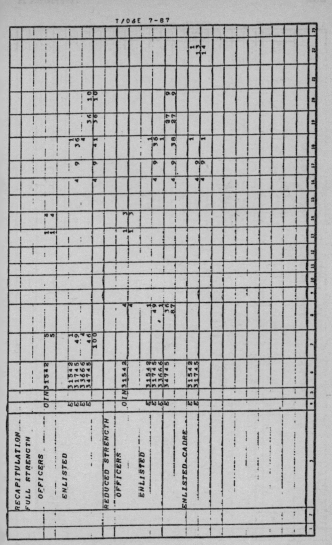

T/O&E 7-87

REMARKS

CADRE AUTHORIZATION OF A SPECIFIC
GRADE AND MOS CODE WILL BE REDUCED
IN TOTAL AND THAT LINE SHOWN IN
REDUCED STRENGTH COLUMN

FOR ENLISTED MOS CODES AND JOB
SPECIFICATIONS SEE SR 615-25-15

FOR ENLISTED CAREER FIELD CLASSIFI-
CATION INSTRUCTIONS SEE SR 615-25-20

01 ALSO LIGHT TRUCK DRIVER
40 AUGMENTATION NOT INCLUDED IN TOTALS -
   MAY BE AUTHORIZED BY DEPARTMENT OF
   THE ARMY WHEN REQUIRED

STANDARD REQUIREMENTS CODES -SRC-
FOR SINGLE SQUADS - PLATOONS-ETC
APPLY TO PARAGRAPHS LISTED BELOW
   PAR 06 SRC 07 087- 0 01-06
   PAR 07 SRC 07 087- 0 01-07

Appendix B

Insignia

At 1900 hours, Tuesday, 10 October 1950, the Department of Defense released a story titled "Army Ranger Infantry Companies, Planned to Be Integral in Army Infantry Divisions, Was Announced Today by the Department of the Army." In terse sentences the plans for the rebirth of the Rangers was revealed. The final paragraph demonstrated that the Army was aware of recent Ranger history and wished to continue the tradition. The paragraph ran: "Ranger Companies now being organized will be authorized to wear the shoulder insignia and otherwise continue the tradition of the Ranger outfits of World War II."

The red, white, and black scroll of the Rangers of World War II was highly respected, and the young men reporting for Ranger training were avid to win and wear the scroll. Plans came to a sudden stop, however, when a Washington-based staff officer discovered that the famous World War II insignia of the Rangers had never been authorized, and that another insignia, little known and less preferred, was what the Army had approved.

The story goes back to the year 1942, when Maj. William O. Darby, commanding officer of the 1st Ranger Infantry Battalion, sought a shoulder insignia worthy of his unit. He announced a contest, with an award of twenty-five dollars for the best design. A member of the Battalion Headquarters Company, Sgt. Anthony Rada of Flint, Michigan, won the prize with a design that featured an arc or scroll with a black background, red trim, and the inscription 1ST RANGER BATTALION in white letters. The shape was based on the "commando arc" and demonstrated the close bond between the Rangers and commandos.

Why the colors black, red, and white were chosen is unknown, but some early reporters thought the black was actually dark blue and the colors of our flag had been selected. The Rangers, however, were insistent the color was black. One former Ranger said the colors were taken from the Nazi flag and were a calculated insult to Hitler. They intended to jam them down the Germans' throats. The 1st, 3rd, and 4th Ranger battalions were proud of their scroll and wore it whenever permitted. They tried to get it approved, but the wheels of bureaucracy turned too slowly and approval did not come through.

On 1 April 1943 at Camp Forrest, Tennessee, the 2nd Ranger Battalion was activated. On 16 July 1943 the War Department's Services of Supply Headquarters published memorandum SPRMD 421.4 (19 June 43), the subject of which was, "Distinctive shoulder patch." The memorandum stated that by order of the Secretary of War, all Ranger battalions in existence or in the future would wear a diamond-shaped blue patch bearing the word "Rangers" in gold-colored letters. The patch was to be also edged in gold. The blue diamond insignia met with disfavor. It resembled the gasoline sign of a blue Sunoco station, and when men wore the patch, other soldiers referred to them as "Gas Troopers." This resulted in frequent fistfights.

When the 2nd and 5th battalions arrived in Europe, they began to wear the unauthorized insignia of the 1st, 3rd, and 4th battalions, adding only their distinguishing number. The 5th Ranger Battalion "liberated" a large number of German marks from a German paymaster, and with these they employed a group of nuns to make their scrolls.

When the 6th Ranger Battalion was formed in the Pacific, it too adopted the red, white, and black scroll designed by Anthony Rada. All the Ranger battalions of World War II wore the scroll, even though it was not authorized.

In 1947 the Army abolished the diamond-shaped insignia, leaving nothing approved for the Rangers. (No Ranger units were then on the Army rolls.) When, in 1950, the need for

Ranger insignia returned, there was no approved insignia to turn to. In the eyes of those who were volunteering, the scroll was the oldest Ranger shoulder insignia and had the approval of the men.

Sometime around 19 September 1950 Colonel Van Houten made a visit to the Pentagon to discuss Ranger insignia with a representative of G-1. Van Houten did not like the diamond-shaped patch—he wanted an arc-type tab. Van Houten was equally opposed to an individual "unit" designation; he sought to build pride in being part of the Ranger family, rather than in being in an individual company. An arc tab was finally agreed upon, but G-1 wanted only a tab that said "Ranger." Van Houten felt that as Airborne was a separate qualification, there should be a tab for each. He specifically desired an insignia with the word "Ranger" in white letters on a black background with red border. Most important to Van Houten was that the approved insignia be ready for issue to the first class of graduating Rangers on 13 November 1950.

The insignia design was done on a rush basis, and on October 30 the Department of the Army, G-1, informed Colonel Van Houten that the approved Ranger arc would be 2 3/8 inches wide and half an inch thick; the base color would be black with a yellow border and yellow lettering (later changed to gold). The word "Airborne" would also be authorized for wear.

The insignia did not find favor with the initial Ranger companies of the Korean War. Orders were that the black and gold Ranger tab would be worn above the division insignia of the division to which the company was attached. Even before the first companies had departed from Fort Benning, the shops of Columbus were selling a red, white, and black scroll that showed the company number and the word "Airborne."

Those companies that served with divisions in the U.S. or that were under close watch by the inspector general wore the black and gold tab over the division (or Army) insignia while on duty. Those in Korea wore the black and gold Ranger tab stitched on their soft caps, but the scroll insignia was procured when men went on leave to Japan and worn on the shoulder.

The colors were not always consistent. The 1st Ranger Company sported a black and gold Airborne Ranger scroll. By the time the units were inactivated, red, white, and black with the company number was the norm. This insignia proliferated when the men were transferred to the 187th Airborne Regimental Combat Team at Beppu, Japan, and men could show their "combat" insignia on their right shoulder.

The red, white, and black scroll was now standard for those Rangers who served in Korea and those elsewhere who could get away with wearing an unauthorized patch. The Japanese merchants made an additional change. They frequently found themselves with a large stock of patches with one company number on it, and out of stock on the number the customer desired. The Japanese resolved this by removing the company number and inserting "INF." Thus the patch read "Airborne Ranger Infantry Company."

Many men who served as Rangers during the Korean War looked upon the black and gold Ranger tab as a qualification badge—a demonstration that they had graduated from a particular form of training—rather then as a unit insignia. The Army reinforced this view when the Ranger Department was formed on 10 October 1951. Army regulations of 23 January 1953 announced the tab, and in its 1965 Army regulation 672-5-1 instructed: ". . . the Ranger tab is a qualification shoulder sleeve insignia, therefore it is not authorized for wear on the right shoulder." Most Rangers who served in Korea wore their red, white, and black scrolls on their right shoulders in defiance of the inspector general. Later, in Vietnam, Rangers would once again wear the red, white, and black scroll.

In 1983 the Ranger veterans of the Korean War began a movement to win official recognition of this traditional Ranger insignia. The Rangers on active duty requested the change be made, and in 1984, and with the formation of a Ranger regiment, the traditional insignia of the Rangers finally became authorized.

Two Ranger companies designed their own insignia. The 7th Ranger Company, while commanded by Captain Eikenberry, designed an oval shoulder patch which featured a parachute badge with a skull centered above crossed bones. At the tip of each of the lower edge of the bones was a die, one showing five spots, the other two spots. The outline of the insignia and the dice, the skull, and crossed bones were in black. The parachute wings, faces of dice, and features of the skull were gray. The background of the patch was gold.

Ranger Thomas Boundurant of the 14th Ranger Company designed a metal unit-crest that consisted of a parachute with a diamond in the center containing the number 14. The diamond was flanked by a lion and unicorn. A scroll near the base of the parachute contained the words "Poison Ivy" (the 14th was attached to the 4th [IV] Infantry Division).

Neither of these company insignia were authorized, and both were short-lived.

Appendix C

Weapons Used by Korean War Rangers

The basic weapons of the ten-man Ranger squad were 4 carbines, 4 M-1 rifles, and 2 Browning Automatic Rifles. Other weapons were available as needed. In combat, men often carried the weapon of their choice. In some circumstances 12-gauge shotguns were used.

Automatic Pistol, .45-Caliber M1911 and M1911 A1 (Ref. Field Manual 23–35)

Known as "The Equalizer" or simply "The 45," this weapon was a recoil-operated, magazine-fed, self-loading hand weapon. The overall length of the pistol was 8.593 inches. The weight of the pistol with magazine was 2.437 pounds. The approximate weight of the loaded magazine with seven rounds was 0.481 pounds. At twenty-five yards, the velocity of the round was 788 feet-per-second with a striking energy of 317 foot-pounds. At twenty-five yards the round would penetrate 6.0 inches of white pine.

.30-Caliber Carbine M-1 and M-2 (Ref. Field Manual 23–7)

The Carbine was a magazine-fed, air-cooled, gas-operated shoulder weapon. Most Rangers carried the M-2 version which could be fired automatically or semiautomatically and used the thirty-round magazine. The weight of the weapon with thirty-round magazine loaded was 6.60 pounds. The cyclic rate of fire on full automatic was 750 to 775 rounds per minute. The weapon had a muzzle velocity of 1,970 feet-per-second. The maximum effective range was listed as 300 yards, but few men would trust the carbine beyond 100 yards.

.30-Caliber Rifle, M-1 (Ref. Field Manual 23–5)
The M-1 was a gas-operated, semiautomatic, self-feeding shoulder weapon weighing 9.5 pounds. A clip of ammunition contained eight rounds. Clips were carried in the cartridge belt and bandoliers. The bayonet weighed one pound. The M-1 had a reputation for reliability.

Browning Automatic Rifle, .30-Caliber M1918A2 (Ref. Field Manual 23–15)
The "BAR" was a gas-operated, air-cooled, magazine-fed shoulder weapon weighing approximately twenty-one pounds without the sling. The magazine contained twenty rounds and weighed one pound seven ounces when full. The weapon fired on slow cyclic rate of approximately 350 rounds or a normal cyclic rate of 550 rounds per minute. The BAR was a heavy brute, subject to frequent jamming. When operating smoothing, it was devastating.

.45-Caliber Submachine Gun M3A1 (Field Manual 23–41)
This was commonly known as the "Grease Gun" from its resemblance to the mechanics' implement. Weighing 10.25 pounds with full magazine, this weapon was an air-cooled, magazine-fed, blowback-operated shoulder weapon. This weapon was sometimes carried by medical-aid men who wanted more protection than their armband.

Crew-Served Weapons

These weapons were pooled at company level and drawn as needed for particular missions. A Ranger company was authorized nine 3.5-inch rocket launchers, nine 60mm mortars, three .30-caliber machine guns, and three 57mm recoilless rifles.

3.5-Inch Rocket Launcher (Ref. Field Manual 23–32)
The launcher was a two-piece, open-tube, smoothbore weapon. When assembled, it measured sixty inches long and weighed thirteen pounds. It fired a high-explosive antitank rocket weigh-

ing nine pounds at a muzzle velocity of approximately 334 feet-per-second. Maximum range was listed at 900 yards, but most antitank actions with the weapon occurred at much shorter ranges.

57mm rifle, M-18 (Ref. Field Manual 23–80)

This air-cooled recoilless rifle could be fired from the shoulder or from a machine-gun tripod. The breech block was manually operated and accepted single-loaded, fixed ammunition. Direct sights were used. The rifle length was 61.60 inches, and its weight with sight and integral mount was 44.40 pounds. The muzzle velocity was 1,200 feet-per-second, and the approximate maximum range was 4.800 yards.

60mm mortar, M-19 (Ref. Field Manual 23–85)

A smoothbore, muzzle-loaded, high-angle-of-fire weapon, the mortar (barrel) was normally used in conjunction with a bipod and base plate and had an overall weight of 45.2 pounds. Maximum rate of fire was thirty rounds-per-minute with a sustained rate of eighteen rounds-per-minute. Maximum range with high-explosive ammunition was 2,000 yards.

.30-Caliber Browning Machine Gun HB M1919A4 (Ref. Field Manual 23–45)

This air-cooled, recoil-operated weapon was fed from woven fabric belts that would hold 150 rounds. The weapon was usually mounted on a light machine-gun tripod M-2. The weight of the gun with tripod was 42.25 pounds. It fired an M-2 ball cartridge with a muzzle velocity of 2,700 feet-per-second. The cyclic rate of fire was 400 to 550 rounds-per-minute, the maximum usable rate of fire 150 rounds-per-minute.

Appendix D

The Rangers Who Gave Their Lives
During the Korean War

Died in Training
Cader A. Bryson, Jack R. Durant, Donald S. Humphrey, Lewis R. Seibert, John J. Daniels, Frederick A. Fuhst, Henry Ayotte, Francis J. Lee, Ronald E. Sullivan

Killed or Missing in Action or Died of Wounds
John Alvis, Tito Angarano, Alexandea D. Arick, Virgil Bach, Harry B. Bagnell, Charles M. Bailey, Issac E. Baker, Charles D. Barcak, Lucien J. Borque, Richard A. Brown, Carroll Broyles, Charley C. Bunch, Robert L. Byerly, Charles L. Carrier, Charles L. Casey, Romeo Castonguay, Howard Chivvis, Wilbert W. Clanton, Owen L. Claycomb, Roy M. Clifton, James F. Clopton, Ralph L. Coufal, Bernard Cummings, James O. Dance, Earl L. Dansbury, Edward J. Durney, Terry Eads, George R. Early, John F. Eddy, Roy B. Evans, James J. Foley, Harrison M. Fraser, Nicholas R. Gallo, Lonnie Garrett, Richard H. Glover, Paul J. Gotney, William J. Graddy, Richard P. Geer, Joe C. Green, Norman A. Grimm, Richard F. Groth, Robert L. Grubb, Carl V. Halcumb, George L. Hall, Glenn M. Hall, Horace Harding, Mayo Heath, Alfred H. Herman, Roger E. Hittle, J. T. Holley, Milton Johnson, Teddy C. Johnson, James E. Jones, Robert N. Jones, Edward J. Keeler, Robert Kettlewell, Frank King, Jr., Reginald W. King, William Kirshfield, John H. Knigge, Sumner J. Kubinak, Fred M. Lang, Jr., Joseph R. Lauzon, Robert P. Laydon, Gordon P. Lewis, Arthur Ligon, Paul J. Lotti, Gilbert Lovato, George Lublinski, Librado Luna, John Lutz, Mackey McKinnon, Walter Madden, Fredrick

Manship, Robert L. Mastin, Walter J. Maziarz, Jr., Edmund Mekhitarian, William T. Miles, John Mitchell, Francisco Misseri, Harry Miyata, Wesley Mohagen, Manuel Moyeda, Jack Murphy, William J. Murphy, Frank A. Nicholson, Ernest G. Nowlin, James Oakley, Micholas O'Brovac, Jerome L. O'Leary, Timothy Ontayabbi, Louis Oulich, Billy L. Parker, James Petteress, Jr., John Pointeck, Jr., Donn F. Porter, Herman L. Rembert, Alvin M. Rhodes, Harold L. Rinard, Herbert E. Robertson, Amon G. Rogers, Joe C. Romero, John D. St. Onge, Robert St. Thomas, Charles D. Scott, Homer I. Simpson, George W. Smith, George G. Smudski, Paul E. Snavely, Jr., John W. Spence, Robert Stewart, Ralph W. Sutton, Alvin R. Tadlock, George Tatarakis, Wayman L. Thomas, Howard S. Thompson, Harry C. Trout, Jr., William G. Vandunk, Antonio Velo, Cecil T. Vesy, Alphard R. Vismor, Eunis G. Waters, William H. Weyland, Donald H. White, Jimmie M. White, William White, Lawrence J. Williams, Ronald C. Wolfe, John W. Wray, Frances E. Young

Appendix E

Korean War Ranger Awards

Distinguished Service Cross
Glenn M. Hall
Romeo Castonguay
Robert L. Mastin
Ralph Puckett, Jr.

Silver Star
Warren E. Allen
Dorsey B. Anderson
Raymond E. Baker
Harold L. Barber
Alfred M. Bukaty
William H. Cole
Norman H. Collins
Curtis E. Courts
Barnard Cummings, Jr.*
John K. Diliberto
James E. Freeman
John D. Girolimo
Michael D. Healy
John A. Jones, Jr.
James E. Kelleher
William Kirshfield*
Fred M. Lang, Jr.*
Walter J. Maziarz, Jr.
Garland McAbee
William R. Miles
Harland F. Morrissey

James Petteress, Jr.
David L. Pollock
Edward Posey
Edward W. Pucel
James C. Queen
George Rankins
John C. Scagnelli
Robert J. Scully
Orvie J. Sharp
Jesse M. Tidwell
Billy G. Walls
Martin R. Watson

Bronze Star Medal (Heroic Achievement)

Andrew J. Adams
Edward D. Adams
Anthony J. Andrade
Gene H. Bigelow
Robert W. Black
Lucien J. Borque*
Harry H. Cagley
James J. Carbonel
James D. Chapman
Wilbert W. Clanton*
Albert Cliette
Earle E. Cronin
Howard K. Davis
James H. Fields, Jr.
Culver V. Gibson
Peter Hamilton, Jr.
William Hargrove
Alfred H. Herman II
Mobert Higginbotham
Roger E. Hittle
Robert N. Jones*
Sumner J. Kubinak*
Librado Luna*
Robert R. Masovcevich
Cleaven McBride
Mackey D. McKinnon*
Harry Y. Miyata*

Michael G. Moriarity
Ernest G. Nowlin*
Ray Pierce
Bernard B. Pryor
Eugene C. Rivera
Joe C. Romero*
Berkeley J. Strong
Stewart W. Strothers
Alvin R. Tadlock*
William E. Thomas
Harry C. Trout*
Thomas M. Uldall
John R. Ulery
Pierre R. Vaporis
Antonio Velo*
Joseph Wells

*Posthumous award

Appendix F

Consolidated History

Eighth Army Ranger Company (8213th Army Unit)
Activated, 24 August 1950. Parent unit, none (TD Unit). Attached to 25th Infantry Division. Campaigns: U.N. defensive, U.N. offensive, CCF intervention, first U.N. counteroffensive. Awards: Korean Presidential Unit Citation, Combat Infantry Streamer. Inactivated 28 March 1951.

Headquarters Detachment 3440 ASU (Ranger Training Center/Command)
Fort Benning, Georgia. Activated 28 October 1950. Inactivated 15 November 1951.

1st Ranger Infantry Company (Airborne)
Activated, 28 October 1950. Parent Unit, Company A 1st Ranger Battalion. Attached to 2nd Infantry Division. Campaigns: CCF intervention, first U.N. counteroffensive, CCF spring offensive, U.N. summer-fall offensive. Awards: Presidential Unit Citation, Hongchon. Presidential Unit Citation, Chipyong-ni. Combat Infantry Streamer. Inactivated, Korea, 1 August 1951.

2nd Ranger Infantry Company (Airborne)
Activated, 28 October 1950. Parent unit, Company A 2nd Ranger Battalion. Attached to 7th Infantry Division. Campaigns: CCF intervention, first U.N. counteroffensive, CCF spring offensive, U.N. summer-fall offensive. Awards: Korean Presidential Unit Citation, Combat Infantry Streamer. Inactivated, Korea, 1 August 1951.

3rd Ranger Infantry Company (Airborne)

Activated, 28 October 1950. Parent unit, Company A 3rd Ranger Battalion. Attached to 3rd Infantry Division. Campaigns: first U.N. counteroffensive, CCF spring offensive, U.N. summer-fall offensive. Awards: Korean Presidential Unit Citation, Combat Infantry Streamer. Inactivated, Korea, 1 August 1951.

4th Ranger Infantry Company (Airborne)

Activated, 28 October 1950. Parent unit, Company A 4th Ranger Battalion. Attached to 1st Cavalry Division. Campaigns: CCF intervention, first U.N. counteroffensive, CCF spring offensive, U.N. summer-fall offensive. Awards: Korean Presidential Unit Citation, Combat Infantry Streamer. Inactivated, Korea, 1 August 1951.

5th Ranger Infantry Company (Airborne)

Activated, 20 November 1950. Parent unit, Company B 1st Ranger Battalion. Attached to 25th Infantry Division. Campaigns: first U.N. counteroffensive, CCF spring offensive, U.N. summer-fall offensive. Awards: Korean Presidential Unit Citation, Combat Infantry Streamer. Inactivated, Korea, 1 August 1951.

6th Ranger Infantry Company (Airborne)

Activated, 20 November 1950. Parent unit, Company B 2nd Ranger Battalion. Attached to 1st Infantry Division. Inactivated, Germany, 1 December 1951.

7th Ranger Infantry Company (Airborne)

Activated, 20 November 1950. Parent unit, Company B 3rd Ranger Battalion. Assigned to 3rd U.S. Army. Inactivated, Fort Benning, Georgia, 5 November 1951.

8th Ranger Infantry Company (Airborne)

Activated, 20 November 1950. Parent unit, Company B 4th Ranger Battalion. Attached to 24th Infantry Division. Campaigns: first U.N. counteroffensive, CCF spring offensive, U.N. summer-fall offensive. Awards: Korean Presidential Unit Citation, Combat Infantry Streamer. Inactivated, Korea, 1 August 1951.

9th Ranger Infantry Company (Airborne)—first cycle
Activated, 5 January 1951. Parent unit, Company E 2nd
Ranger Battalion. On completion of training, company was
disbanded and used as replacements for Ranger companies
in Far East Command.

9th Ranger Infantry Company (Airborne)—second cycle
Parent Unit, Company E 2nd Ranger Battalion. Attached to
31st Infantry Division. Inactivated, Fort Benning, Georgia,
5 November 1951.

10th Ranger Infantry Company (Airborne)
Activated, 5 January 1951. Parent unit, Company F 2nd
Ranger Battalion. Attached to 45th Infantry Division. Inac-
tivated, Japan, 15 September 1951.

11th Ranger Infantry Company (Airborne)
Activated, 5 January 1951. Parent unit, Company C 3rd
Ranger Battalion. Attached to 40th Infantry Division. Inac-
tivated, Japan, 21 September 1951.

12th Ranger Infantry Company (Airborne)
Activated, 1 February 1951. Parent unit, Company D 3rd
Ranger Battalion. Attached to 28th Infantry Division. Inac-
tivated, Camp Atterbury, Indiana, 27 October 1951.

13th Ranger Infantry Company (Airborne)
Activated, 1 February 1951. Parent unit, Company E 3rd
Ranger Battalion. Attached to 43rd Infantry Division. Inac-
tivated, Camp Pickett, Virginia, 15 October 1951.

14th Ranger Infantry Company (Airborne)
Activated, 27 February 1951. Parent unit, Company C 2nd
Ranger Battalion. Attached to 4th Infantry Division. Inacti-
vated, Camp Carson, Colorado, 27 October 1951.

15th Ranger Infantry Company (Airborne)
Activated, 27 February 1951. Parent unit, Company D 2nd
Ranger Battalion. Attached to 47th Infantry Division. Inac-
tivated, Fort Benning, Georgia, 5 November 1951.

Headquarters Detachment (Trainees) and Ranger Trainee Companies A and B

Activated, HQ DET (Trainees) organized 5 January 1951, changed to Trainee Company A and B 17 April 1951. Activated, 22 April 1951. Parent unit, none (Table of Distribution Units). Trainee Company B inactivated, Fort Benning, Georgia, 4 October 1951. Company A inactivated, Fort Benning, Georgia, 5 November 1951.

Appendix G

Those Who Served

Note: Many Rangers served in more than one company. Where known they are listed in all companies they served with.

Eighth Army Ranger Company

LAST NAME	FIRST NAME	MIDDLE INITIAL
ALBRECHT	CHARLES	J
ANDERSON	JESSE	E
ARNSTRONG	JOHN	N
AUTEN	EDGAR	W
BALDWIN	CHARLES	I
BARDSLEY	JOHN	G
BEARDEN	BOBBY	R
BEATTY	JAMES	D
BEAUREGARD	RNARD	F
BELL	FRANCIS	
BELL	ROBERT	H
BENT	CHARLES	K
BESSONEN	EARL	W
BLUE	KENNETH	L
BOLGRIN	FLOYD	E
BORQUE	LUCIEN	J
BRANHAM	RICHARD	D
BRANKO	GEGICH	
BRANSON	WILLIAM	M
BRENNAN	EUGENE	B JR
BRISTER	BERYLE	D

BRUZ	RICHARD	G
BROWN	DONALD	H
BUNN	CHARLES	N
CAGLEY	HOWARD	H
CASNER	MERRILL	S
CASSATT	ELMER	H
CATINO	EDMUND	
CHARETTE	PETER	E
CHILDERS	DONALD	D
CIAMBRONE	JOSEPH	A
CLANTON	WILBERT	E
CLARK	CHARLES	C
CLARK	CLAUDE	D
COLEMAN	ALFRED	L
COMBS	FRANKLIN	D
CONTRARES	RANDOLPH	
CORSETTE	ROBERT	A
COSTELLO	JOSEPH	S
CRESON	ROBERT	
CROMER	RALPH	
CRONIN	EARL	
CROWE	GORDON	M
CRISPINO	FRED	
COUFAL	RALPH	L
CUMMINGS	BERNARD	
CURTIS	CHARLES	H
CUTSHAW	ROBERT	JR
DANIELS	GLENN	W
DELIBERTO	JOHN	K
DIXON	EDGAR	
DODD	GERALD	R
DONAHUE	KENNETH	A
DOYLE	EARL	W
DUNN	JOHNNIE	
DURUM	SIDNEY	L
DZURCANIN	JOHN	
FAULKENBERRY	ROBERT	E
FAZENBAKER	ELVON	
FIGLER	JOHN	C
FINNIE	NELSON	E
FLUMMER	RALPH	

FOX	JAMES	L
FRACCULA	ANTHONY	R
FRAZIER	OWEN	M
GASKILL	CALLIAS	E
GEGICH	BRANKO	
GODDARD	NORMAN	
GROVES	RAYMOND	
GUSTAFSON	ROLF	
HACKLER	JOHN	P III
HAUGHT	ROBERT	G
HESS	RAYMOND	H
HICKERSON	MORRIS	L
HIGGINS	GRADY	D
HITTLE	ROGER	E
HOFFMAN	RANTER	L
HONEYCUTT	HAROLD	F
HORSLAND	MELVIN	L
HUNT	VIRGIL	P
JARDINE	JERRY	D
JAROSKY	CHESTER	M
JENKINS	FRANK	J
JEWELL	THEODORE	P
JOHNSON	GRAYDON	W
JOHNSON	LEONARD	F
JONES	IVAN	B
JONES	ROBERT	E
JONES	ROY	V
JUDY	WILLIAM	L
KAAPUNI	CLARENCE	R
KALISH	MIKE	
KEMMER	WILLIAM	R
KILPATRICK	CHARLES	L
KIMBALL	CHARLES	C
KIMURA	HARUTUKU	S
KLEIN	LAVERNE	H
KNUDSEN	WILLIAM	K
KOCH	VERNON	S
KOHLBECKER	JAMES	R
KOONCE	JAMES	L
KORN	FRANK	E
KUBINAK	SUMMER	J

IAEA	SHERMIAH	K
IRWIN	LOUIS	G
LAGRAND	DALLAS	
LANDERS	BILLY	S
LANIER	JAMES	C
LAUDERMAN	GLEN	R
LAUZON	JOSEPH	R
LEE	PAUL	E
LEWIS	JOSEPH	
LILLARD	PAUL	
LORBECK	EUGENE	D
LOUDNER	CLIFFORD	
LUNA	LIBRADO	
MANNING	BERNARD	
MATTISON	DARIUS	C
MAX	WILLIAM	E
MAY	LEROY	N
MCGEE	JOHN	H
MCKINNON	MACKEY	
METCALF	GLEN	W
MIKEZ	GEORGE	G
MITCHELL	JOHN	
MITCHUM	THOMAS	L
MIYAIA	HARRY	Y
MOON	JAMES	W
MORRISSEY	HARLAND	
MURPHY	WILLIAM	J
NORBURY	MICHAEL	A
NOWLIN	ERNEST	G
O'BROVAC	MICHOLAS	
OLSON	HARVEY	S
O'NEILL	TERRY	E
PAPLACZYK	STANLEY	L
PARKER	BILLY	L
PATTERSON	BALDO	A
PATTERSON	WILBUR	
PETERSON	BRUCE	A
PITTS	CHARLES	L
POLLOCK	DAVID	L
PUCKETT	RALPH	
PUNTSAKUS	DIMITREE	

REVELS	GEINON	
ROBINSON	BERNARD	J
ROBINSON	JOHN	E
ROCCO	RICHARD	
ROMERO	JOE	C
ROSS	CHARLES	G
RUSSELL	FRED	W
SALAS	CARLOS	J
SARAMA	ROBERT	
SAVIO	AUGUST	
SHELLY	RAY	V
SHIGIEMOTO	HAROLD	T
SIMPSON	MERLE	W
SINCLAIR	JOHN	R
SKERKOWSKI	WILLIAM	L
SLIGHTER	VERNE	A
SMATHERS	JOHN	M
SMITH	ALEXANDER	
STRACHER	RICHARD	D
STEELE	CANNON	R
STEWART	BILLY	M
STEWART	JAMES	L
STILES	DICK	M
STRICKER	JAMES	
SUMMERS	JOHN	A
SWEIGART	DONALD	G
SYLVA	EDMUND	K
SZARUGA	MARTIN	P
TABATA	SADAMU	
TADLOCK	ALVIN	R
TAYLOR	EVERETT	R
TAYLOR	LEON	
TERRY	O'NEILL	E
THOMSON	JOSEPH	L
TINGLE	LEONARD	E
TIDWELL	CLYDE	
ULERY	JOHN	R
VANCE	EDWARD	
VANN	JOHN	P
VAPORIS	PIERRE	R

VICKROY	MARVIN	K
WALLS	BILLY	G
WARREN	KENNETH	
WATERS	ALLEN	JR
WEIBEL	WILLIAM	U
WEINBERG	THOMAS	H
WELLS	CHARLES	L
WHITE	LEROY	
WHITE	WILBUR	
WHITE	WILLIAM	
WIGGINS	EARL	
WILKINSON	JOHN	
WINTERS	HARRY	M
WILLIAMS	IRVING	L
WILLIAMS	JOHNNY	C
WORMAN	BILL	E
WRIGHT	CHARLES	

Ranger Training Center/Command

ADAMS	JAMES	Y
ANORGA	JOE	
BAKER	THOMAS	V
BECK	EARL	P
BELFORD	WARREN	C
BISSONNETTE	AIME	J
BLACKBURN	CLYDE	B
BRENNAN	THOMAS	S
BRENTLEY	HAROLD	R
BRIGGS	EDWIN	
BROWN	LEROY	C
BULWINKLE	ALFRED	L
CHACOS	JAMES	M
COKER	HORTON	S
CONDON	JOHN	J
CONGER	WILLIAM	E
COPLEY	LEWIS	D
COPPING	CHARLES	G
COULTER	JACK	W
CROOK	WILBURN	
DAWSON	FRANCIS	W

DAY	LESLIE	H
DELGADO	PAUL	
DOQUEMIN	GORDON	J
FOSHEE	RUDOLPH	P
FRIEND	HOWARD	W
GAINOR	CHARLIE	W
GALLAGHER	DANIEL	P
GARDNER	GEORGE	M
GOODPASTURE	JOHN	R
GRAHAM	JOHN	
GRAY	ROBERT	W
GRIFFIN	MARVIN	
HABICHT	MICHAEL	
HAMER	JOHN	A
HAMRICK	PAUL	
HANCOCK	FRANK	J
HARRINGTON	JAMES	R
HARRIS	WILLIAM	
HARVEY	JOHN	H
HEARD	JOHN	C
HENDEE	DON	C
HIBDON	JAMES	E
HIGGINS	DAVID	D
HILL	ALFRED	
HODNETT	JOHLIAM	J
HOLLEY	HORACE	E
HUGHES	WILLIAM	W
IVEY	GEORGE	
JONES	RAY	E
JUNG	GORDON	C
KELLY	JAMES	
KILKUSKIE	THEODORE	
KINNEY	WILLIAM	J
KOEPCKE	HENRY	
KOON	CHARLES	E
KRIEGER	HENRY	
KUHN	CHARLES	
LAMBERT	LUCIEN	
LEE	JOHN	A
LESLIE	BEN	

MACKEY	WILLIAM	
MARSHALL	OSCAR	E
MASKEW	JACK	
MATTEO	CHARLIE	
MEEK	CHARLES	A
MOCK	JAMES	W
MONSARRAT	GEORGE	
MOON	MORRIS	P
MOORE	HILTON	E
MORROW	JESSE	L
MOXLEY	LUCIUS	C
NEVSETA	RONALD	G
OSTEEN	JOHN	L JR
PARNELL	GEORGE	A
PAZANOWSKI	BERNARD	
POOLE	ELVERTT	E
RAZE	DALTON	D
SANDERS	ROBERT	C
SAVAGE	ROY	C
SCHUSTER	EDWARD	A
SEAMAN	WILLIAM	
SHAHAN	VERNON	
SHIPMAN	CLARENCE	
SINGLAUB	JOHN	K
SMITH	GEORGE	
SNYDER	JACK	A
STREET	JACK	B
STUART	ROBERT	M
TASSEY	GEORGE	
TAYLOR	DAVID	
THOMPSON	MARTIN	W
ULIASZ	JOHN	I
VAN HOUTEN	JOHN	G
WALKER	EDWIN	A
WEAVER	LAURY	K
WELSH	REDMOND	B
WHITE	WALTER	JR
WHITEHEAD	CHARLIE	
WILHELMSON	LARRY	A
WILSON	WILBUR	

| WOOD | JOHN | S |
| ZIMMERMAN | HERMAN | |

1st Ranger Infantry Company (Airborne)

ADAMS	ANDREW	J
ADAMS	WILBUR	L
ADKINSON	HAROLD	P
ANGLIN	JOHN	P
ARAGON	CARKOS	
ARKELL	LYLE	J
AVERY	JOHN	C
BACH	VIRGIL	
BAGNELL	HARRY	
BAILEY	CHARLES	M
BAKER	EARL	RAY
BARCROFT	CURTIS	L JR
BAXLEY	MARCUS	L
BAYNE	ROBERT	D
BEDDINGFIELD	TRUMAN	
BLACK	CHARLES	J JR
BLACKMON	EARL	G
BODROGHY	ROBERT	F
BORLLOU	ROLAND	A
BORUSIEWICZ	STANLEY	
BOWDEN	JOSEPH	
BOWEN	WILLIAM	J III
BRADY	WILMONTE	A
BRAMONTE	SEBASTIANO	N
BRIGHTWELL	ROBERT	H
BRILLA	THOMAS	J
BRUCE	NELSON	E
BUCKELEW	ALVIN	H
BUCKLES	HOMER	L
BUKATY	ALFRED	M
BUNCH	CHARLES	
BURDETT	JAMES	
BURGESS	HERSHELL	L
BURTON	JAMES	F
BURNS	PAUL	F
BYERLY	ROBERT	L
CANON	EARL	

CARPENTER	JAMES	E
CARRIER	CHARLES	L
CARROLL	JOSEPH	B JR
CARVELL	RICHARD	F
CASHMAN	RICHARD	J
CASTONGUAY	ROMEO	
CLIFTON	JAMES	H
CLOPTON	JAMES	
COFFEY	ROY	E
COLBERT	CLEATUS	L
COLE	GAIL	R
COLE	WILLIAM	H
COLEMAN	JAMES	N
CORRAL	IGNACIO	B
COSMAN	EARL	R
COJDIK	JOSEPH	D
DAHL	GLENN	L
DAILEY	JOHN	D
DANCE	JAMES	
DANSBERRY	EARL	
DAVIS	HOWARD	K
DELFINE	NICK	
DEVERY	JAMES	J JR
DEWITT	HOWARD	H JR
DOBBIE	WALLACE	P
DOBBSON	JAMES	H
DOBSON	ALBERT	L
DOUGHERTY	WENDELL	N
DUBREUIL	EDMUND	J
EARLY	GEORGE	R
EDDY	WALTER	E
EVANS	DONALD	E
EVANS	JOHN	H JR
EVANS	ROY	
FENLEY	STEVEN	G
FIORI	CHARLES	
FOLEY	GERALD	F
FOLEY	JOHN	F
FOSTER	CHARLES	E
FOTI	JOHN	G
FRASER	HARRISON	M

FULLER	ROBERT	N
GALEY	JAMES	D
GARSIDE	LORRIN	
GEER	RICHARD	P
GEER	ROBERT	
GILLAND	RICHARD	B
GIROLMO	JOHN	D
GLASKOX	WILLIAM	B JR
GOODWIN	RUFUS	L
GOYEN	MARK	
GRADDY	WILLIAM	J
GREEN	JAMES	
GRIM	NORMAN	A
GRUBB	ROBERT	L
HALCUMB	CARL	V
HALL	GLENN	M
HARDING	HORACE	A
HAYDEN	ERNEST	J
HEATH	MAYO	S
HEEDT	FRED	W
HERMAN	ALFRED	H
IMPERIAL	JOSEPH	L
JENKINS	MORRIS	H
JONES	EVAN	E
JUDKINS	JOHN	A
KETTLEWELL	ROBERT	
KING	REGINALD	
KINSLSEY	CHARLES	F JR
KLOKE	HARLYNN	H
KNIGGE	JOHN	H
LAFONTAINE	JOSEPH	R
LANG	ALLEN	
LAVALLEY	ROBERT	P
LAYDON	ROBERT	P
LEWIS	GORDON	P
LISI	JOSEPH	P
LOCKIE	CHARLES	G
LOTTI	PAUL	J
LUBLINSKI	GEORGE	
LUKASIK	ANTHONY	
LUTZ	JOHN	W

MADDEN	WALTER	J
MANSFIELD	HENRY	W
MARX	FRANK	C
MASTIN	ROBERT	L
MCCUNE	HERBERT	F
MCMAHON	JOSEPH	P
MCCORMACK	DENNIS	H
MCCONE	HERBERT	P
MCNEELY	EARL	P
MEANLY	GORDON	W
MEEKS	ROY	E
MEGINNESS	KENNETH	E
MEKHITARIAN	EDMUND?	
MEYER	EUGENE	A
MEYERS	EDDIE	
MICHAELSON	MIKE	
MIESSE	JOHN	W
MORGAN	ROBERT	W
MORIARITY	MICHAEL	G
MORSE	LONNIE	J
NICKELS	FRANK	C
NICHOLS	ALBERT	E
NYLAN	RALPH	A
OATLEY	JOHN	
O'LEARY	JEROME	L
OLSON	DORAL	D
OLUICH	LOUIS	
PARKS	CALVIN	
PATERSON	HORACE	
PENNELL	ROBERT	L
PHILLIPS	JOSEPH	E
PIERSALL	OSCAR	L
PITTMAN	BILLY	
PITTMAN	RUFUS	
POINTECK	JOHN	JR
POOLE	FRANCIS	K
RAMATOWSKI	ALEXANDER	I
REARDON	WILLIAM	
REEDY	JOHN	H
REILLY	JAMES	J JR
REVOK	GEORGE	

REYNOLDS	JIMMY	A
RHATIGAN	WILLIAM "RIP"	C
RINARD	HAROLD	L
ROBERTSON	EVERETT	E
ROBERTSON	HERBERT	E
ROBINSON	FRANKLIN	D
ROBINSON	HARRY	P
ROGERS	DAVID	P JR
ROMERO	ROBERTO	R
ROSS	CHARLES	G
RUIZ	VICTORIANO	
SAFRAN	ROBERT	J
SCHROEDER	EDWIN	J
SCHROEDER	HARRY	J
SEYKA	RICHARD	
SHARP	WAYNE	E
SHATZKY	RICHARD	
SHELLEY	ROBERT	A
SHINGLETON	ROBERT	I
SHULER	EDWIN	D
SIMMONS	JOSEPH	V
SIMONSON	GALE	C
SIMPSON	THOMAS	J
SMITH	GEORGE	C
SPENCE	JOHN	W
STEVENS	RICHARD	C
STEWART	ROBERT	J
STREDER	EMIL	
STRIEGEL	JOHN	
SUMMERS	RONALD	
THERIAULT	PAUL	E
THIBODEAUX	LAWRENCE	P
THOMPSON	HOWARD	S
THOMPSON	STANLEY	C
TROCHE	VINCENT	JR
ULRICH	GEORGE	P
VALENZUELA	HECTOR	
VESY	CECIL	
VILLA	LEWIS	J
VISMOR	ALPHARD	R
VOSS	GORDON	M

WARNER	BENNY	L
WARREN	ROBERT	F
WATERS	CHARLES	F
WATERS	EUNIS	G
WELLS	JAMES	R
WILSON	JACK	
WISNIESKI	WILLIAM	
WISPERT	WILLIAM	J
YATES	CHARLEY	
ZALETA	ARTHUR	
ZAVESKY	FRED	C

2nd Ranger Infantry Company (Airborne)

ADAMS	EDWARD	D
ADAMS	LOUIS	M
ADELL	ALLEN	
ADKINS	KIRK	P
AIKENS	LEGREE	
ALLEN	DONALD	
ALLEN	WARREN	E
ALSTON	MARION	A
ANDERON	JESSIE	
ANDERSON	JESSIE	
ANDRADE	ANTHONY	
ANDREA	TEEDIES	P
ANTHONY	ANTONIO	M
ARNOLD	EUGENE	B
BAKER	ISAAC	E
BANKS	NELSON	L C
BARTON	RICHARD	E
BEDLEY	BETHEL	
BELL	JOHN	M JR
BEVERLY	WILLIAM	I
BIVENS	GEORGE	E
BOATWRIGHT	DANIEL	
BROWN	JAMES	W
BRISCOE	RICHARD	
BUFORD	DAVID	T
BURSE	THOMAS	M
BUSH	HOMER	
BYNUM	GEORGE	JR

BYRD	LLEWELLYN	C
CAMPBELL	MACK	W
CAMPOS	VICTOR	
CARRELL	JAMES	E
CLARKE	DAVID	A
CLEVELAND	CLINTON	W
CLEAVELAND	VARLEY	
CLIETTE	ALBERT	
COCKAYNE	JOHN	D
COLEMAN	EUGENE	C
COLEMAN	WILLIE	L
COLLINS	NORMAN	H
COLLINS	VIRL	J
COURTS	CURTIS	E
CREW	MORRIS	B
DANIELS	SHERMAN	
DAVIS	JAMES	R
DAVIS	RICHARD	E
DEFRAFFINREED	PAUL	M
DIAS	HERCULANEO	G
ENGLEMAN	HARVEY	G
ESCARELA	JOSE	A
ESTELL	LAWRENCE	L
EVANS	JAMES	
FELDER	DONALD	L
FEREBEE	ROBERT	L
FIELDS	JAMES	H JR
FLETCHER	HENRY	
FORD	JOHN	JR
FOSTER	ALBERT	
FREEMAN	JAMES	E
FULTON	ROBERT	A
GALINGTON	OLIVER	W
GARLAND	LESTER	
GERMAIN	GERARD	
GIBSON	CULVER	
GLOVER	RICHARD	H
GORDON	ANDREW	
GORDON	MORGAN	S
GOULD	JOHN	W
GRAHAM	EARL	

GRASTY	ISAAC	JR
GRAY	WALTER	S
GREEN	HERMAN	J
GUDE	JAMES	H
GURIA	JOHN	
HALL	CARL	D
HARDY	JIM	
HARGROVE	WILLIAM	
HARRIS	ELLSWORTH	
HARRIS	WILLIAM	J
HARRISON	HERMAN	O
HARVEY	JAMES	E
HAWKINS	WILLIE	C
HENDERSON	JAMES	
HIGGENBOTHAM	MCBERT	
HILL	ROLAND	
HODGE	ROLAND	
HOLLAND	FLOYD	S
HOLLEY	J	
HOLLINGER	WILLIAM	
HOSEY	LEE	
HOWARD	BENNIE	
JACKSON	EARL	
JACKSON	GEORGE	
JACKSON	HERMAN	
JACKSON	WINSTON	
JENKINS	GLENN	JR
JOHNSON	BRUCE	A
JOHNSON	EMMET	L
JOHNSON	HAROLD	A
JOHNSON	MILTON	
JONES	JOHN	H
JULIUS	VICTOR	
KELLEY	JOSEPH	
KING	FRANK	JR
LAND	ELMORE	
LANIER	WILLIAM	M
LEARY	FRED	L
LEE	HOSEY	
LEGGS	RALPH	JR
LESURE	DAVID	

LEWIS	CHARLES	U
LEWIS	GORDON	
LOFTON	MATTHEW	
LOUNDES	JOHN	
LUCAS	ERNEST	L
LYLES	PAUL	
MASON	JACOB	J
MATHIS	WILLIAM	
MCBRIDE	CLEAVEN	
MCLEAN	LESLIE	J
MCPHERSON	WILLIAM	J
MILLER	NED	
MITCHELL	GEORGE	H
MOLSON	GEORGE	
MONTE	JAMES	L
MOORE	KENNETH	R
MORRIS	OTHEL	
MORSE	CALVIN	A
MURPHY	JACK	
MURRAY	JAMES	R
NEEL	GORDON	J
NEWMAN	RICHARD	L
NIXON	SAMUEL	
NUNLEY	JOHN	E
OAKLEY	JAMES	S
OLIVER	HOWARD	
OLIVER	JOE	
OWENS	GLEN	
PARKS	NATHAN	
PAULDING	CRAIG	
PAYNE	SAMUEL	L JR
PETTERESS	JAMES	JR
PLATER	JAMES	M
POPE	JAMES	J
POSEY	EDWARD	L
PRYOR	BERNARD	
QUEEN	JAMES	C
RACALERA	JOSE	A JR
RANKINS	GEORGE	
REESE	EARNEST	
REMBERT	HERMAN	L

RHODES	WILLIAM	E
RHONE	RAY	
RIDDELL	WILLIAM	H L
ROBERTSON	SMEAD	
ROGERS	MONTELL	M
SCOTT	CHARLES	D
SCOTT	SAMUEL	
SHADE	WILLIAM	
SIMMS	WILLIAM	S
SMALL	WHEELER	S
SMITH	ROBERT	L
SMITH	SCHERRELL	L
SMITH	SUMERRELL	
SQUIRES	HOWARD	
ST MARTIN	JUDE	P
ST THOMAS	ROBERT	
STROTHERS	STEWART	
SUTTON	RALPH	W
TATE	BILLIE	
TAYLOR	JAMES	
TERRELL	JOHN	JR
THOMAS	GEORGE	
THOMAS	WILLIAM	E
TUCKER	ORRIE	
TUCKER	WILLIAM	
VAILS	ROBERT	A JR
VALERY	CLEVELAND	
VAN DUNK	WILLIAM	G
VICTOR	JULIUS	
WADE	VIRGIL	E
WALKER	JAMES	I
WASHINGTON	WILLIAM	
WATKINS	ROBERT	
WEATHERSBEE	WILLIAM	
WEBB	BURKE	
WELLS	JOSEPH	
WEST	DONALD	
WEST	LAWRENCE	D
WEST	RAMON	
WHITE	LEROY	
WHITMORE	JOSEPH	

WILBURN	VINCENT	
WILLIAMS	AIKINS	
WILLIAMS	LAWRENCE	
WILLIAMSON	OTIS	
WILSON	HENRY	
WILSON	WILLIAM	
WODDARD	ISAIAH	
WRIGHT	WILLIAM	H C

3rd Ranger Infantry Company (Airborne)

ACOSTA	JOSEPH	M
ADAMAITIS	WILLIAM	L
AKINS	LAVERNE	
ALDRIDGE	JAMES	E
AMBURN	THOMAS	S L
ANDREWS	WILLIAM	T
ARENS	JOHN	W
BALLOU	ROLAND	M
BARBER	HAROLD	L
BASS	DAVID	P JR
BATCHELDER	HARRY	J
BATEMAN	JAMES	W
BEDDINGFIELD	TRUMAN	L
BERK	BILL	
BILOTTI	NINU	
BLACKWELL	ATLEY	B
BOUVET	ANSELM	U
BROWN	ROBERT	L
BURKE	WILLIAM	P
CAMPBELL	GEORGE	W III
CARMICHAEL	HENRY	A
CARPENTER	ROYCE	L D
CASERES	JUAN	
CHANNON	ROBERT	I
CHILLION	MARTIN	E
CISNEROS	ARTHUR	
CLIFTON	ROY	M JR
COLE	GAIL	R
COLLETT	BURCHELL	JR
COLLINS	DONALD	C
COMER	BRAUDIS	A

CONTRERAS	ROBERT	U
COPELAND	AUBY	
CORTEZ	JOSE	E
COURNOYER	JOSEPH	R M III
DALTON	ALFRED	O
DAVIS	CHESTER	M
DAVIS	FRED	E
DAY	DONALD	L
DELUCA	RALPH	F
DEMLOW	GEORGE	W
DESMORE	ERNEST	J
DIAZ	ROBERT	A
DROST	CARL	W
EATON	RICHARD	J
EDWARDS	WILLIAM	F
ELLMERS	RICHARD	D
ESTEP	ROBERT	
ESTERLINE	THOMAS	J
ETHEREDGE	KENNETH	O
EWING	GORDON	C
EXLEY	ROBERT	L
FEHSER	RICHARD	M
FELIX	CONRAD	F
FERGUSON	JOHN	S
FITZGERALD	PATRICK	S
FORREST	JOSEPH	R
FRIESS	DALE	L
GAITHER	CHARLES	R
GILLESPIE	HAROLD	C
GEORGIOU	CONSTANTINO	C
GRACE	JAMES	E
GRAHAM	CHARLES	L
GREEN	JACK	A
GREENWOOD	HAROLD	A
GRILLS	FRANK	M
GROSSMAN	ALBERT	H
GUNNING	GERALD	
HAMILTON	PETER	
HEATH	JAMES	T
HENDZEL	FRANK	R

HERHOLZ	EGON	
HICKMAN	MARION	L
HUTCHESON	WILLIAM	M
JACKSON	KENNETH	L
JENKINS	JOHN	B
JOHNSON	LLOYD	G
JOHNSON	WILLIAM	A
JONES	JAMES	E
KENNARD	ROBERT	S
KENT	WILLIAM	A
KING	CARL	V
KIRKLAND	CHARLES	W JR
KNOEBEL	BENNY	L
KOSMAS	NICK	
KOTHE	LESLIE	M
KUCK	DANIEL	F
LEE	DONALD	E
LEWIS	JULIAN	D
LOEWEN	EUGENE	
LOWEN	CURTIS	E
LOWE	WILLIAM	P
MAILHOT	JOSEPH	P
MANGES	LEWIS	B
MARSHALL	CLINT	R
MARTINEZ	ALONZO	E
MASTERS	REX	G
MAYS	PAUL	K
MAZUR	VLADIMIR	W
MCCLOSKY	GERALD	
MCCORMICK	WILLIAM	J
MCCULLOUGH	ELMER	E JR
MCLESKEY	BROADUS	L
MILLER	JACK	L
MINKA	WALTER	
MIOTKE	THOMAS	F
MISSERI	FRANCISCO	
MOHEGAN	WESLEY	
MOODY	ALFRED	L
MORRIS	WILLIAM	T
MORTON	EDWARD	D

MULLIN	JERRY	F
MULLINS	JARRILL	
MURPHY	CHARLES	M
MURRAY	DONALD	B
NAKAJO	MAS	M
NICHOLSON	FRANKLIN	A
NIEMI	KENNETH	E
NORRIS	JOHN	C
O'NEILL	HARRY	B
OSBORN	WILLIAM	C
OWENS	KENNETH	E
PAGANO	FRANK	
PALOMBI	ROCCO	A
PARKER	ROBERT	L
PARRISH	CHARLES	
PASSINI	PRIMO	L JR
PEKAY	STANLEY	P
PELLON	FREDERICK	
PENA	EARNEST	
PERCIVAL	JACK	K
PIERCE	RAYMOND	L
PIETROGEORGE	MICHAEL	C
PIETROWSKI	EDWARD	F
PIKE	EUDORSEY	
PORTER	JAMES	A
POTEMPA	EDWARD	J
POWELL	CHESTER	F
PRONIER	ROBERT	A
RACINE	RONALD	A
RANCO	NICHOLAS	C
RAWLS	DAVID	
RAY	ERNEST	A JR
RENZ	LEONARD	W
REPP	ROBERT	L
RHYNE	DAVID	W
RICHARDS	HAROLD	A
RIDENHOUR	CHARLES	L
ROBERTS	EDGAR	T
ROBERTS	FLOYD	
ROST	ELMER	L

RUMAGE	JOHNNIE	L
SAMS	BURGESS	
SARTORI	JOHN	W
SAYLOR	RICHARD	E
SCULLY	ROBERT	
SEIBERT	ELMER	O
SHAFER	JACK	
SHEEHAN	ROBERT	J
SHERRY	EDWARD	C
SIMMONS	JAMES	E
SIMPSON	HOMER	I
SMITH	CHARLES	E
SMITH	LEONARD	D
SMUDSKI	GEORGE	B
SMYTH	ROY	E
SPICER	MARION	A
STAMPER	JAMES	M
STANEK	VICTOR	F
STEVENS	JULIUS	P
STEVENSON	WALLACE	L
TANONA	CHESTER	P
TATARAKIS	GEORGE	G
THERRY	RUSSELL	G JR
THOMAS	ROBERT	R
TIDWELL	JESSIE	C
TIMMONS	JOHN	B
TOBIN	JOHN	L
TOEPKER	NORMAN	U
TRACY	EARL	A JR
TROJCHAK	FRAN	
TWIGG	DAVID	
VALVERI	JOHN	
WAIKSNORIS	ANTHONY	J
WALKER	CARLETON	P
WARD	NEAL	F
WILKINSON	CALVIN	M
WILLIAMS	JOE	P
WILLIAMS	LARRY	M
WILLIS	OLAN	F
WILSON	GORDON	D

| WORKENS | PAUL | W |
| WYATT | NEAL | H |

4th Ranger Infantry Company (Airborne)

ACKLEY	DONALD	C
ALARID	MAXIMINO	
ALVARADO	PEDRO	
ALVIS	JOHN	C
ANDERSON	DORSEY	B
ANDRCZEYCK	FRANK	J
ANGARANO	TITO	
ANGELL	JOHN	
ANGLIN	ROBERT	B
ANDZALDA	MOISES	
ATKINS	ALBERT	E
ATWOOD	BUELL	D
AYERS	JOHN	C
BAKER	RAYMOND	E
BARTHOLOMEW	RALPH	J
BATEMAN	JAMES	M
BAUER	JAMES	A
BIGELOW	GENE	H
BINK	JACK	G
BLACKABY	JOHNNY	O
BLACKBURN	KENNETH	C
BLACKETTER	CLAUDE	P
BOWER	KENNETH	J
BRASSEUR	RONALD	A
BREXEL	CHARLES	
CAMACHO	RAY	
CAPONE	RICHARD	F
CARBONEL	JAMES	J
CARPENTER	FRANCIS	I
CHADA	WILLIAM	
CHAPMAN	JAMES	D
CHICKAUL	JOHN	
CHORD	WILBUR	J
COX	CHARLES	H
CRESON	ROBERT	F
CREWS	THOMAS	L
CRITCHLEY	JOHN	J

DAHLHEIMER	GENE	D
DE ROUCHEY	DELOS "DICK"	R
DEXTER	LEWIS	
DICKENS	TROY	L
DILLAN	JOHNNY	M
DOSS	BILLY	J
DUTKO	WALTER	
ELDER	JAMES	S
FALKENSTEEN	CLINTON	
FISH	VINCENT	
FISHER	KENNETH	
FORBES	FRANK	M
FOHST	FREDERICK	A
GAMPBILL	CLAY	JR
GARCIA	RICARDO	
GARRET	RICHARD	G
GIBSON	KENNETH	W
GILMORE	JOHN	
GOLDEN	ROBERT	D
GOOLSBY	WILLIAM	V
GORMAN	DAVID	P
GUINEY	PAUL	J
GRAHAM	EMERY	B
GREGORY	WILLIAM	A
GROOMS	RICHARD	R
GROTH	RICHARD	P
GUSTAFSON	BENJAMIN	
HALL	LEONARD	E
HALL	ROY	I
HAMLIN	FRED	
HAMPEL	JEROME	A
HEALY	MICHAEL	D
HEFFERNAN	JAMES	M
HIGGINS	EARL	A
HILBERT	ELLSWORTH	F
HILTON	JIM	M
HOLOHAN	PATRICK	J
HOLLIS	BILLY	
HORNER	BILLY	J
JOHNSON	JAMES	L
JOHNSON	WILLIAM	R

KLINGENSMITH	JOHN	
KNOBEL	BENNY	L
KOOP	ALFRED	E
KOOP	LEONARD	V
KRISKO	ROBERT	
LAMM	ROBERT	L
LAMUTHE	DONALD	
LANDIS	MARVIN	T
LANGAN	GERALD	J
LANGHAM	RAY	
LA RUE	DOUGLAS	J
LAVERTY	DONALD	C
LEE	FRANCIS	I JR
LESTER	EUGENE	
LIGON	ARTHUR	
LOPEZ	JOSE	A
LOPEZ	RAUL	
LYONS	LESLIE	L JR
MACIEL	DAVID	E
MACK	RICHARD	F
MACUMBER	JOHN	
MADDRY	JOHN	A
MANSHIP	FREDERICK	
MARQUESS	ELMER	
MARSHALL	TED	
MARTIN	JAMES	
MASOVCEVICH	ROBERT	
MATTEO	GREGORY	A
MAYNARD	WILLIAM	P
MCCLENNEN	HENRY	
MCDONOUGH	EDWARD	T
MCGUINNESS	THOMAS	P
MCINTOSH	LOUIS	
MCPHERSON	GEORGE	C
MCPHERSON	LESTER	V
MILES	WILLIAM	I JR
MILLER	WILLIAM	G
MOORE	JOSEPH	C
MOORE	WILLIAM	M
MURPHY	DAVID	P
MYERS	LOYS	F JR

NEAL	LOUIS	M
NELSON	ROBERT	W
NESTLER	JOHN	A
NORRIS	JAMES	E
OAKES	HERMAN	I
OGLE	WILLIAM	R JR
O'KAIN	ROBERT	P
OLIVERI	RAYMOND	P
OZGA	JOHN	M
PATTERSON	THOMAS	
PINCKNEY	MILES	M JR
POINTECK	JOHN	JR
POWELL	THOMAS	W
PUCEL	EDWARD	W
PURCELL	PATRICK	J
PUTNAM	WILLIAM	E
RAMUS	RAYMOND	R
RAUBACH	JAMES	B
REDGATE	GEORGE	B
REDGATE	PAUL	
REEVES	GROVER	E
REISCH	JEROME	R
REPACK	JOSEPH	
RIGGS	ROY	V
ROBINSON	KENNETH	A
RODRIGUES	JOSEPH	A
ROSE	THOMAS	E
SALAS	CARL	J
SANCHEZ	MIQUEL	J
SANCHEZ	RALPH	V
SCHROEDER	GEORGE	E
SCHUSTEFF	ROBERT	
SMITH	ALFRED	H
SMITH	CARLIN	
SMITH	JACK	L
SMITH	LEO	B
SOMMERS	HAROLD	A
STEPP	LESLIE	G
STILES	JESSE	M
STOVER	DEBRA	E
SULLIVAN		D

SULLIVAN	JOHN	W
SUNCHILD	JOHN	
SZCZEPANIAK	KAZIMIERZ	
TAKACH	FRANK	A JR
THRASHER	BILLY	J
TONNIGES	TONY	
TRITZ	CYRIL	E
VECCHIO	DOMINIC	I
VIDRINE		A
VOYTKO	ANDREW	G
WAKEMAN	ROBERT	B
WARD	TOM	
WARREN	JOHN	
WATERBURY	JOSEPH	W
WATSON	MARTIN	R
WATTS	JOSEPH	C JR
WAY	JAMES	H
WAYMAN	THOMAS	L
WHITFIELD	ROBERT	W
WILCOXSON	JESSIE	M
WILLIAMS	GERALD	E
WILSON	DEVERN	E
WINDER	CHARLES	R
WOELFEL	LOUIS	H
WOLFE	RONALD	
YOUNG	FRANCIS	E
YOVICH	STANKO	

5th Ranger Infantry Company (Airborne)

ADKINS	JACK	D
ADKINS	LEONARD	A
ALDRICH	CLAIR	E
ALLEN	ARTHUR	H
AMBORN	THOMAS	S
ANTROBUS	CHARLES	M
ARENA	PAUL	H
ARNOLD	JOHN	H
BAILEY	ROY	L
BALLARD	ALFRED	J
BARCAK	CHARLES	D
BARTHOLOMEW	RALPH	J

DRINKWATER	JAMES	L
DULANEY	ROBERT	A
DYKE	DONALD	M
ECKHARDT	WALTER	
EDDY	JOHN	P
EDWARDS	EVERETTE	L
EDWARDS	RAYMOND	H
EDWARDS	THEODORE	M
EISMAN	JOHN	V
ELKINS	JOHNNY	L
EMERSON	JOHN	
EMERSON	MARVIN	T
EVANS	ALBERT	G
EXLEY	ROBERT	L
FAVORS	JOSEPH	H
FIGUREL	JOHN	
FORCIER	EDGAR	M
FRANKO	JOSEPH	
FRANKS	DONALD	G
FRYE	MARVIN	H
FULLER	ROBERT	N
GAGNON	JOSEPH	R
GALLO	NICHOLAS	R
GALLOWAY	RICHARD	W
GARCIA	HENRY	G
GEORGIA	BILL	
GILMORE	ROBERT	W
GLISSON	OTIS	D
GODFREY	GEORGE	W
GOLDBAUM	LOUIS	G
GONZALES	JESSE	
GRAMBILL	CLAY	JR
GROSS	GERALD	D
GUSTAFSON	THOMAS	
HALE	JOHN	H
HAMMOND	JOHN	
HANNON	WILLILAM	B
HARDAWAY	ROBERT	G
HARGETT	RICHARD	A
HATCH	JAMES	L
HAYDEN	ANDREW	

HAYDEN	JOHN	T
HILPERT	EDWARD	T JR
HOLLINGSWORTH	JAMES	D
HOMER	DALE	
HOMER	WALLACE	D
HOY	FRED	R
JOHNSON	CLAUDE	D
JONES	BOBBY	L
JONES	EVIE	L
JOBECK	JOHN	G
KAHL	DONALD	H
KALAKAUSKIS	EDWARD	A
KANDZIURA	GREGORY	
KEELER	EDWARD	J
KELCH	HOWARD	
KELLEHER	JAMES	E
KELSO	MINOR	L
KELSO	MYRON	M
KESTLINGER	ROBERT	S
KIRSHFIELD	WILLIAM	JR
KOROWSKI	RICHARD	L
LAIRD	REGIS	C
LANG	FRED	M
LEWIS	CLARENCE	V
LUDDEN	EDWARD	W
MACDONALD	KIRBY	P
MAHRT	WILLIAM	E JR
MAILHOT	MAURICE	J
MARIN	LUCADIO	G
MARTINEZ	ALONZO	H
MARTINEZ	CARIOS	Z
MATHIS	ROBERT	
MAY	WINFRED	L
MAYNE	ROBERT	L
MAZIARZ	WALTER	J JR
MCABEE	GARLAND	J
MCANDREWS	JOHN	J
MCANDREWS	JOHN	J JR
MCCLOSKEY	WILLIAM	J
MCGEE	MICHAEL	
MCGINNIS	MACK	

MCGLOTHLIN	BILLY	
MCKENNA	DONALD	K
MCMILLIAN	JACK	D
MEEHAN	MICKEY	J
MIDKIFF	LON	
MIZER	GLEN	L JR
MONTOYA	LOUIS	C
MOODY	WILLIAM	
MOORE	JESS	
MORRIS	JACK	D
MOTT	RONALD	H
MULLINS	EMMITT	
MURDOCK	BERNARD	E
NEAL	ALBERT	S
NEAL	THOMAS	L
NEAULT	GERARD	A
NEMECHECK	JOHN	T
NETTLES	ROBERT	A
POWELL	WILLIS	G
ROBERTS	MARION	A
ROBLES	LUGARDO	S
RODRIGUEZ	MANUEL	A
ROMAGNULI	ALBERT	A
RYAN	WILLIAM	H
SAMS	BURGESS	
SANSALONE	GOLFREDO	D
SCAGNELLI	JOHN	C
SCARBORO	LEONARD	H
SCHULTZ	ANSEL	C
SHAMALY	LOUIS	R
SHARP	ORVIE	J
SHEMITZ	FRANK	G
SIMS	WILLIAM	S
STANKICH	MICHAEL	
SZARNIAK	RALPH	E
TEEL	RAYMOND	T
THATCHER	IRWIN	
ULATOSKI	JOSEPH	R
VARELA	HENRY	
WALKER	CARROLL	K
WALKER	DENZEL	H

WESTMORELAND	LONER	B
WHITE	DONALD	H
WHITEHEAD	WILLIAM	
WILSON	ROBERT	I
WINKLES	ORBAN	S
WOFFORD	E	G
WOODS	HARVEY	J
WORDEN	LEONARD	R
WRAY	JOHN	G
YBANEZ	LOREN	D
YBARRA	TONY	S
ZAMBOS	THEODORE	
ZELLER	VIRGIL	L

6th Ranger Infantry Company (Airborne)

AKERS	ISHMAEL	W
ARKELL	LYLE	J
AYERS	ROBERT	N
BARTLETT	ANDREW	V JR
BEBEAU	HOWARD	C
BESS	HAROLD	M
BROWN	LAWRENCE	R
BOZEMAN	JIM	JR
BURNS	WILLIAM	F
BURT	J	F
CADENA	MARCELLO	S
CAIN	JAMES	S
CARLL	FREDRICK	J
CAROZZA	GIOVANNI	
CATLETT	BILLY	F
CHAPMAN	FORREST	D
CHESTNUT	WILLIAM	K
CHIKI	RUDOLPH	L
CLARK	WILLIAM	L
COOPER	BEN	W JR
CORNELIUS	ROBERT	V
COTTER	LOUIS	M
COX	NORMAN	T
CULPEPPER	WILLIAM	S
CURRY	WILLIAM	H
DA SILVA	JACK	

DAUGHERTY	DARREL	W
DAVIS	FLOYD	H
DAWSON	MAX	
DEBUSSCHERE	ROBERT	C
DONALDSON	CHARLES	N
DYE	JOSEPH	SR
EDGE	ZANE	G
ELDEN	GEORGE	W
ELLIS	GEORGE	B
ESTRADA	JESUS	
FLEMING	RALPH	L
FLORES	ALFRED	H
FORD	CHARLES	R
GALA	FRANK	
GEORGE	HARLEY	E
GIACHERINE	ALFRED	J
GIARD	DAVID	L
GLENN	JOHN	M
GREENMON	FRANCIS	E
GRIFFIN	JOE	R
GRIGGS	HOWARD	
GRUETZMACHER	WILLIAM	F
GUTHRIE	THOMAS	F
HAMANN	EDWARD	J
HAUGEN	RICHARD	N
HEIL	JOSEPH	G
HENNESSY	PAUL	K
HILL	VIRGEL	R
HOFFMAN	WALTER	R
HOGE	CLARENCE	L
HORINE	JAMES	R
HORN	DONALD	R
HORNBEAK	JOE	D
HOY	FREDERICK	T
HUFFINE	JONATHAN	F
HUMPHREY	DONALD	S
HURST	KENNETH	J
HUX	DAVID	F
JACKSON	RUSSEL	L
JACOBI	ROBERT	R
JARRETT	THOMAS	H

JAYNES	BILLY	J
JOHNSON	VALENTINO	A
JUDGE	CHESTER	P
KAMM	WILLIAM	F
KAUFFMAN	ALBERT	L
KEELER	CHARLES	I
KELLY	ALFRED	
KERVIN	JOSEPH	C
KERVIN	THOMAS	W
KIMMEL	WALTER	E
KLUEGEL	JOSEPH	C
KOBILIS	ROBERT	J
KOLBY	EDMUND	
KONOPKA	JOHN	
KUTA	EUGENE	A
LACATENA	MARCANTONIO	M
LAFERTY	HAROLD	W
LANZILLO	JOSEPH	G
LAVOIE	PHILIP	J
LAWRENCE	JOSEPH	L
LEYRER	ERNEST	JR
LINARDAKIS	ANTANASIO	
LINZELL	CLINTON	F
LIVINGSTON	HARRY	J
LUNA	MANUEL	J
LUNA	RUBEN	JR
LUNSFORD	JOHN	E
LUTTRELL	JOHN	J JR
LUX	HARRY	E JR
LYNCH	JOSEPH	F
MACK	J	B
MADISON	EUGENE	H
MALONE	RAYMOND	P
MANDRELL	BILLY	D
MANDRELL	JIMMIE	
MARCISZEWSKI	STANLEY	M
MARIK	RAYMOND	L
MARTINEZ	HECTOR	H
MATTESON	MARTIN	P
MCDONALD	JESSE	E
MCDONALD	WILLIAM	G

MCGRATH	THOMAS	V
MCKENNA	DONALD	F
MCCLAIN	HENRY	K
MEHRLE	JOHN	R
MICHOLA	DANIEL	S
MIDDIONE	ANGELO	
MOORE	WILLARD	
MURPHY	BERNARD	G
NEAL	JAMES	S
NELSON	ROBERT	B
NICHOLS	GEORGE	N
PAHL	IRVING	C
PYBURN	ALLEN	R
REAMES	WILLIAM	K
ROBERTS	LEROY	R
SAXTON	CHARLES	R
SCHULZE	FREDERICK	W
SIMMERMAN	JAY	E
SKOIEN	CLARENCE	E
SMITH	R	B
SNAVELY	GEORGE	R
SNOWDEN	ROBERT	L
SPARKS	JAMES	C
SPRATLIN	ROBERT	J
SUKNATCH	JOHN	
SULLIVAN	ROBERT	J
SURFACE	MARTIN	L
SWANSON	ROBERT	B
TRAYNOR	DONALD	
WEBER	ELDRED	E
YNCLAN	ANIBAL	J

7th Ranger Infantry Company (Airborne)

ALVAREZ	ARTHUR	
ANDRUS	HERBERT	B
ANWEILER	ROBERT	
ATKINS	CLEM	
BAKER	ADAM	L
BAKER	MARVYN	E
BALES	ELDON	
BASTIAN	RANDOLPH	

BATTLES	CALVIN	
BEECHER	THOMAS	A
BENTZ	GEORGE	A
BETZ	EDWARD	J
BLUNT	ALBERT	
BOELTER	RICHARD	W
BOHIN	HARRY	JR
BOWERS	MARVIN	A
BOYNTON	ALLEN	R
BRADLEY	EDWARD	J
BRANDER	FRED	C
BREEDLOVE	BARNELL	
BREWER	HERBERT	J
BROWN	LEE	E
BROWN	THOMAS	
BRYSON	KENNETH	L
BYERLY	ERNEST	L JR
CAMP	WALTER	H
CAMPBELL	VINCENT	
CAPPELLETTI	VICTOR	JR
CARD	WILLIAM	R JR
CARLSON	DOUGLAS	W JR
CARMONA	GEORGE	L
CAVANAUGH	JAMES	
CHARTIER	RAYMOND	A
CHESTER	JOHN	
CRESTMAN	CHARLES	
CHRISTMAS	MERRY	L
CLARK	ROBERT	P
CLARK	ROOSEVELT	B
CLEMENT	ALBERT	V
COLEMAN	LONNIE	
COLLINS	DEWEY	P
CORBIN	CLARENCE	R
CREAGER	ROBERT	E
CULPEPPER	JOHN	N
DANZI	DOMINIC	P
DAVIS	ALBERT	H
DEAVER	ALLEN	
DE SILVA	JAMES	I
DUNHAM	FRANCIS	W

DOTY	PAUL	L
EALY	HAROLD	O
EDWARDS	RAYMOND	H
ELLSEY	ROBERT	H
FAISTENHAMMER	LUDWIG	
FERGUSON	BERNARD	
FIZUR	ROBERT	
FLAHERTY	RAY	
FLEISHMAN	JERRY	
FOUNTAIN	CECIL	
FRAZIER	WILLIAM	J
GASKINS	JERRY	
GAULT	CHADBORNE	W
GENTRY	LAVERNE	
GIBSON	WILLIAM	V
GODWIN	JOHN	F
GRAY	THOMAS	JR
GREEN	JOSEPH	C
GREENFIELD	JAY	L
GRIFFITH	KENNETH	S
GUNDERSON	JUNIOR	
HANNING	OSCAR	
HANNOCK	JOHN	W
HANSTON	ROBERT	
HATHAWAY	ROBERT	C
HATHCOAT	HOWARD	C
HEAD	BENNIE	
HENDLEY	BILLY	
HILL	ALOYSIUS	
HILL	ROLAND	
HINES	GENE	A
HUDSON	HOWARD	
INMAN	LOUIS	
JACOBSON	LOUIS	
JOHNSON	HENRY	
JOHNSON	ROBERT	
KELSO	MINOR	L
KLOBCAR	WILLIAM	
KNIGHT	RAY	
LAFFERTY	HAROLD	
LAWTON	ELWYN	

LAWRENCE	RAPHAEL	
LAWRENCE	WESLEY	
LAYNE	PHILIP	
LEWIS	BILL	
LEWIS	JULIAN	D
LEWIS	MANUEL	
LEWIS	SAMUEL	C
LEWIS	WILLIAM	J
LINNEAR	LEROY	E
LOVEGROVE	JOHN	E III
LUBUDZINSKI	GEORGE	
LYKKEN	DONALD	L
MALONE	CECIL	
MAHER	RUSSELL	E
MANLEY	CHARLES	L
MANTHEY	JOHN	H
MARCOTTE	WILLIAM	J
MARSHALL	DOUGLAS	G
MCENTEE	JOHN	P
MCKINNEY	SAMUEL	L
MCNAUER	HERMAN	
MEDLIN	EDWARD	J
MEDRANO	RALPH	
MILLER	COLMORE	
MILLER	ROLAND	A
MOLOCK	JOHN	R
MORGAN	RICHARD	D
MORI	RIKIO	
MOUNCE	MAC	D
MULAC	ANTHONY	
MYERS	CHARLES	E
MYERS	PAUL	F JR
NAGLE	DENNIS	F
NICHOLS	BOBBY	
O'KAIN	ROBERT	P
PACCIO	DONALD	M
PARKER	ARTHUR	C
PATTON	HOLLIS	M
PEREA	GILBERT	
PIETMONTESE	JOSEPH	
PODESKI	RONAN	

PRUITT	JAMES	
RASH	WESLEY	E
REAVES	JACK	
REEVES	ROBERT	R
REINHART	DONALD	
RESTOFER	LAWRENCE	
REYNOLDS	JACK	
RHOADS	RICHARD	R
ROY	JOHN	W
SALZMAN	ROBERT	P
SCHEPANIAK	MARCELLOS	
SHAW	EUGENE	
SHAW	LELAND	J
SHEPARD	GEORGE	
SHIRES	JAMES	C
SIEGLER	LOUIS	M
SIMMONS	HERBERT	W
SIMPSON	CHARLES	B
SLOAN	WILLIAM	C
SMART	JOHN	
SMITH	DAVID	
SMITH	EARLIE	
SMITH	WAYNE	L
STEPHENS	DONALD	
STRICKLER	HUGH	
STROMAN	FRED	
STUART	PERRY	E
SURBER	WILLIAM	G
SZAPANUS	LOUIS	S
TAYLOR	THOMAS	A
THATCHER	IRWIN	F
THERENS	EDWARD	J
THOMAS	LLOYD	K
THOMPSON	DONALD	C
TRACY	EARL	
TRAVERS	CHARLES	E
TRIMBLE	GRADY	U
TRUMBLE	LEROY	
VERONESI	NORMAN	R
WAGNER	LARRY	
WALSTEN	DAVE	

WATTS	JOSEPH	C
WELTON	WALTER	
WEGENER	CARL	J
WENAGE	VERNON	G
WHEELER	CARL	C
WILKINS	JOSEPH	E
WILSON	KENNETH	C
WINTER	ROYAL	
WOODWORTH	WALTER	L
WYNNE	DAVID	L
WYSINGLE	PRESTON	
ZAVALNEY	MARK	J

8th Ranger Infantry Company (Airborne)

ABLE	LEE	R
ALLEN	JOHN	C JR
ALMEIDA	JOE	
BAKER	JACKIE	L
BALDRIDGE	ORAL	L
BARLEY	JAMES	L
BAXTER	GEORGE	B
BEAUREGARD	JOSEPH	A
BELKNAP	ALVIE	J
BELLUOMINI	RUDOLF	G
BERRY	CHARLES	J
BIRTCHER	RICHARD	L
BISHOP	JOHN	H
BLACK	ROBERT	W
BOCK	KARL	M
BOLIN	GEORGE	E
BOECHE	KENNETH	V
CARR	HARRY	B
CHAGNON	PAUL	O
CHANEY	JOE	D
CISNEROS	JESSE	
COLEMAN	JAMES	H
COOK	HERSCHEL	H
COX	WILLIAM	P
CRAIG	CHARLES	R JR
CRAIG	CLARENCE	W
DASILVA	JAMES	J

DIAZ	MANUEL	M	
DRUM	CONNIE	M	
EIKENBERRY	ROBERT	W	
ELLIS	GAYLE	H	
ERB	NORMAN	F	
FEIGLEY	ROY	L	
FINKE	JOHN	A	
FIORE	ANTHONY	S	
GAY	THOMAS	J	
GIACHERINI	ALFRED	J	
GILSTRAP	ROBERT	G	
GREEN	LOWELL	A	
GREGORY	GILL	M	JR
HAGUE	GEORGE	E	
HALE	HERMAN	J	
HALL	GEORGE	L	
HARDGROUND	THOMAS	M	
HATHAWAY	ROBERT	C	
HEMMING	NORBERT	G	
HENRY	RONALD	G	
HERBERT	JAMES	A	
HODAK	PARK	A	
HOLBERT	CHESTER		
HOOKS	HAROLD	J	
HOSCH	JOSEPH	E	
INGRAM	BILLY	H	
INGRAM	ROBERT	C	
INGRAM	THOMAS	E	
JOHNSON	WILLIAM	A	
JORGENSON	VICTOR	E	
KENNEDY	JAMES	N	
KESTLINGER	ROBERT	S	
KILEY	ROBERT	G	
LANGNER	STANLEY		
LAWSON	ULAND	G	
LENZ	CHARLES	N	
MAYFIELD	MURRELL	D	
MCFARLAND	JAMES	R	
MCGREGOR	JOSEPH	P	
MCNEELY	JAMES	W	
MCNULTY	WALTER	J	

MIOTKE	THOMAS	F
MOODY	WILLIAM	
MOORE	PHILIP	D
NICHOLSON	THOMAS	W
OGBURN	HOWARD	
OGBURN	JOHN	H
OHS	KENNETH	L
OKON	WERNER	H
OSBORNE	RICHARD	
OUIMETTE	CHARLES	E
PARKER	GENE	W
PIERSZA	ROBERT	
PLACKIS	JAMES	J
POPPY	CLIFFORD	L
POTTER	HAROLD	
POWELL	THOMAS	W
PRESTON	RICHARD	B
RADFORD	HERSCHELL	K
RAMIREX	SANTIAGO	C
RAY	CHARLES	
RAULS	ARTHUR	W
RAYMOND	RAY	
REYNOLDS	JAMES	R
RIDEL	WILLIAM	G
RISH	EMANUEL	P
RIVERA	DANIEL	C
RIVERA	E.	CONRAD
ROBERTS	FLOYD	
ROLLO	KENNETH	
ROSEN	MIKE	
RYAN	JOHN	P
SAVOIE	ROY	J JR
SCHILLING	GEORGE	N
SEDGWICK	ERNEST	JR
SETTLES	RICHARD	E
SHAW	WALLACE	
SHINAVIER	ROBERT	A
SHORT	RAYMOND	
SHORTS	CLIFFORD	J JR
SHUGRUE	DANIEL	P
SILKA	HARRY	P

SIMON	RALPH	H
SIMPSON	MILBURN	D
SLAUGHTER	DELBERT	W
SLAVINSKI	JOSEPH	P
SMITH	EDWARD	D
SMITH	JAMES	F
SMITH	KEITH	W
SMITH	RONALD	F
SNAVELY	PAUL	E JR
SNYDER	CLIFFORD	E
SPARKO	MARKO	R
SPEGAL	EDDIE	W
SPRAGINS	CHARLES	E
STANKICH	MICHAEL	M
STARCHER	RICHARD	D
STEELE	ARTHUR	J
STOKES	THOMAS	E
STOUT	EDWARD	T JR
STRAND	RICHARD	S
STRONG	BERKELEY	J
STROUSE JR.	MILFORD	E
STUBES	VICTOR	JR
STUPKA	THOMAS	
SULLIVAN	RONALD	E
SWAMP	WARREN	J
SWICEGOOD	HAROLD	H
TAUNTON	CHARLES	
TEAGUE	JAMES	H
THOMAS	LAWRENCE	V
THORSTEINSSON	PETER	J E
TIEMEYER	WILLIAM	P
TILLMAN	WILLIAM	G
TISAK	NICK	
TORRES	PETER	F
TROUT	HARRY	C JR
ULDALL	THOMAS	M
UTTS	EDWARD	B
VARNELL	WILLIAM	E
VELASCO	ISMAEL	
VELO	ANTONIO	
WALDECKER	JOHN	F

WALTERS	GENE	H
WARREN	JAMES	W
WASHBURN	WENDELL	W
WATSON	ERNEST	L
WEHLAND	WILLIAM	H
WEITZELL	HOWARD	E
WEST	JOHN	B
WESTENHEFFER	ROBERT	L
WEYENT	DONALD	W
WHEAT	CHARLES	B
WHITE	JIMMIE	M
WHITE	JOHN	D
WIGGINS	LEONARD	W
WILLIAMSON	LEROY	JR
WILLIS	OLAN	F
WOLFE	CHESTER	A
WOLFORD	CRAIG	B
WOOD	CALVIN	E
WYANT	JAY	W
ZAGO	NUNZIO	
ZAGURSKY	HARRY	
ZEIGLER	ARTHUR	
ZENISKY	LEON	

9th Ranger Infantry Company (Airborne)

ACKMAN	WESTON	L JR
ADCOCK	LEWIS	
ARMISTEAD	ROBERT	E JR
AYOTTE	HARRY	
BAETEN	RICHARD	M
BALL	J.	NOEL
BARBER	WALLACE	R
BARNETT	PAUL	W
BASTIAN	RANDOLPH	
BERRY	ROBERT	C
BENNETT	WILBUR	L
BOATNER	CARY	
BOCAN	SAMUEL	M
BODROGHY	ROBERT	F
BOHIN	HARRY	JR
BOOKER	DAVID	L

BORELLA	WILLIAM	
BOWLES	DELBERT	D
BOYKIN	SAM	M
BRANDT	RICHARD	C
BRITTON	JOSEPH	D
BRIDGES	JAMES	
BROOKS	DONALD	E
BROWN	HOWARD	G
BROWNE	EDWARD	A
BUCEY	PAUL	E
BURAS	FRANK	I
BURCE	DENSON	
BURNHAM	ERNEST	D
BURNHAM	RALPH	E
CAMPBELL	GRADY	B
CASTO	CLIFFORD	E
CHANDLER	JOHN	C
CRESTMAN	CHARLES	G
CHRISTENSON	JACK	
CLARK	MARION	F
CUNNINGHAM	MAURICE	G
CUZART	JACK	D
CRUNKLETON	JAMES	M
DAVIS	ALBERT	H
DEAN	MURRIEL	E
DEFOUR	JAMES	A
DEMENT	ROLAND	
DERRYBERRY	LARRY	
DUFFY	GERALD	
EMPANIE	ROBERT	V
ENGLISH	RANDY	
EVANS	DONALD	I
FEIGLEY	ROY	C
FETNER	MELVIN	B
FLANAGAN	EDWARD	G
GALLAGHER	ROBERT	
GAMBLE	CHARLES	B
GODWIN	RICHARD	
GONZALES	ROBERT	
GORDON	HERBERT	L
GOZA	ROBERT	

HAMILTON	WILLIAM	
HAND	HENRY	J
HANLON	JIM	
HARRIS	CLAUDE	
HART	BEDFORD	
HARVEY	ALTON	H
HASKEW	WILLIAM	D
HATHAWAY	ROBERT	C
HAYWOOD	ROBERT	S
HESTER	ERNEST	W
HILL	FELIX	JR
HILPERT	EDWARD	I JR
HUGHES	ARCHIE	
INGLE	RALPH	
JACKSON	KENNETH	R
JENNINGS	CURTIS	M
JOHNSON	CHARLES	W
JOHNSON	JULIUS	D
JOHNSTON	WALDON	K
JONES	EDWARD	E
JONES	FRED	M
KING	FRANCIS	W
KOSKI	EDWIN	S
LAKEY	DONALD	L
LANGHAM	CLARENCE	
LARKIN	JAMES	H
LARSCHEID	ROBERT	A
LAWRENCE	FRED	
LEONARD	EUGENE	
LEVIN	ROBERT	
LEWIS	STANLEY	
LOHSE	WILLIAM	
LOLLAR	CLIFF	D
LUBINSKY	JOSEPH	JR
LUBY	CHESTER	A
LUHMANN	GEORGE	H
LUJACK	JOHN	D
MANNING	CLYDE	L
MARBURY	DAVID	H
MARCOTTE	WILLIAM	J
MARNET	RICHARD	J

MARTINEZ	GEORGE	G
MCCLAIN	JOSEPH	
MCCLAIN	LOUIS	W
MCDOWELL	CLYDE	
MCDOWELL	DELMER	C
MCLOUTH	FRED	P
MCKIMMENS	MARK	
MCLOUTH	FRED	P
METZLER	ROBERT	
MICCICHE	JOE	
MILES	BOBBY	C
MITTS	FIELDEN	W
MOORE	JAMES	
MOORE	JOHN	
MORGAN	GRADY	
MORRISON	ARTHUR	M
NICHOLSON	DARL	
O'DOWD	LEO	L
ORYSIEK	HENRY	E
PALMER	MICHAEL	B
PARKER	EARL	B
PARSONS	EARL	
PAYNE	JAMES	
PETERS	THOMAS	A
PIETMONTESE	JOSEPH	
PORTER	DUNN	
REDECKER	WARREN	C
REESE	CHARLES	
REESE	RICHARD	K
REINHART	DONALD	
RODERICK	EDWARD	
ROGERS	EUGENE	
ROSE	JAMES	JR
ROWE	JAMES	A
SAGER	GERALD	
SCHLOSS	IRWIN	
SIMEK	DOUGLAS	
SIMMONS	RALPH	E
SIMMS	JOSEPH	I
SIMS	GERALD	H
SKELTON	BILLY	W

SONNIER	WHITNEY	J
SOUTH	JERYUL	D
SPENCER	ODIS	H
SPEYERER	EDWIN	M
STANFORD	ALTON	
STEVENS	THOMAS	
STRICKLER	HUGH	
SULLIVAN	VIRGIL	
SWAN	RICHARD	L
TAYLOR	NESBY	
TEAGUE	BURRELL	L
TEANER	RICHORD	L
TERANISH	YOSHIO	
THOMLINSON	JOHN	H
THOMAS	THEODORE	C
THOMPSON	ROBERT	J
THOMPSON	SILAS	M
TIMMIS	JAMES	A
TREMAINE	DUNCAN	R
TRIBBLE	RICHARD	G
TUCKER	ROBERT	A
UNDERWOOD	RICHARD	E
URIBE	MARCO	
VALDERRAMA	ALFRED	C
VICK	PHARES	
VICK	WALTER	
WALDROP	WINFRED	P
WALKER	BILLY	
WATSON	TOM	J
WATSON	WILLIAM	U JR
WATTS	BOB	A
WEBSTER	STANLEY	L JR
WESSON	GEORGE	W
WEST	ROBERT	JR
WHITE	BENJAMIN	
WHITE	WALTER	D
WHITLEY	JAMES	
WILLIAMS	CHARLES	E
WILLIAMS	HENRY	
WOOD	KENNARD	G

| YATES | THOMAS | |
| YOUNCE | HAROLD | D |

10th Ranger Infantry Company (Airborne)

ABBOTT	RALPH	P
ALEXANDER	PAUL	W
AMES	WARREN	H
ANDERSON	RICHARD	E
BALL	ALFRED	L
BALOMENOS	ARTHUR	C
BARBOE	HOWARD	L
BARGSLEY	RODNEY	M
BARNETTE	JAMES	R
BARWIN	WILLIAM	A
BASHAM	W	S
BASHAN	WILLIAM	L
BAXTER	RALPH	E
BELL	DONALD	K
BELL	TOMMY	L
BENJAMIN	DONALD	G
BORRIELLO	RALPH	L
BOWIEN	MONROE	
BRITTAIN	FRANK	W
BROOKS	CARL	G
BROWNLEE	LOUIS	C
BRYLOWE	NORMAN	
BRYSON	CADER	A
BURNHAM	ELMER	JR
CANTWELL	BILL	
CAPE	BUSTER	J
CASEY	CHARLES	L
CASTELLO	ALFONSO	G
CATES	BEN	A
COOK	JAMES	D
CORREA	EDWARD	
COURTNEY	ROBERT	L
CRABTREE	CHARLES	F
DAMRON	VERNON	R
DANIELS	JOHN	J
DEHART	NOLAN	
DELK	CHARLES	A

DESMUKES	RAY	L
DOERR	WAYNE	C
DONNELLY	HARRISON	C
DUNCAN	LAWRENCE	C
DUNN	EDWIN	L
DUNN	JAMES	B
DURANT	JACK	R
DUREN	KENNARD	R
DYER	FREDDIE	A
EDWARDS	JERRY	D
EUSTICE	RAYMOND	JOE
FERRALL	LYAL	R
FERRALL	RICHARD	R
FICK	LEROY	G
FIKE	EMMETT	E
FIORITO	JOHN	J
FOLEY	JAMES	L
FOOTE	OSCAR	H
FOX	GEORGE	P
FURRY	LOYAL	W
GABOSSI	TONY	
GAUNT	ELDON	S
GAY	EDWARD	H
GILL	BARNEY	A
GLENDENNING	CHARLES	F
GOODE	MONTE	H
GOWER	GENE	
GOWER	RAY	E
GREEN	JOE	C
GREENWAY	RICHARD	D
GAUDOLUPE	RAMUS	
HALL	BERNARD	E
HAMILTON	WELDON	W
HAMMACK	DARRELL	W
HANES	PHILIP	D
HARVEY	JACK	H
HAYNES	ROBERT	J
HENRICKSON	HILBERT	J
HILL	ROBERT	H
HOLMAN	HURSHEL	
HURD	BENNY	E

HYATT	RICHARD	D
JACKSON	MERLE	P
JOHNSON	CARL	W
JOHNSON	HAROLD	E
JONES	CALVIN	P
JONES	NEIL	
JONES	RAYMOND	A
JORDAN	BILL	E
KASKASKE	ADAM	
KELLY	FLOYD	E
KELTNER	JAMES	L
KEMMERER	ROSS	
KEMP	JOHN	T
KLEINDORF	SAMUEL	
KOSS	MICHAEL	S
LANGSTON	JAMES	W
LAW	ROBERT	E
LEONARD	T	J
LOUGEE	DONALD	E
LOWELL	CARL	R
MACAULAY	WILLIAM	A
MACRI	ANGELO	C
MARINO	RALPH	Q
MATHIS	BILLY	
MCKELVEY	BILLY	J
MCPHERSON	JACK	D
METHENEY	DELBERT	J
MILES	RICHARD	O
MILLER	FRANK	
MILLER	SAMUEL	C
MORRIS	TROY	E
NASH	JOHN	H
NELSON	HAROLD	M
NYKIEL	EDWIN	C
OWEN	H. DREW	
PARISH	RONALD	G
PARKER	THOMAS	P
PATERSON	FREDDIE	J
PEASE	LAWRENCE	H
PETERS	JIM	R
PETERSEN	ELWYN	B

PETERSON	FREDDIE	J
PIPKIN	THOMAS	A
PONCE	ALFONSO	
PREWITT	HAROLD	G
PRICE	WELDON	R
RAMOS	GUADALUPE	
RAVEN	DONALD	W
REES	DONALD	E
REEVES	PAUL	W
RICH	MICHAEL	D
ROGERS	AMON	G
ROTAN	JAMES	H
SCHRAGE	URBAN	A
SCOTT	BOYCE	R
SCOTT	ROBERT	D
SEALS	RAY	E
SHARP	JAMES	M
SHINE	PAUL	W
SHINPAUGH	GRADY	G
SHIRLEY	JERRY	L
SHUTT	LADDIE	D
SINOR	BILLY	G
SLAUGHTER	JERRY	D
SMITH	LESLIE	A
SPEIGHTS	JAMES	E
SPIESS	JAMES	C
SPRAGINS	CHARLES	E
STEELE	DEAN	L
STEPHENS	CARL	
STEPHENS	JERRY	R
STEVENS	CARL	E
SULLENGER	OVERTON	G
SWINNEY	ROBERT	R
THOMPSON	RALPH	A
TOCK	ROBERT	H
TOMKIEWICZ	LEO	
TURNER	ALLAN	P
TURNER	ARMAND	K
TURNER	BOBBY	J
TURNER	MARION	P
TWILLEY	ROBERT	F

VOLTON	FRANK	M
VON WINDEGUTH	DONALD	L
WAINWRIGHT	LEONARD	L
WALL	LEO	W
WEARING	LESTER	F
WEINRICK	RODNEY	D
WITT	JAMES	H
YEAGER	PETER	
YOWELL	HOMER	C
ZIMMERMAN	BOBBY	L

11th Ranger Infantry Company (Airborne)

AHR	EDWIN	R
ARNER	BOB	
ASHMORE	JAMES	W
BANBURY	JACK	L
BARR	ROBERT	C
BARTLETT	ARMANDO	
BATES	HUGH	M
BEAUCHAMP	RONALD	G
BLIXRUD	ALDEN	M
BOLSTER	GERALD	P
BOOTH	JERRY	
BRASE	ROBERT	D
BRINEGAR	TERRY	E
BRITT	JIM	E
BUCHANAN	ROBERT	G
CALDERHEAD	JAMES	
CARAWAN	HENRY	B
CARUTH	CHARLES	W
CAULLEY	GERALD	F
CHAMPION	ROGER	
CHEEK	RALPH	
CHIVVIS	HOWARD	E
COLEMAN	CLINTON	E
COOK	ROBERT	A
CROSBY	ROY	
CRUZ	TRINO	
DAVIDSON	ANDREW	D
DAVIS	JAMES	
DAVIS	WILLIAM	

DELGADO	JOSE	A
ESTRADA	FERNANDO	
ESTRADA	RICHARD	
EVANS	BEN	M
FABRE	MICHAEL	D
FICK	DORSEY	R
FORSETH	RICHARD	
FRANKLIN	JAMES	A
FRENCH	THOMAS	
FULWILER	HAROLD	K
GARCIA	THOMAS	SR
GARDNER	RICHARD	
GARRETT	LONNIE	
GEARY	ROBERT	D
GOBBLE	JAMES	H
GOMEZ	JOHN	
GREEN	ROBERT	F JR
HAGAN	EDWARD	B
HAMMER	JOHN	
HARRIS	DAVE	A
HENNESSY	JOHN	
HENSLEY	JACK	B
HOLGUIN	HERACLIO	B
HOLMES	THEODORE	S
HUFFAR	WALTER	E
HUNYADY	LESLIE	C
HURLEY	RICHARD	F
HUSS	JOHN	R
HUTTO	SIDNEY	L
JACOBY	PHILIP	A
JOHNSON	TEDDY	C
JOHNSON	THOMAS	W
JONES	RUDOLPH	M
KEEGAN	FRANCIS	
KEEGAN	JOHN	P
KEIR	ROGER	L
KIEFER	BYRON	D
KILGORE	RILEY	
KOMISAREK	JOHN	R
KUAHMEW	KEITH	M
KUNAU	ROBERT	L

LA PORTE	JOSEPH	
LAW	MONTE	K
LAWRIE	WILLIAM	L
LEWALLEN	WILLARD	
LISH	VERL	K
LOOMER	WALTER	S
LOSKA	WILLIAM	
LOZA	EDWARD	C
LUNDBERG	RICHARD	
MALLORY	WILLIAM	
MANNION	THOMAS	F
MANRIQUEZ	EUGENE	
MCCAULLEY	GERALD	E
MCCAULLEY	KENNETH	H
MCFARLAND	JACK	
MCCOY	JAMES	F
MCWHIRTER	RICHARD	A
MILES	RALPH	G
MIXON	MARION	E
MOONEY	GARY	
MONJE	HECTOR	
MORENO	LOUIS	J
MOSES	RICHARD	
MUIR	WILLIAM	H
MUNOZ	JOHN	J
MURPHY	WALTER	L
NEAL	GERALD	D
NELSON	WILLIAM	S
NICHOLLS	EUGENE	C
NIXON	DONALD	B
NOLLAU	STEVAN	
NOWAK	CASMER	
OLIVER	ERNEST	L
ONGE	JOHN	D
OWENS	BURTON	B
PETERSON	CARMEN	R
PINEDO	AUGUSTINE	R
PITCHER	ARTHUR	Y
PORIE	JOSEPH	C
PORTILLA	RICK	W
RAMUS	VICTOR	E

RASENS	ROBERT	J
REICHMAN	WALDON LEE	
REMER	FORREST	H
RICHARDS	LARRY	K
RIDDLE	JACK	
ROBINSON	DOUGLAS	J
ROBITAILLE	EDWARD	G JR
ROMANIO	MICHAEL	M
SAITES	LOUIS	N
SALO	JAMES	R
SAMPSON	EARL	
SCHOCK	GEORGE	R
SCHULTZ	THEODORE	
SHARE	PETER	
SHEDD	JOHN	J
SHINE	PAUL	W
SHULER	HAROLD	G
SHUSTER	MANUEL	A
SHUTES	MALCOLM	D
SISO	GEORGE	
SMITH	BENNY	A
SODENKAMP	FRANK	
SODENKAMP	LEONARD	F
SOUNIA	DONALD	L
STEWART	PAUL	A
STIVER	ROBERT	A
SUTHERLAND	LESTER	A
TOVES	ALFRED	B
UNDERWOOD	STAN	
VAN ALSTINE	KENNETH	
VAN CISE	ROBERT	
VAUGHAN	BILLY	D
VERITY	FRED	
WEST	PAUL	D
WHYTE	ROBERT	M
WILLIAMS	WILLIAM	L
WOLLERY	LLOYD	A
WOOLETT	WILLIAM	
WUEST	EDGAR	J JR
YBARRA	DANIEL	E

YOUNGER	ESIUS	A
ZIMMERMAN	DONALD	A E
ZWICKL	JOSEPH	E

12th Ranger Infantry Company (Airborne)

ALEXANDER	FRANK	R
ARCHAMRAULT	ROBERT	
BARTO	JOSEPH	W
BERRY	WARREN	C
BIGART	ROBERT	H
BODEMER	HENRY	P
BORK	WALTER	E
BRENNEN	ARTHUR	J
BRYCE	WALTER	J
BURBIE	PATRICK	J
CHRISTJOHN	JOHN	E
CICUZZA	SISTO	M
CINICULA	TUNY	JK
COLE	HAROLD	O SR
COLE	ROBERT	L
COLEMAN	ROBERT	JR
COLLINS	WILLIAM	A
CONWAY	EDWARD	J
COOMBS	ROBERT	T
COOPER	ERNEST	J
DECRISTOFARO	JAMES	R
DOLIN	LOUIS	D
DUDA	JOSEPH	M
EASTIN	GLEN	R
EDMUNDS	JAMES	H
EIDELL	KURT	
FALVO	JOSEPH	N
FORSMARK	ARTHUR	
GARDJULIS	JOHN	W
GAUNT	ROBERT	W
GRASSO	ANTHONY	
GRUNDON	JAMES	P
HASS	JACK	D
HANDLEY	HARRY	B
HANSON	WILLIAM	G JR

HEASLEY	ALFRED	D
HICKS	MELVIN	L
HOWELL	FRANK	D
IDELL	ROBERT	F
JACKSON	ASHBY	W
JORDAHL	MERLE	O
KAUFFMAN	CHESTER	E
KAYLOR	JOHN	R
KAYS	HAROLD	V
KAYS	JACK	
KILDAY	JAMES	F
KING	FRANK	L
KUZMA	JOHN	
LABROZZI	ANTHONY	
LADNIER	HERMES	M
LANT	ROBERT	
LEONARD	BARRETT	
LEVAN	DONALD	E
LEWIS	ALBERT	
LOVETTO	VINCENT	V
MAINES	PHILLIP	D
MARSHALL	SETH	
MARTIN	LEVI	
MCDERMOTT	JACK	A
MEDEIROS	FELIX	L
MEISENHEIMER	ROBERT	C
MISTURA	BERNARD	S
MITCHELL	JEROME	L
NETHERLAND	GEORGE	E
O'DONNELL	ED	Z
PALMER	ROBERT	A
PATTERSON	LAWRENCE	
PAYNE	JOE	A
PEJACK	EUGENE	C
POGREBA	LAWRENCE	J
RAMSEY	WILLIE	D
RANF	CARL	V
REHMEL	GLENN	B
REISS	HOWARD	C
RHODES	CLAIR	L

RICHARDSON	THURMAN	L
RUSSELL	FRANKLIN	
SCHNELL	MERLYN	W
SCOTT	ADRIAN	V
SHAFFER	GERALD	H
SHEEHAN	FRANCIS	V
SISK	MARTIN	J
SISK	PATRICK	H
SMITH	BERYLE	
SMITH	DONALD	V
SNYDER	DON	
SOWELL	ELMER	P
STELLATO	TONY	P
STEPHENS	DUANE	A
STINNARD	DON	B
STOKES	JOSEPH	J
STRICKLAND	SAM	U
TARR	SHERMAN	B
TAUFER	DONALD	P
TAUFER	RONALD	L
TAYLOR	JACK	B
TAYLOR	ROBERT	D
THORN	HAROLD	A
TUCKER	ANDREW	
WADSWORTH	CHARLES	G
WADSWORTH	ROBERT	E
WALSH	PATRICK	J
WELSH	TEDD	A
WESTFALL	JOHN	C
WETZEL	PERRY	H
WETZEL	RICHARD	S
WILLIAMS	JACK	L
WILLIAMS	ROBERT	P
WILLIAMS	WILLIAM	
WISE	DONALD	
WITCZAK	HENRY	
WOOD	MANUAL	A JR
WOOLEY	JOHN	G JR
WRIGHT	J WARD	
ZIMMERMAN	JACK	A

| ZOOK | HARVEY | J JR |
| ZUCHNIK | EDWARD | L |

13th Ranger Infantry Company (Airborne)

ATWOOD	WILSON	R
BALLOU	SELAH	
BARRETT	ROY	C
BEERS	HARRY	D
BERG	ROBERT	W
BETIT	CHARLES	W
BIRD	RALPH	
BLODGETT	JOSEPH	D
BOLDT	HERMANN	L
BRADY	JOHN	P
BRIGGS	JACK	H
BROWN	ROBERT	L
BUNGARZ	FRANK	
BUREL	THOMAS	F
BUTCHKO	JOSEPH	J
BYRON	THOMAS	F
CATINEAULT	ROGER	G
CHAMPAGNE	ROBERT	G
CHARPENTIER	MELVIN	R
CLEMENT	JAMES	
CLOUSE	THOMAS	F
CLOW	ROBERT	L
CORNELL	WALTER	F
CORYELL	DAVID	C
COTE	ROGER	J
COUILLARD	RAYMOND	J
CZERNIEWSKI	STANLEY	F
DAVIS	FRANK	J
DAY	JAMES	M
DELUKEY	GEARY	F
DELMASTRO	MICHAEL	
DELVALLE	CLEMENT	
DERWIN	JAMES	M
DEVINE	JOHN	F
DEWBERRY	OSCAR	H
DIERKS	JOHN	H
DIMODICA	CUNCETTO	

DODGE	RUSSELL	E
DOUGLAS	WILLIAM	
DRAHEIM	JOHN	J
DUNN	DONALD	E
DVORAK	JAMES	A
EDWARDS	EDWIN	
EGBERT	HAROLD	R
ESEPPI	PAUL	J
FANNING	JOHN	V
FITCH	ROBERT	M
GAINER	RICHARD	E
GALLOWAY	DAVID	
GANTT	ROBERT	F
GELINAS	WILLIAM	P
GIBLIN	THOMAS	F
HAND	DONALD	A
HARRIS	FRANK	B
HARRIS	MERLE	E
HARWOOD	VICTOR	K
HAWES	EGBERT	D
HEFFERMAN	DONALD	
HELIN	WAYNE	H
HENDRIX	RALPH	W
HICKEY	EDWARD	J
HOBBS	ROBERT	N
HODGKINSON	HAROLD	J
HOWE	THOMAS	
HOLAPPA	FRED	C
HUDSON	REMUS	A
HURLEY	ROBERT	J
ILLUZZI	JOHN	
JACOVONE	THEODORE	
JORGENSON	PETER	C
KAVOLIUS	VYTAUTUS	J
KENDALL	JACK	L
KIBBIE	CARLTON	R
KIDD	HOWARD	W
KURTZ	RICHARD	W
LABRIE	RICHARD	M
LA DOW	ROBERT	P
LAMICA	STANLEY	B

LANE	ELMER	
LANEY	LUTHER	
LEATHERS	GENE	
LEWIS	EDWARD	L
LUVARA	JOHN	J
MADURA	JOHN	C
MAINEY	JAMES	
MANGRUM	EPHRIAM	F
MARKS	WALTER	S
MARR	LEONARD	V
MATTHEWS	ROY	A
MCCULLUM	CLARENCE	E
MCALLISTER	MAURICE	E
MCDONALD	FRED	S
MCENROE	JAMES	P
MCGETRICK	DONALD	J
MCNEVIN	EDWARD	F
MCCOLLUM	CLARENCE	
MILARDO	VINCENT	J
MILLER	ROBERT	R
MONTAGUE	LAWRENCE	E
MORDENTE	JOSEPH	D
MORRISON	RONALD	A
MOSS	KENNETH	M
MULVEY	WILLIAM	
MUNK	WAYNE	M
MURPHY	JAMES	M
NELSON	CLOYTON	E
NETTLES	WILLIAM	R
NICE	JOSEPH	W
NICHOLSON	DAVE	
O'BRIEN	ARTHUR	W
O'BRIEN	EDWARD	F
O'BRIEN	SIMON	
O'CONNOR	MICHAEL	J
PALMER	ANDREW	A
PALMER	ROBERT	C
PARKER	ROBERT	M
PARMENTIER	GERALD	
PATTERSON	ALTON	H
PATTERSON	LLOYD	I

PEASE	THOMAS	H
PEPIN	JOHN	L
PFIELSTICKER	RICHARD	M
PHILLIPS	ALBERT	L
PITTENGER	RICHARD	A
PRATT	CARL	R
PROVOST	NORMAN	J
QUIGLEY	ROBERT	J
RAMSDELL	LAWRENCE	
RECLA	JACK	
RHODES	ALVIN	M
SCHENKER	FRED	W
SHEA	JOHN	E
SHOEMAKER	CLYDE	
SIEBERT	LEWIS	R
SILVERIO	ANTHONY	
SIMON	STEVE	R
SIMMONS	DONALD	
SLOAN	GEORGE	R
SMITH	JAMES	
SMITH	THEODORE	W
ST JOHN	JAMES	JR
STEVENS	EDWARD	A
STRIZ	EDWARD	
STROM	ANTHONY	P
SULLIVAN	WILLIAM	P
SUTHERLAND	JAMES	
SUTHERLAND	WILLIAM	Y
TAYLOR	ROYCE	E
TEUBER	RONALD	W
THERLAND	JAMES	
THOMAS	HARLEY	J
TONER	THOMAS	E
TRAINOR	DONALD	
TURNER	WALTER	E
TWINING	JOHN	
URBANO	JOSEPH	A
VASQUES	DOMINICK	J
VERHAGEN	GERALD	L
WALSH	JOHN	
WARD	THOMAS	J

WILLEY	ANDRE	
WILLIAMS	JOHN	A
WISNIEWSKI	RICHARD	W

14th Ranger Infantry Company (Airborne)

ALBARO	ERNEST	V
ALLEN	FARRELL	J
AMATO	SAM	
ANDERSON	FRANCISCO	
ARNAUD	HARRY	
BABCOCK	ROBERT	M
BEERS	WARREN	
BITTLE	JOHN	C
BOGARDOS	CHARLES	
BONDURANT	THOMAS	E
BORDELON	LAURY	J
BREWER	LUCIAN	L
BROOKER	ROLAND	K
BROTHERS	ISRAEL	J
CAMERON	RUSS	
CARNEY	JONATHAN	D
CHAMBERLAIN	COLLIN	C
CHAVEZ	TONY	
CLARK	DAVID	
CLEVENGER	WALTER	R
CLOUSE	THOMAS	
COLE	FRANZ	E
CROW	WILLIAM	
CROWDER	KENNETH	
DE LEON	VICTOR	
DUBE	LEONARD	
DUNLAP	JAMES	JR
DURHAM	CHARLES	R
EGELER	WARREN	L
ESPINOZA	TORIBIO	L
EVANISKO	GREGORY	G
FAIOLA	HENRY	
FATLAND	EVAN	
FOLKS	SOLOMAN	J
FRANCO	EMELIO	L
GAUT	DON	P

GIBSON	WILLIAM	D
GILLILLAND	WILLIAM	S
GOLDWORTHY	JAMES	L
GRANT	W	E
GREER	EDWARD	B
GRISWOLD	DONALD	E
GUYOT	BOB	
HAYES	ERNEST	I JR
HAYNES	JAMES	D
HELMEL	FRED	P
HERRING	EVERETT	L
HESS	FRED	G
HINTZ	H	J
HODEN	NEEDHAM	JR
HOFFMASTER	GENE	
HOFFMASTER	JACK	
HOLDEN	NEEDHAM	C
HOLLOWAY	JOE	JR
HOOPER	FRED	
HOUSE	EARL	JR
HOWARD	LARRY	J
HUBBARD	EZRA	
HUDSON	ED	L
JENNINGS	RANDOLPH	D
JOHNSON	LELAND	
KAFRAL	DANIEL	
KINDER	STANLEY	S
KOSINSKI	ANTHONY	
LARKIN	LEROY	
LEVIN	CLARENCE	
LIEBL	GEORGE	M
LOPEZ	JOSE	A
LUTTRELL	BOB	G
MAHLER	WILLIAM	
MARTINEZ	EDUARDO	R
MCCAFFERTY	THOMAS	J
MCGILL	ROY	T
MCGINTHY	ALFORD	JR
MEDDERS	TRUMAN	L
MULT	ROBERT	J
MONTGOMERY	KEN	

MOORE	DAWSON	C
MOORE	DWAYNE	
MOORE	GORDON	L
MORLEY	ADRIAN	
MORRISON	WILLIAM	
NIGH	GLENN	
PACE	LONNIE	D
PERRA	ENRIQUE	R
POLICICHIO	ANTHONY	
PORTER	ROBERT	E
PORTERFIELD	WILLIAM	A
PRON	LOUIS	
PUMPHREY	RICHARD	I
PURCELL	JOHN	K
RAMIREZ	RICARDO	M
RAYMOND	RAWLIN	R
REGAN	THOMAS	C
RHODES	HORACE	C
RITCHIE	BRYON	JR
ROBINSON	JAMES	D
RODARTE	GILBERT	
SANCHEZ	SAM	H
SEAVEY	RICHARD	R
SERPAS	CLAUDE	J
SHANKE	GERALD	C
SHARPLESS	HARRY	M
SHEW	JOHN	R
SHORE	NED	J
SICKO	GEORGE	
SIMMS	BENJAMIN	
SIMONS	ROBERT	B
SKELTON	JOHNNY	
SKIVER	LEO	
SNYDER	JAMES	E
SOTUYU	GILBERT	
SPAULDING	ROBERT	L
SPEARS	GEORGE	H
STAR	MOSES	
STIMMLER	GEORGE	L
STOWELL	PAUL	J
STROCK	STANLEY	

SULLIVAN	EDWARD	J
SWAILS	PALMER	L
THOMAS	WILLIAM	A
TOTH	JOHN	A
TURLEY	ALONZO	E
VAN METER	OKEY	
VANAMAN	ROBERT	J
WARD	ALLEN	P
WEAVER	MARVIN	C
WEBB	CARL	O
WHEELER	JOCKO	
WILLARD	ORIN	L
WRIGHT	GEORGE	C
YBARRA	RAYMOND	
YOUNG	HAROLD	E

15th Ranger Infantry Company (Airborne)

ANTHONY	NICHOLAS	C
APPULGLIESE	JAMES	V
ARNOLD	GERALD	
ATCHISON	THOMAS	G
BAKER	DARYLE	J
BANKERT	ANTHONY	D
BARRIO	EDWARD	G
BEATTY	ROY	
BEAUDETTE	THOMAS	J
BELTER	RONALD	D
BELTON	HENRY	I
BEST	EUGENE	E
BIRD	J	C
BISHOP	DANIEL	R
BLINKWITZ	KENNETH	
BLOCK	LENOARD	
BOLK	PHILLIP	
BORDON	EMIL	
BORETTA	LEON	D
BOYLE	ROBERT	V
BRENT	ROBERT	H
BRYER	EDWARD	
BUCK	RICHARD	R
BURNS	JOHN	F

BUZA	WILLARD	J
CALLIGAN	TERRANCE	J D
CASSIDY	HENRY	D E
CHRISTENSON	LLOYDS	
CLEAR	JOHN	W
CLINGER	WILLIAM	S
COLLERT	JACK	L
COSTARO	JOSEPH	J
COSTIN	ELDRED	A
COURTNEY	JOHN	
CRICK	ROBERT	G
CULVER	STANLEY	H
DALLMAN	DONALD	P
DEHAVEN	JAMES	D
DELANEY	RICHARD	
DEL TORO	MARIO	
DELUCA	JOHN	
DICKS	JEROME	P
DI GUSU	LOUIS	P A
DOFFING	SYLVESTER	F
DYE	RONALD	
EBEL	GORDON	J
EDWARDS	CLIFTON	J R
ENGSTROM	JOHN	W
FISH	DEAN	
FITCH	LESTER	L
FREDLUND	JAMES	R
FRITZ	DANIEL	L
GATES	EMERSON	A
GOCHA	GEORGE	L
GOETTE	JAMES	A
GROVE	ERNEST	R
HALLIGAN	JOHN	P
HANSCOM	WILLIAM	E
HANSEN	EDGAR	L
HARLOW	GILES	D
HEADLINE	RUSELL	H
HERBERT	DONALD	B
HINCKLEY	JOHN	
HUNT	JOSEPH	
HUPP	FORREST	JR

JABBOUR	ALBERT	
JAMES	ROBERT	D
JARVIS	GEORGE	S
JEWELL	ROBERT	M
JOHNSON	CHARLES	R
JOHNSON	HARLAN	C
JOHNSON	JOHN	A
JOHNSON	MERLYN	R
JOHNSON	WILLIAM	
JONES	WILLIAM	R
JULIAN	FREDERICK	M
KAPITZKE	PAUL	W
KELLY	FREDERICK	J
KELLEY	RAYMOND	H
KENT	J	W
KENYON	KENNETH	E
KINDER	WILLARD	H
KING	EUGENE	W
KLEIN	DANIEL	A
KLITZKE	MERLE	E
KUFKAS	JOHN	
KOVALCIK	JOHN	N
KRICK	BURTON	J
KRUPNICK	ROBERT	D
KURTZ	EUGENE	D
LAURSEN	ROBERT	L
LEGE	DENNIS	R
LEVACK	LEN	
LIND	OTTO	J
LOAKAKUS	ANDRO	M
LOVING	JOSEPH	S
LOWENSTEIN	JOSEPH	V
LOWENSTEIN	LEE ROY	S
MAACK	ELROY	V
MAPP	JAMES	H
MARTIN	THOMAS	
MARTINOVICH	THOMAS	J
MATISCHUNSKI	THOMAS	
MACDONALD	WILLIAM	J
MACNAMARA	ROBERT	J
MCNAMARA	LAWRENCE	

MCNAMARA	ROBERT	J
MCQUIEN	RICHARD	
MCTEAGUE	J	P
MENA	JESUS	
MILLETT	ROBERT	A
MIMM	ARNOLD	
MITCHELL	JOSEPH	
MITCHELL	DONALD	
MOORE	HARRY	
MURPHY	THOMAS	A
MURRAY	KENNETH	A R
NIBLER	WILLIAM	N
NIMS	DONALD	F
NOWICKI	EUGENE	
OLSON	ROLLAND	E
OPP	ORVILLE	
PANEK	RICHARD	
PEDLEY	RICHARD	A
PETERSON	LEE	E
PHILLIPS	BERNARD	
PICURRO	BERNARD	
PLATTNER	JOHN	C
POPE	JAMES	A
PRITTS	ROBERT	
RAMOS	VICTOR	E
REAMER	GLENN	E
REDDIES	HENRY	W
REGAN	DONALD	B
REGAN	ROBERT	J
REMILLONG	ROLAND	H
RICE	WILLIAM	J
RIDENHOUR	HOWARD	P
RIMS	DONALD	
ROSEGRANT	EDWARD	J
SANDERSON	ROY	D
SCOTT	JACK	I
SHAW	WARREN	
SIPE	FRED	L
SMITH	ROGER	D
SNEVA	ROBERT	
SOUERS	DONALD	C

STOBERT	WILBERT	N
STROMAN	FRED	L
SWANK	MARCEL	G
SWINGLE	RONALD	N
TATE	LAWRENCE	
THOMPSON	KENNETH	W
TOMEI	ALBERT	
TRAXLER	CLIFF	
TRIPP	JAMES	W
VOLLECA	FRANCIS	H
WAGAMAN	CHARLES	R
WALTERS	GENE	A
WELCH	CHARLES	E
WILLIAMS	CHRISTOPHER	R
WINN	ARNOLD	B

Ranger Training Company A (Airborne)

AMMERMAN	JAY	F
ANDERSON	WILLIAM	E
BAGBY	EDWIN	C
BASSETT	GEORGE	E J
BATCHA	GEORGE	M
BENNETT	JOHN	C
BOWERS	ROMAN	L
BREWER	HERBERT	J
CAMPBELL	RICHARD	C
CARGAN	JOHN	J
CARSTENS	EARL	M
CARTLEDGE	JAMES	C
CENTOFANTI	VINCENZO	
CHALMERS	JOHN	
CHANEY	DON	
CHESTER	JOHN	A
CLEAR	JOHN	W
CONNALLY	WILLIAM	
DALY	JOSEPH	R
DAVIDSON	HOMER	
DAVIS	NOAH	F
DESMOND	TIMOTHY	G
DOWLING	ROY	M
ERIEKSON	ROY	E

FONESCA	RAUL	N
FRYSON	RAYMOND	
GALLAGHER	PATRICK	J
GALT	CHADBORN	W
GARRETT	CARLOS	W
GAYLORD	WESLEY	
GILSDORF	RONALD	B
GOODWIN	JOHN	JR
HAGGERTY	ROBERT	J
HAMLIN	JAMES	L
HARDY	RICHARD	I
HARL	GEORGE	D
HARMON	JOSEPH	W
HARTNETT	JAMES	F
HASKEW	WILLIAM	D
HICKS	FREDERICK	J
HUCAL	MICHAEL	
JOHNSON	BOBBY	
JOHNSON	CLARENCE	
JOHNSON	CURLEE	
KASKUSKIE	STANLEY	L
KELLBACH	CLARENCE	L A
KENDALL	CLAUDE	A
KENNEDY	DONLEY	C
LARKIN	HOWARD	E
LAYNE	PHILLIP	E
LEYBA	RICHARD	
LONGO	JOHN	R
LUPO	JOHN	
MALONEY	JERRY	
MURPHY	FREDERICK	
NALOR	WILLIAM	H
NORRIS	JAMES	E
OLIVER	HOWARD	
PAPPAS	JOHN	
PERRY	ALVIS	
PERRY	ROBERT	M
PULLON	MELVIN	
RAEIN	WILLIAM	N
RASSMUSSEN	WAYNE	
RUSSLER	LEE	W

SASSER	GARLAND	G
SHAW	EUGENE	D
SHEVLIN	FRANCIS	
SIMMS	TOSCO	J
SILVERS	JAMES	
SNIPES	JOHN	M
SPENCER	JOE	
STANTURF	JACK	A
STAUDE	RICHARD	
THOMAS	GEORGE	
WALSH	LEWIS	G
WARREN	JAMES	E
WELBORN	CARL	
WELTON	WALTER	B
WILLIAMS	FINA	
WILLIAMS	ROBERT	H
WOODWORTH	ROY	
YORK	CURTIS	W

Ranger Training Company B (Airborne)

ARENDT	ROBERT	
BITTORIE	JOHN	H
BRANDENBURG	JAMES	G
BRAYMAN	WILLIAM	R
BRYANT	CARL	
BUDYNKIEWICZ	ROBERT	C
BURAS	FRANK	T
CASELLA	EMIL	
CLARK	ROBERT	
DUGAN	JAMES	
FEDORCHAK	WILLIAM	
FLOYD	JAMES	
GAVIN	JOHN	RYAN
GREYSHOCK	DONALD	G
GURZYNSKI	JOHN	G
HANDLEY	MERLIN	J
HAY	GILBERT	E
HAYS	ROBERT	J
HILBORN	VIRGIL	D
HILL	ARNOLD	
HILTON	MEDFORD	

HOOVER	JAMES	D
KATSIKARIS	ARISTOTELUS	
LAROUCHE	ALDON	
LANNUM	R	L
MAHER	RUSSELL	E
MARTIN	PERRY	J
MCGUIRE	WILLIAM	G
MCMAHON	ROBERT	L
MILLER	COLMORE	
NEEL	GORDON	J
PIRES	GILBERT	
POWELL	CECIL	P
RAMEY	TRACY	A
READY	ARCHIE	
REEDER	EDWARD	M
SILAS	AUSTIN	JR
WELBORN	CARL	U
WELTON	WALTER	B
WILLIAMS	FINA	P
WILLIAMS	ROBERT	H
WITHERITE	TERREL	V
WILSON	DONALD	N
WOODWORTH	ROY	
WRIGHT	HAROLD	
YESTER	JOSEPH	A

End Notes

Chapter 1

1. The 38th parallel which separated North and South Korea was a compromise proposed by American Rear Admiral Matthias Gardner.
2. In 1950–51 few American soldiers had confidence in their South Korean allies, but given proper training and equipment, they eventually developed into a strong and capable force. The South Koreans suffered nearly 845,000 casualties during the war.

Chapter 2

1. John H. McGee headed the Miscellaneous Division, G-3 Section, Eighth U.S. Army. According to McGee, in a letter written to the author, this was originally "a cover name for a G-3 commanded unit organized to conduct guerrilla warfare." Under McGee's direction a variety of Army units with designations in the 8000s were formed to perform deep reconnaissance and support guerrilla operations behind enemy lines.
2. Ralph Puckett, Jr. would win the Distinguished Service Cross and lose a toe. Of the latter he said, "It doesn't matter, it had corns anyway." Puckett ended his service career as a colonel.

Chapter 3

1. From the initial order, officers familiar with Ranger operations were opposed to the concept of attaching companies of Rangers to infantry divisions. They wanted assignment to battalions so they could be controlled at theater level. Col. Jack Street, who fought as a Ranger in World War II and was on the staff of the Ranger Training Command, told the author, "All of us knew it would not work."
2. The raid was a principal style of warfare of the American Indian. It was from this skilled foe that Americans learned the techniques

which, when combined with the superior firepower and discipline of a conventional army, made the Rangers a force to be reckoned with.

3. In the early days of the war, the 2.36-inch rocket launcher, with which the American troops were equipped, was not effective against the T-34 Tank. The arrival of the 3.5-inch rocket launcher, along with American armor and air superiority, deprived the North Koreans of this edge.

4. John Gibson Van Houten eventually reached the rank of major general and his service after the Rangers included division commander, 8th Infantry Division, Fort Carson, Colorado, and commander of the Military District of Washington. He died in February 1974.

5. Edwin Walker ultimately achieved the rank of major general. During World War II he was commanding officer of the 3rd Special Service Force in the Aleutian islands; the 1st Special Service Force in Italy, France, and Germany; and the 474th Infantry Regiment in Germany and Norway.

6. The depth of knowledge in the Ranger companies in Korea was astounding. A rifleman may have been a communications specialist; a machine gunner, a former medic; the company clerk, an expert in demolitions. Whatever task needed to be accomplished, there were men with the skills to do it.

Chapter 4

1. The 2nd Ranger Infantry Company (Airborne) was the only all-black Ranger unit the United States Army has ever had. In late July 1951, when integration was in full swing, several white Rangers were assigned to the 2nd, but before they could join the unit the Rangers were deactivated.

2. BAR. The Browning Automatic Rifle was the weapon that most symbolized the Rangers of the Korean War—a Ranger squad had two, the line infantry squad one.

3. Maj. (later Colonel) Jack Street was one of the most popular instructors at the Ranger Training Center. He was known as "Tricky Jack" for the many tricks of war he knew. Street had been an original member of Darby's Rangers in World War II. As a staff officer involved in the invasion of Normandy, he played a heroic role in assisting Ranger units by ferrying ammunition and supplies and removing wounded. When my wife Barbara was dying of lung cancer, my friend and brother Col. Jack Street told me he also was dying of cancer. Our conversation that day touched many things, and the kindness of this gentle warrior will never leave me while I live. Col. Jack Street and Barbara Nell Black died the same day—March 10, 1987.

4. During the Korean War the policy was for soldiers to save the water in their canteen. With the war in Vietnam, the Army realized it was

healthier to replace body fluids. In Vietnam, infantrymen often wore two or more canteens.

5. The goal for Korean War Rangers was to march cross-country a distance of fifty miles in twelve to eighteen hours. The marches were brutal, but no documentation is available that the goal was achieved. World War II British Commandos considered a forty-two-mile march in nineteen hours achievable.

6. James A. Herbert, USMA class of 1945, survived being wounded in Korea, achieved the rank of brigadier general, and served with distinction during the Vietnam War. He was senior province adviser in Long An province in Vietnam in November 1967 when the author reported for duty under his command. We had not seen each other since 25 April 1951 and the battle on Hill 628.

7. A quartering party is a small group of officers, communicators, and guides that goes forward to the new location and makes arrangements for the main body of troops to follow.

Chapter 6

1. John Paul Vann served as a lieutenant colonel in Vietnam in 1962. Dissatisfied with the progress of the war, Vann left the service in 1963. In 1966 he returned to Vietnam as a civilian adviser. He was killed when his helicopter crashed in 1972. At that time he was the director of the second regional assistance group in the central highlands of Vietnam, with rank equivalent to a major general.

2. TO&E 7-87: To be a Table of Organization and Equipment unit normally was a higher form of acceptance. The unit would have military ancestors, and its battle honors and campaigns would accrue to the parent regiment. Unfortunately for the Eighth Army Ranger Company and the Ranger family, the authority making them a TO&E unit came from the general headquarters of the Far East Command's message CX50251, 2 December 1950. Men fought, bled, and died in the campaigns of this unit, but because the authority did not come from the Department of the Army, their campaign streamers are not permitted to fly from Ranger colors. The men of companies A and B also served in Table of Distribution units. For these volunteers, this was a subject that caused resentment throughout their lives. They served as well as the men in TO&E units, but felt their units were denied recognition. "We were treated like 'bastard' units," one Ranger grumbled.

3. DUKW stood for Detroit United Kaiser Works and was an amphibious vehicle developed in World War II.

4. Mark Goyen, while physically not large, is a "big man." He lost a leg at the battle of Chipyong-ni, then made over 1,600 free-fall parachutes jumps. One of the most memorable interviews for this work was with Mark in a motel room in Carlisle, Pennsylvania, with his artificial leg propped in a corner, a silent remembrance of Korea.

5. John K. Singlaub achieved the rank of major general. He disagreed with President Carter's intention to withdraw American forces from Korea and had the courage to speak his views. After resigning from the Army, he devoted his life to assisting those people and nations who fight communism.

Chapter 7

1. After the Korean War, Howard K. Davis became a gentleman adventurer throughout Latin America, operating as an anti-Communist, anti-dictator agent. Davis, who was a superb pilot, was involved in plots and counter-plots. In 1958 he was the military chief of a guerrilla band in eastern Cuba, and in 1969 he and several others bombed the palace of the Dictator "Papa Doc" Duvalier. He was for a time under sentence of death. During the Vietnam War he was a contract pilot flying various cargo in and out of Vietnam.

2. Charles E. Spragins served as a company commander with the 23rd Infantry in Korea, and commanded a brigade in Vietnam. He achieved the rank of major general, and operates a real estate firm in South Carolina.

3. Emmett Fike returned home to Warrior, Alabama, and had the name of the road leading to his home changed to "Ranger Trail." In 1985–86 Emmett, Jim Britt of 11th company, and other Rangers traveled thousands of miles searching out surviving family members and the burial places of Korean War Rangers. A graveside memorial service would be held and a bronze Ranger scroll attached to the gravestone. Fike was the third president of the Korean War Ranger Association.

4. On a trip to Fort Carson, Colorado, in 1985, the author found an Army mule stuffed and on display in the Fort Carson Museum. It was like finding a friend in the same condition. For those interested in learning more of this valiant creature, the 20 March 1951 issue of *Life* magazine contains an article "Last of the Quadrupeds in the U.S. Army."

Chapter 8

1. After his experience as a Ranger and POW, Anthony "Luke" Lukasik chose the hazardous profession of being a motorcycle police officer on the streets of Warren, Michigan.

2. Glenn Hall, who was awarded the Distinguished Service Cross for his actions at Chipyong-ni, was killed by friendly forces as he tried to reenter friendly lines on 19 May 1951.

3. The raid on the Saint Francis Indians put an end to years of suffering by the colonists at the hands of a fierce band of Abenakis. Robert Rogers and two hundred Rangers embarked by whaleboat on the night of 13 September 1759. Enduring great hardships, the Rangers arrived at the Saint Francis encampment on the evening of October 5. At three A.M. they attacked and destroyed the enemy camp. With

the enemy countryside aroused, Rogers and his men survived much hardship, arriving safely home on October 31. Rogers and his men had covered approximately four hundred miles of wilderness. For further reading see *Robert Rogers of the Rangers* by John R. Cuneo.

Sened Station: In February 1943, during the Tunisian campaign, the 1st Ranger Battalion was ordered to raid enemy outposts. The objective was the Sened Station outpost, manned by crack Italian troops. The Rangers made a twelve-mile night march to close on the objective, hid out during daylight hours, then made a night assault with three companies on line. In less then half an hour the enemy position was destroyed. For further reading see: *The Spearheaders and/or Darby's Rangers* by James Altieri.

Chapter 9

1. 82mm mortar was a Communist-bloc mortar designed so that it could fire American 81mm mortar ammunition.

2. Earl Baker, along with Lew Villa and Fred Heedt, are among the many Rangers who made successful careers with the post office after their military service.

3. Robert Morgan had a successful Army career, then entered the import/export business in Taiwan.

4. Robert Bodroghy, after the breakup of the Rangers, joined Colonel McGee and became an expert in clandestine operations. He achieved the rank of colonel.

5. Sam Amato continued his Ranger ways in Vietnam, where he did much to establish Vietnamese Ranger battalions.

Chapter 10

1. Charles Ross had the distinction of being the last company commander of both the Eighth Army Ranger Company and the 1st Ranger Infantry Company (Airborne). He achieved the rank of colonel.

2. John W. Thornton survived captivity and received the Navy Cross. He continued a distinguished naval career and achieved the rank of captain. His story is told in his book *Believed to Be Alive*.

3. Marty Watson lived a life of travel and adventure. When I met him in 1983, he was dying of cancer. Ernest Hemingway would have understood Watson. He personified "grace under pressure." Marty would not talk of his experiences except when I asked him the difference in his treatment as a captive of the Germans and as a captive of the Chinese. His eyes flashed as he said, "If you must endure captivity, it is better if your race and culture is similar."

4. Eugene Kuta did all a man could do to get into battle. Badly wounded, he lay between the lines for many hours before being rescued. His courage carried him through to become a success in the business world.

5. Donn Porter of the 9th Rangers, born 1 March 1931 at Sewickley,

Pennsylvania, volunteered for combat after the breakup of the Rangers. As Sgt. Donn Porter of Company G, 14th Infantry Regiment, 25th Infantry Division, he earned the Medal of Honor. The citation reads in part:

Sgt. Porter, a member of Company G, distinguished himself by conspicuous gallantry and outstanding courage above and beyond the call of duty in action against the enemy. Advancing under cover of intense mortar and artillery fire, 2 hostile platoons attacked a combat outpost commanded by Sgt. Porter, destroyed communications, and killed two of his three-man crew. Gallantly maintaining his position, he poured deadly accurate fire into the ranks of the enemy, killing 15 and dispersing the remainder. After falling back under a hail of fire, the determined foe reorganized and stormed forward in an attempt to overrun the outpost. Without hesitation, Sgt. Porter jumped from his position with bayonet fixed and, meeting the onslaught in close combat, killed six hostile soldiers and routed the attack. While returning to the outpost, he was killed by an artillery burst, but his courageous actions forced the enemy to break off the engagement and thwarted a surprise attack on the main line of resistance.

Donn Porter is buried at Arlington Cemetery, and there is a firing range named after him at Fort Benning, Georgia. It is believed there are no next of kin, as his Medal of Honor was sold at auction in London by Sotheby's in March 1983 for $5,000.

6. A wide variety of knives accompanied the Rangers of the Korean war. The most popular were the Sykes-Fairbirn, a stiletto-type Commando knife used in World War II, and the more practical Randall fighting knife. Most combat occurs beyond knife range, and a knife's key functions were to open cans, cut brush, dig, or otherwise serve as a construction tool.

7. Herman "Herm" Boldt achieved the rank of chief warrant officer, and, with his wife Lois, is living in Pennsylvania. In 1983 they began the monumental task of determining the names of all those who had served in the Rangers during the Korean War and locating and reuniting these men. It was a masterful piece of detective work and a service that brought joy to many.

Chapter 11

1. Mike Stankich became a military artist. His work is displayed at the Ranger Regiment and at the U.S. Army Military History Institute.

2. Robert Channon achieved the rank of colonel. He was the second president of the Association of the Ranger Infantry Companies (Airborne) of the Korean War.

3. John B. Jenkins of the 3rd Rangers became a minister, as did Ben Simms of the 14th Rangers.

4. Robert L. Exley kept a diary of his wartime experiences. He is retired from the FAA and now runs a travel agency in Florida.
5. Richard J. Eaton commanded a battalion in the 1st Infantry Division in Vietnam and a brigade in the 3rd Infantry Division in Europe. He achieved the rank of brigadier general.
6. Mae West: A malfunction caused by suspension lines passing over the parachute canopy as it is opening, giving the chute a bosom effect.
   Cigarette Roll: A malfunctioned parachute that forms a vertical roll streaming upward.

Chapter 12

1. Michael D. Healy commanded a battalion of the 173rd Airborne Brigade and the 5th Special Forces Group (Airborne) in Vietnam. He achieved the rank of major general.

Chapter 13

1. The nickname "the Devils" for the 8th Airborne Rangers came from an infantry officer who saw the company moving out with blackened faces for a night raid.
2. Nick Tisak returned to Ambridge, Pennsylvania, raised five sons, became a millwright, and established a reputation for decency and kindness that is a model for his comrades.

Chapter 14

1. 6th Medium Tank Battalion. These M-46 (Patton) tanks, painted with tiger stripes and claws, performed magnificently with the 24th Division. For further information see *Armor in Korea* by Jim Mesko.

Chapter 16

1. Joseph R. Ulatoski commanded a battalion and a brigade in Vietnam, and eventually achieved the rank of brigadier general.

Chapter 17

1. For General Ridgeway's views, I recommend reading his book, *The Korean War*.
2. Fred R. Hoy of the 5th Rangers became a successful building contractor in Pennsylvania. He has a dog named "Pabst" that will growl at any man introduced as a member of the 1st Ranger Company.
3. Cain's March: The author could find no documentation to verify the length and time of this march. Members of the 6th Rangers feel strongly that it occurred as stated.
4. *The Ranger* was published on 11 April, 1 May, 23 May, 12 June, 3 July, and 25 July 1951.
5. Joe Holloway, Jr. became an award-winning photographer whose work made the cover of *Life* magazine. After graduating from the

University of Alabama, he joined the staff of United Press International in 1959, serving in Atlanta, Raleigh, and Miami. In the 1960s he covered the civil rights marches. In 1967 he joined the staff of the Associated Press and covered the war in Vietnam, where he was wounded. In Long An Province, Vietnam, 1968, while I waited for a helicopter, a man loaded down with photographic gear saw the Ranger scroll on my right shoulder and gave a Ranger yell. It was Joe Holloway. We had never met till then, but we were, and are, brothers.

Chapter 18

1. 187th Airborne Regimental Combat Team: There was high-level concern that the Russians might threaten Japan to relieve pressure on their allies in Korea. The 187th was removed from Korea and positioned at Beppu on the Japanese island of Kyushu. Its Airborne mobility made it readily available for a variety of missions. It played a major role in putting down the disgraceful events at Koje-do Island, Korea, when Communist prisoners were permitted to get out of control and seize an American general.

Chapter 19

1. The Rangers had the last laugh about being assigned as replacements. In most companies the final act before disbanding was to promote every man one grade. This meant the noncommissioned officer leadership of the 187th was heavily weighted with Rangers.

Chapter 21

1. Tom Ward of the 4th Rangers returned to his native North Carolina and the foundry business. Married, with two sons and a daughter, he is the patriarch of the Southeastern Foundry Company of Greensboro, North Carolina.

Bibliography

Books

Adleman, Robert H., and Col. George Walton. *The Devil's Brigade*. Philadelphia: Chilton Books, 1966.

Appleman, Roy E., *South to the Naktong, North to the Yalu*. Washington, D.C.: Department of the Army, Chief of Military History, 1956.

Cagle, Commander Malcolm W., and Commander Frank A. Manson. *The Sea War in Korea*. Annapolis, Maryland: United States Naval Institute, 1957.

Esposito, Vincent J., ed. *The West Point Atlas of American Wars*, Vol. II 1900–53. New York: Frederick A. Praeger, 1959.

Gruenzner, Norman. *Postal History of American POW's: World War II, Korea, Vietnam*. State College, Pennsylvania: The American Philatelic Society, 1979.

Jackson, Robert. *Air War Over Korea*. New York: Charles Scribner's Sons, 1973.

Leckie, Robert. *Conflict, the History of the Korean War*. New York: G.P. Putnam's Sons, 1962.

Ogloblin, Peter. "The Korean War." Center for International Studies, American Project, Working Paper III.

Ridgeway, Matthew B. *The Korean War*. Garden City, New York: Doubleday, 1967.

Thornton, John W. *Believed to Be Alive*. Middlebury, Vermont: Paul S. Eriksson, 1981.

War History Compilation Committee. *History of U.N. Forces in Korean War*. The Ministry of National Defense, Republic of Korea, 1975.

Whiting, Allen S. *China Crosses the Yalu*. New York: The Macmillan Company, 1960.

Monographs/Historical Reports

Action on Hill 628, the 8th Ranger Infantry Company (Airborne). Headquarters, Eighth U.S. Army Korea (EUSAK), 4th Historical Detachment.

Hwachon Dam. Headquarters, Eighth U.S. Army Korea (EUSAK), 3rd Historical Detachment.

Special Problems in The Korean Conflict. Department of the Army, Chief of Military History, p. 138. Headquarters, Eighth U.S. Army Korea (EUSAK).

Unit Histories

The First Cavalry Division in Korea. Atlanta: Albert Love Enterprises.

"Second to None." The Second United States Infantry Division in Korea, 1950–51, 1951–52.

7th Infantry Division in Korea. Atlanta: Albert Love Enterprises, 1954.

3rd Infantry Division in Korea. Tokyo: Toppan Printing Company Ltd., 1953.

25th Infantry Division. The Tropic Lightning in Korea. Atlanta: Albert Love Enterprises.

24th Forward. Pictorial history of the Victory Division in Korea. Tokyo: Koyosha Printing Company.

Newspapers

The Ranger, The Columbus Ledger Enquirer, The Atlanta Constitution. Newspaper File of the Ranger Training Center.

Archival Sources

The Diary of the Ranger Training Center, Unit Data Cards, Morning Reports, Division and Regimental Combat and After-Action Reports, Company Histories.

Personal Sources

Personal diaries of Robert Exley, 3rd Ranger Company; and James Way, 4th Ranger Company. Letters and cassette tapes from and personal interviews with over 100 Ranger veterans.

Index

About the Author

Robert W. Black is a retired U.S. Army colonel who served in Vietnam and with the 8th Ranger Infantry Company (Airborne) in the Korean War. He is a member and past president of the Airborne Ranger Association of the Korean War and is currently working on a history of the Rangers in World War II. He lives in Carlisle, Pennsylvania.

$$\begin{array}{r} 65.4 \\ 11\overline{)720} \text{ min} = 654 \text{ m/hr} \\ 66 \\ \hline 60 \\ 55 \\ \hline 50 \end{array}$$

$12 \text{ min} = 1 \text{ m}^i$

12 MIN	1
	2
24 "	4
48 "	
12	5

$1\frac{L}{5}$

54 m^i

55

$$\begin{array}{r} 24 @ 10 \text{ min} \\ 20 \\ \hline 240 \text{ min} \end{array}$$

$$30\overline{)480} \mid 12.5$$
$$\begin{array}{r} 30 \\ \hline 80 \\ 60 \\ \hline 20 \end{array}$$

4

48^7